Understanding European Foreign

Understanding European Foreign Policy

Brian White

palgrave

First published 2001 by
PALGRAVE
Houndmills, Basingstoke, Hampshire RG21 6XS and
175 Fifth Avenue, New York, N.Y. 10010
Companies and representatives throughout the world

PALGRAVE is the new global academic imprint of
St. Martin's Press LLC Scholarly and Reference Division and
Palgrave Publishers Ltd (formerly Macmillan Press Ltd).

ISBN–13: 978–0–333–94988–7 ppc
ISBN–10: 0–333–94988–9 ppc
ISBN–13: 978–0–333–94989–4 paperback
ISBN–10: 0–333–94989–7 paperback

This book is printed on paper suitable for recycling and
made from fully managed and sustained forest sources.

A catalogue record for this book is available
from the British Library.

Library of Congress Cataloging-in-Publication Data

White, Brian, 1947–
   Understanding European foreign policy/Brian White.
      p. cm.
   Includes bibliographical references and index.
   ISBN 0–333–94988–9 (cloth) – ISBN 0–333–94989–7 (pbk.)
   1. Europe—Foreign relations—1945– 2. European
   cooperation. 3. Security,
   International. I. Title.

D843 .W453 2000
327.4—dc21   00–046875

Editing and origination by
Aardvark Editorial, Mendham, Suffolk

10 9 8 7 6 5 4
10 09 08 07 06 05

Printed in China

To my mother and
in memory of my father

Contents

List of Abbreviations   ix

1 Europe and the World   **1**
European Cooperation and Integration: From Dunkirk to
   Amsterdam   4
Key EU Institutions Outlined   11
What is 'Europe'?   18
The Approach and the Structure of the Book   23

2 Making Sense of Europe's Global Role   **27**
Contending Approaches   27
The Adaptability of Foreign Policy Analysis   32
What is European Foreign Policy?   36
An FPA Framework of Analysis   39

3 External Relations: Community Foreign Policy   **47**
Context   47
Actors and Policy-making   50
Capabilities and Instruments   53
Community Foreign Policy in Action: The Community and
   the GATT   58
Context   59
Process   61
Conclusion   69

4 European Political Cooperation   **71**
Context   71
Actors and Policy-making   74
Capabilities and Instruments   80
European Political Cooperation in Action: The Community
   and South Africa   84
Context   85
Actors and Policy-making   86
Conclusion   92

5 From EPC to CFSP: Union Foreign Policy **94**
Context 94
Actors and Policy-making 97
Capabilities and Instruments 102
CFSP in Action: The EU and the Former Yugoslavia 106
Context 107
Process and Action 110
Conclusion 115

6 The Europeanization of National Foreign Policies: The
Case of Britain **118**
Britain: The Exceptional Case? 119
Context 122
Actors and Policy-making 127
Capabilities and Instruments 131
A Europeanized British Foreign Policy? 134
New Labour, New Europeans? 136
Conclusion 141

7 Security and Defence: Towards a Common
European Defence Policy? **142**
Towards a Common European Defence Policy? 143
Security, Defence and Actorness 152
Conclusion 154

8 After Maastricht and Amsterdam: A Common
European Foreign Policy? **156**
Context 157
Actors and Policy-making 159
Capabilities and Instruments 161
Towards a Common European Foreign Policy? 162
The View from Foreign Policy Analysis 166

9 European Foreign Policy and Foreign Policy
Analysis **170**
Foreign Policy Analysis in Crisis? 171
Foreign Policy Analysis and the State 173
Foreign Policy Analysis, Identity and Social Meanings 174

Foreign Policy Analysis, Ideas and the Formulation
  of Policy   177
Conclusion   178

Bibliography   179

Index   191

List of Abbreviations

ABM	Anti-Ballistic Missile
ACP	African, Caribbean and Pacific [countries]
ASEAN	Association of South-East Asian Nations
CAP	Common Agricultural Policy
CCP	Common Trade or Commercial Policy
CDP	Common Defence Policy
CEECs	Central and East European Countries
CET	Common External Tariff
CFP	Comparative Foreign Policy
CFSP	Common Foreign and Security Policy
CJTF	Combined Joint Task Force
COREPER	Comité des Représentants Permanents (Committee of Permanent Representatives)
COREU	Correspondants Européens (European correspondents)
CSCE	Conference on Security and Cooperation in Europe
DFA	Department of Foreign Affairs
DG	Directorate-General
DGER	Directorate-General for External Relations
DOP	Defence and Overseas Policy Committee
DSS	Department of Social Security
DTI	Department of Trade and Industry
EC	European Community
ECJ	European Court of Justice
ECMM	European Community Monitoring Mission
ECSC	European Coal and Steel Community
ECU	European Currency Unit
EDC	European Defence Community
EDF	European Development Fund
(E)DOP	Sub-committee [of the DOP] on European Issues
EEA	European Economic Area

EEC	European Economic Community
EFP	European Foreign Policy
EMS	European Monetary System
EMU	Economic and Monetary Union
EP	European Parliament
EPC	European Political Cooperation
EPRD	European Program for Reconstruction and Development in South Africa
EPU	European Political Union
EQ	European Questions
ERM	Exchange Rate Mechanism
ESDI	European Security and Defence Identity
EU	European Union
EURATOM	European Atomic Energy Community
FCO	Foreign and Commonwealth Office
FPA	Foreign Policy Analysis
G7	Group of Seven
GAC	General Affairs Council
GATS	General Agreement on Trade in Services
GATT	General Agreement on Trade and Tariffs
GNP	Gross National Product
HR	High Representative
IFOR	Implementation Force
IGC	Intergovernmental Conference
IO	International Organization
IR	International Relations
ITO	International Trade Organization
JHA	Justice and Home Affairs
MAFF	Ministry of Agriculture, Fisheries and Food
MEP	Member of the European Parliament
MFN	Most Favoured Nation
NAFTA	North American Free Trade Agreement
NATO	North Atlantic Treaty Organization
NPT	Nuclear Non-Proliferation Treaty

OECD	Organization for Economic Cooperation and Development
OPEC	Organization of Petroleum Exporting Countries
OSCE	Organization for Security and Cooperation in Europe
PPEWU	Policy Planning and Early Warning Unit
PoCo	Political Committee [of National Political Directors]
QMV	Qualified Majority Vote/Voting
SBIRS	Space-Based Infra-Red System
SEA	Single European Act
SEM	Single European Market
SFOR	Stabilization Force
TEU	Treaty on European Union
TOA	Treaty of Amsterdam
TRIPS	Trade-related Aspects of Intellectual Property Rights
UK	United Kingdom
UKREP	United Kingdom Permanent Representation
UN	United Nations
UNHCR	United Nations High Commission for Refugees
UNPROFOR	United Nations Protection Force
UR	Uruguay Round
US	United States [of America]
USA	United States of America
USSR	Union of Soviet Socialist Republics
WEU	Western European Union
WTO	World Trade Organization

1

Europe and the World

One of the striking features of commentaries on world politics in the last decade of the twentieth century was the growing number of references both in the media and in academic texts to Europe as a major player of global significance. Indeed, it was increasingly difficult to find any area of international activity, whether area denotes a geographical region or an important issue, in which Europe was not thought to feature prominently in interactions with other major players such as the United States. The clear implication is that an understanding of what Europe does in relation to the rest of the world is one key focus that might help us to understand the workings of contemporary world politics as we begin the twenty-first century.

Many of the stories that hit the headlines in the 1990s saw Europe in conflict with other players and not infrequently the target appeared to be the United States. Transatlantic 'trade wars' over, for example, bananas, genetically modified maize or hormones in beef were overt signs of a fundamental change in transatlantic relations after the end of the cold war. While Europe and the United States had been strategic partners in the NATO alliance throughout the cold war period, the removal of the Soviet threat in 1991 focused attention less upon partnership and more upon the competitive aspects of their economic relationship. Behind the headlines lay two trade-related issues that triggered both conflict and a growing realization, particularly in the United States, that Europe was now a 'big hitter' in global politics and a serious competitor of equal stature to the USA.

The first was the Uruguay Round (UR) of the General Agreement on Trade and Tariffs (GATT), which lasted from 1986 to 1993. Not only were Europe and the United States the key players in this largest ever multilateral set of trade negotiations, but the attempts to negotiate a global reduction of trade barriers across an unprecedentedly wide range of goods and services also dramatically expanded the range of transatlantic issues in conflict. Only an 'eleventh hour' deal between European Trade Commissioner Leon Brittan and his opposite number

US Trade Representative Mickey Kantor enabled an agreement to be finalized in December 1993. From this perspective, the establishment thereafter of the World Trade Organization (WTO) in 1995 as a replacement for the GATT has only provided a permanent, institutionalized forum for further trade disputes across the Atlantic.

A second major 'trigger' of transatlantic trade conflict was the Burton-Helms and D'Amato legislation in the US, which sought to impose economic sanctions upon firms trading with Cuba, Iran or Libya. The problem with this legislation was its 'extra-territoriality' provisions that sought to use US law to punish not only US companies but also non-US companies, including those based in Europe. Not surprisingly, this caused anger in Europe and the European Union (EU) threatened to take the case to the WTO to have the measures declared illegal. The issue was finally resolved by negotiation and eventually the Clinton Administration backed down in the face of determined and united European opposition. But a succession of trade disputes through the 1990s provided a worsening climate of mistrust as Americans viewed with considerable suspicion European plans towards the end of that decade to develop a European defence force. While this force is to be 'separate but not separable' from NATO, the Americans became concerned that the Europeans were expanding their global role into the defence sphere possibly outside the transatlantic relationship. Suspicion and concern about European plans, it must be said, was also tempered by scepticism about the credibility of such a force. After all, one of the important reasons for Europeans seeking a more or less autonomous European defence capability was their woefully inadequate military performance in the series of conflicts in the former Yugoslavia. The Americans were not slow to point out that the Europeans had signally failed in the Balkans to demonstrate that they were now unified around their much vaunted Common Foreign and Security Policy (CFSP). A relatively high degree of European unity over external economic policy was clearly not being matched in the foreign and security policy fields.

But if we look below the headline stories, there have been plenty of other examples of Europe not only developing a global role but seeking to extend areas of cooperation rather than conflict with a growing network of other international actors. This global push began in the early 1990s with a huge programme of European Community (EC) aid and support to the former countries of the Soviet empire, a programme organized by the European Commission and supported by the United States and the other members of the Group of Seven (G7) most industrialized countries. This was followed after 1993 by an intensification of relations with countries outside Europe, in the Mediterranean, South America, the United States and Asia. The results in terms of new cooperation agreements, 'among others the New Transatlantic Agenda [1995, with the USA], the Barcelona Declaration [following an EU summit with all the Mediterranean states except Libya in 1995], the EU-Mercosur Agreement [an interregional agreement in 1995 with the Southern Cone Common Market – Mercado Comun del Sur – comprising Argentina, Brazil, Paraguay and Uruguay] and the Euro-Asian summit in Bangkok [in 1996] – have shown the European Union to be an international actor as never before' (Piening 1997: 199). (For the full range and substance of relationships between Europe and the rest of the world now covering virtually every state and international organization, the reader is recommended to consult the headings under CFSP and external relations on the official EU website at http://www.europa.eu.int.)

At the beginning of the twenty-first century, Europe is preoccupied with three major issues, all of which have the potential dramatically to expand Europe's global reach and global influence in the near future. The first of these, developing a more or less autonomous defence capability, we have already touched on and will be looking at in detail in a later chapter. The second issue is enlargement. At the beginning of 2000, no fewer than twelve European countries were at various stages of negotiating entry to the EU, with a thirteenth, Turkey, finally accepted as a candidate member. The end result of this process will be to expand the geographical boundaries of an ostensibly unified Europe to include almost every European state, which cannot but reinforce Europe's 'clout' on the world stage. The third issue is the completion of the Economic and Monetary Union (EMU) project across the EU. The planned adoption in 2002 of the Euro as the single European currency is likely to underline its significance as a major global currency in competition with the US dollar and the Japanese yen.

If we accept that Europe is a key player in contemporary world politics, the first problem that confronts anyone trying to understand Europe's global role is that it is not at all clear who or what 'Europe' is. Depending upon the issue, references are variously and confusingly made (as above) to the EU, or the EC, or the institutions of the EU such as the European Commission, or to one or more of the 15 member states of the EU. Sometimes commentators seem to assume that Europe is a single integrated entity in world politics, acting internationally, rather like the United States, as another global 'superpower' perhaps.

But, at other times, references suggest that the whole (Europe) is little more than the sum of its parts (the member states), which are rarely united on anything! Clearly, before we can begin to make sense of Europe in relation to its global role, we need a basic understanding of the process of cooperation and integration in Europe to discover why 'Europe' so often appears to be constituted by different combinations of players. In the process of recounting a brief history of European integration, we must also identify the key institutions within the EU that have a role in global policy.

European Cooperation and Integration: From Dunkirk to Amsterdam

For more than 50 years, the states (primarily although no longer exclusively) of Western Europe have been involved in a process of cooperation and integration with varying degrees of success. But one result of this can be flagged at the outset. The outcome has been to change fundamentally the nature of Europe and European politics and therefore the nature of relationships between Europe and the rest of the world. The process began almost immediately after the Second World War when fears of a resurgent Germany prompted the **Dunkirk Treaty** (1947) of mutual defence between Britain and France, a collective defence agreement that was extended to include the three Benelux countries (Belgium, the Netherlands and Luxembourg) the following year with the signing of the **Brussels Treaty** (1948). No sooner had this treaty been signed, however, when fears about German intentions were replaced by fears about the Soviet Union following the Berlin crisis, the first major East–West crisis of the cold war. Negotiations began with the United States and Canada to extend the Brussels Treaty into a transatlantic defence agreement. The result was the **North Atlantic Treaty** (1949) and the birth of NATO with 12 founding members.

Both the onset of the cold war and the establishment of NATO were crucial to the next stage of European cooperation, which represented a move beyond intergovernmental cooperation towards an integrated (Western) Europe. The cold war established a new enemy, the Soviet Union, and set up a competition between East and West in terms of political, economic and social systems. But it also concentrated minds in Western Europe on the internal as well as the external dangers of another world war. NATO provided a response to the external threat in the form of transatlantic security guarantees, which enabled European governments to focus on economic recovery and reconstruction aided by US financial assistance in the shape of Marshall Aid. The form that recovery took addressed both external East–West competition and unresolved internal security issues, the historically hostile relationship between France and Germany in particular. Supported by the United States for strategic East–West reasons, economic recovery began with limited economic integration.

First, a European Coal and Steel Community (ECSC) was established in 1952, the first of the European Communities, which put coal and steel production under the partial control of a supranational body called the High Authority. Six states signed the **Treaty of Paris** (1951) setting up the ECSC (France, Germany, Italy and the Benelux countries). The central objective was to pool the key war-making resources of France and Germany and to prevent the production of unauthorized German armaments. If ECSC had security as well as economic objectives, a more clearly focused strategic objective underlined the next, highly ambitious attempt to extend European integration. The immediate stimulus was pressure from the United States following its costly involvement in the Korean War (1950–53) to persuade European members of NATO to shoulder a greater burden of defence. Their plan involved German rearmament and the establishment of a European defence force under NATO command, to include sizeable West German contributions. Not surprisingly, this prospect so soon after the Second World War horrified the Europeans, and the French in particular. The French response was a counter-proposal for a European Defence Community (EDC) in which a fully integrated European army would be linked to a politically united Europe. The **European Defence Community Treaty** was signed in 1952 and ratified by five of the six ECSC members but, ironically, it was the failure of the proposal's author, the French Government, to ratify the Treaty that ended this federalist scheme in 1954. While, as detailed in Chapter 7, the defence problems that ensued were quickly resolved, the dramatic collapse of the proposed EDC ensured that European integration thereafter focused until the 1970s on the more limited objective of building upon ECSC to achieve further integration of European economies.

A way forward was provided by a 1952 plan proposed by J.W. Beyen, Foreign Minister of the Netherlands. His view was that the sectoral integration of coal and steel only was insufficient to promote economic recovery and development. He thus proposed a more wide-ranging customs union and a common market embracing the six members of ECSC. This would mean abolishing barriers to 'internal' trade and establishing a common 'external' tariff for incoming goods. These ideas together with Jean Monnet's plan for integrating atomic energy were discussed at an ECSC foreign ministers' meeting in Messina, Sicily in June 1955. A decision to explore both ideas led to a favourable report (from a committee chaired by Paul-Henri Spaak, the Belgian Foreign Minister), which was followed in turn by intensive intergovernmental bargaining and eventually the signing of the **Treaties of Rome** in March 1957. One Treaty signed by the six ECSC members established the European Economic Community (EEC) and the other established the European Atomic Energy Community (EURATOM).

The EEC treaty outlined the principles of a common market that when completed would enable the free movement of goods, persons, services and capital within the market. Significantly, it also established in treaty form the aspiration 'to lay the foundations of an ever closer union among the peoples of Europe'. Some elements of the common market were relatively easy to put in place. A customs union, for example, was established ahead of schedule (in July 1968). But other elements were much more politically sensitive. The setting up of a Common Agricultural Policy (CAP) was particularly controversial and led to major conflicts between member states and the European Commission. A dispute between the French President Charles de Gaulle and the Commission over the funding of CAP produced a major crisis in the process of European integration. In July 1965, to avoid the possibility of France being outvoted, de Gaulle withdrew the French representatives from the Council of Ministers and the Committee of Permanent Representatives, thus creating the so-called 'Empty Chair Crisis'. This was resolved in January 1996 with agreement on the 'Luxembourg Compromise'. This involved acceptance of the principle of majority voting in the Council but also the agreement that 'when very important issues are at stake, discussions must be continued until unanimous agreement is reached'. But behind this immediate issue lay the crucial question of whether the EEC would be governed along intergovernmental lines (with member governments making the important decisions) or along supranational lines (with governments sharing sovereignty with transnational institutions whose laws and policies are binding upon those governments).

A second problematic issue for the integration process in the 1960s was enlargement following the 1961 applications to join the EEC from Britain, Denmark, Ireland and, in 1962, Norway. The general problem here was the question of 'widening' versus 'deepening'. In simple terms, could the Community expand its membership ('widening') *and* take further steps to extend the process of integration ('deepening'), or did the one process preclude the other? The focus of this problem in the 1960s was the British application and again it featured the French President as a key player. As a convinced intergovernmentalist, de Gaulle was less concerned that British membership might hold back the process of integration, but he did take the view that the very close British links with the United States would undermine the prospective political unity of Europe. On this basis, he vetoed the British application on two occasions, in 1963 and 1967. It was not until the resignation of de Gaulle in 1969 that the enlargement problem could be resolved. At the instigation of de Gaulle's successor Georges Pompidou, a special summit of member states took place at The Hague in December 1969 that explicitly linked widening to deepening by agreeing in principle to enlargement but also agreeing to extend Community cooperation into new areas. Two major reports were endorsed the following year.

The first set up a procedure called European Political Cooperation (EPC) for coordinating the foreign policies of member states (see Chapter 4). As this new process was explicitly established on intergovernmentalist lines, it extended European cooperation into a significant new area of activity rather than extending Community control (or 'competence' as it is called in 'Euro-jargon'). The second report, on the the other hand, envisaged a dramatic deepening of European integration as it outlined a plan for EMU. This apparent recovery of momentum after the problems of the 1960s was underlined by an ambitious political commitment made at the Paris summit in October 1972 (with Britain, Denmark and Ireland signed up to join the EEC the following year). The member states declared their intention 'before the end of the present decade to transform the whole complex of their relations into a European Union'. But, as Dinan notes, 'as the decade progressed – and the EC became bogged down in high inflation rates, soaring unemployment, and low economic growth, prospects for European union grew more and more remote' (Dinan 1998: 184). The reaction to the Middle East War in October 1973 and the ensuing oil embargo and price rises typified the problem. With their economies in chaos, member states reacted individually rather than jointly despite facing common problems. What became known as 'eurosclerosis', economic stagnation and little or no progress on European integration, lasted until the early 1980s.

A more sustained recovery of momentum in the 1980s had three interacting elements that propelled the Community forward. First, a second stage of enlargement to the South of the continent was success-fully negotiated with Greece joining the EEC in 1981 and Spain and Portugal thereafter in 1986. Second, the holding of the first direct elections in 1979 led to a more assertive European Parliament (EP). A revised constitution for the Community, *The Draft Treaty Establishing the European Union*, was passed by the EP in February 1984. Third, and most significantly, moves towards a genuinely integrated Single European Market (SEM) were set in train. The important stimulus here was the launch of the European Monetary System (EMS) in 1979. Despite several exchange rate crises and the loss of members from the system, EMS did effectively stabilize the exchange rates of member states over time and, equally important, it provided the confidence to reactivate the idea of economic and monetary union beginning with a sustained SEM programme. These moves were also stimulated by a sense of failure to move beyond a customs union to a genuinely free flow of goods, persons, services and capital across the EEC and also by a growing concern that, in the absence of further integration, European economies were becoming less and less competitive with the United States and Japan.

Once the long running crisis over Britain's contributions to the Community budget had been resolved at the Fontainebleau summit in 1984, the way was open to revise the Rome Treaty provisions to facilitate a single market. This was necessary because it was apparent that the removal of all barriers was unlikely to occur without breaching the unanimity rule and introducing the principle of majority voting (staunchly resisted by de Gaulle in the 1960s). However, not all member states were prepared to agree to this fundamental change in decision-making. Ironically, it took an unprecedented vote at the Milan European Council in June 1985 (with Britain, Denmark and Greece outvoted) to set up an Intergovernmental Conference (IGC) to revise the Treaty of Rome. This resulted in the **Single European Act** (signed in February 1986 and ratified in July 1987), which set a target date of December 1992 for completion of the SEM programme and established that most of the decisions to implement the single market would be taken by majority voting in the Council. With the SEM on track, the European Commission President Jacques Delors strongly supported by German Chancellor Kohl and French President Mitterrand pushed for a relaunch of EMU. The ensuing Delors Report which proposed a three-stage plan to achieve EMU – promoting economic convergence, establishing a European Central

Bank, and finally creating a single currency – was accepted by the European Council at its June 1989 meeting in Madrid.

It was at this point that the history of European integration intersected with the history of the cold war. The revolutions in Eastern Europe that initiated the end of the cold war and opened up the possibility of German reunification suddenly impacted on the whole process of integration. In general terms, these changes had a positive impact and served to extend the boundaries of a European union. Not only was the planned economic and monetary union boosted by Kohl's wish for his partners to accept German reunification, but their wish in turn to contain a reunified Germany within a new, unified Europe added political union to the immediate agenda. During 1990, member states decided to hold two parallel IGCs, one on EMU and the other on European Political Union (EPU), both of which reported to the Maastricht summit in December 1991. While much progress was made on EMU, 1999 being set as the definitive date for establishing a single currency (the Third Stage of the Delors Plan), much less progress was made on EPU. The **Treaty on European Union** (1991) was signed at Maastricht and established a Union, but the substance of that treaty bore all the hallmarks of a compromise between the intergovernmentalists and the integrationists.

Attempts by the Dutch presidency in the second half of 1991 to bring all aspects of European policy into a unitary union structure failed because of the determination of other members to ensure that foreign policy, defence and home affairs would continue to be handled on an intergovernmental basis and therefore outside Community competence. What was agreed in the Treaty on European Union (TEU) was a Union based – deploying a rather loose Greek temple analogy – on three 'pillars'. Pillar 1, by far the most powerful pillar, contains the three established Communities now referred to as the European Community (EC). It deals by Community methods of decision-making (detailed in the next section) with all the major internal areas of policy together with external areas falling within Community competence, such as trade and cooperation agreements with third parties. In contrast, the issue areas contained within Pillars 2 and 3 are decided by intergovernmental agreement. Pillar 2 contains a Common Foreign and Security Policy (CFSP), a determined attempt to build upon and improve the procedures for coordinating the foreign and security policies of member states (see Chapter 6). Pillar 3 deals with cooperation in areas related to justice and home affairs (JHA).

If, with the formal establishment of the EU in 1993, it looked like the Europeans had finally fulfilled long-held aspirations for European integration, any celebrations were short lived. The process of integration thereafter again went through one of its 'down' periods marked by frustration and setbacks rather than achievement. Significant achievements there undoubtedly were. The first enlargement of the new Union (the fourth round overall) was successfully negotiated, with Austria, Finland and Sweden converting 'the Twelve' into 'the Fifteen' in 1995. The complex process of admitting a potential host of new members from Central and Eastern Europe was started by the December 1997 decision to include the Czech Republic, Poland, Hungary and Slovenia in the first phase of negotiations. The single market was largely completed on schedule by 1993. The Third Stage of the Delors EMU plan was also completed broadly on schedule at the beginning of 1999 with the adoption (initially in 11 member states) of the new Euro currency in parallel with other national currencies, with a single currency projected to start in 2002.

But problems followed immediately after the signing of the TEU in 1991. The rejection of the treaty in a referendum in Denmark created a ratification crisis over the next 18 months that, although resolved in the short term by a process of agreed 'opt-outs' for certain members (the TEU was eventually ratified in November 1993), in the longer term cast serious doubts upon the credibility and the legitimacy of the Union and certainly sapped the confidence needed to reform the structures and processes hastily agreed at Maastricht. Nevertheless, a review IGC was held in 1996–97, if only because it was mandated by TEU. But the **Amsterdam Treaty** (1997) that emerged from this IGC was a disappointment largely because it retained the inadequate 'pillar' structure and failed to make any radical changes. The ratification of Amsterdam in 1999 was followed by the decision to set up yet another IGC in 2000 to focus more narrowly on agreeing the institutional changes that will be needed following enlargement to 25 or more members. As the new millennium began, many observers, while accepting that much had been achieved in the process of European cooperation and integration over a relatively short historical period, were looking for signs of a new momentum to regenerate the process.

Key EU Institutions Outlined

Our brief history of European cooperation and integration has necessarily touched on the role played by European states in that process but it has also made references to the various EU institutions that have played and continue to play a key role in structuring and managing relationships between Europe and the rest of the world. It might be useful, particularly for those readers who are unfamiliar with these institutions, to identify them and their functions more explicitly here. These 'pen portraits' will also serve as an introduction to more focused references to them in a foreign policy context in the main body of the text.

The European Council

We start with the institution that, although not legally an institution of the EC, may be regarded as the pinnacle of the EU system. The European Council consists of regular meetings (often referred to as summit meetings) of heads of government and/or heads of state of the 15 member states together with the President of the European Commission. While informal summits were held from the early 1960s, the Council idea emerged at the suggestion of the French President Giscard d'Estaing in 1974 and the first formal European Council was held in Dublin in March 1975. It was officially recognized as a Community body by the 1986 Single European Act (SEA), which noted that it should meet at least twice a year either in the country holding the presidency of the Council or in Brussels. Since 1986 it has been normal for foreign ministers of member states also to attend.

The role of the European Council is twofold. First, it provides overall political direction to the EU. Second, it serves as a 'clearing house' to resolve problems that have proved to be intractable at Council of Ministers level. Decisions are usually taken by consensus and are embodied in statements of the presidency, referred to as 'Conclusions of the Presidency'. More than any other institution perhaps, as Dinan suggests, the European Council has shaped the European integration process since the 1970s. It has done this in three related ways. First, it has served as a 'constitutional architect', making major decisions on, for example, enlargement and economic and monetary union, which have 'significantly enlarged the scope and magnitude of joint activities'. Second, it has set the agenda of the integration process by adopting general guidelines on a widening range of issues. Finally, it has made important decisions often in summit-style 'package deals' across a range of issues. While these decisions have no status in Community law they have nevertheless provided a framework for Community legislation (Dinan 1998: 188–9).

The Council of Ministers (Council of the European Union)

Despite the important decision-making role played by the European Council with respect to particularly intractable issues and decisions that have 'constitutional' implications, the Council of Ministers (which should not be confused with the European Council) is the principal decision-making body in the EU. The members of the Council are government ministers of member states who represent the views of their governments. Actually there is no single 'Council' as such, rather the 'Council' meets in 20 or more different Councils depending upon the subject matter being discussed. The 15 Economic and Finance ministers meet in the Economic and Finance Council (popularly known as Ecofin), the 15 agriculture ministers meet in the Council of Agriculture Ministers, the foreign ministers in the Council of Foreign Ministers, and so on. The latter is often referred to as the General Affairs Council (GAC) to indicate its wider ranging brief to look at general policy questions as well as external relations, and also to indicate its seniority, although in recent years, with the EU focusing more and more on economic and monetary union, Ecofin has been challenging GAC's position of seniority.

The Council collectively has extensive legislative and executive powers. It has the power to take legally binding decisions and to make other decisions that are not legally binding. Legislative decisions in the Council are taken either unanimously or, since the 1986 SEA, by qualified majority voting (QMV) on some issues. QMV works by each member state being allocated a numerical weighting (Germany has ten votes, Luxembourg only two, for example) totalling 87 votes in all. For a proposal to be adopted, a 'qualified majority' normally means 62 votes must be cast in favour (with 26 votes constituting a 'blocking minority'). Currently, with further enlargement in prospect, QMV weightings are being reviewed together with the number of commissioners appointed by each member state. In some areas, under the power of 'co-decision', these legislative powers are shared with the EP. The Council also shares with the EP the authority to approve and adopt the Community budget. Finally, the Council is responsible for authorizing, overseeing and concluding negotiations and agreements with non-member governments and international organizations. While the Council is the most powerful of all the Community institutions, many of its decisions are structured by decisions taken at the lower level of COREPER and various working groups.

The presidency

On a rotating six-monthly basis, each member state acts as president of the Council, which means that country is responsible for organizing all the business of the Council of Ministers and the European Council: chairing nearly 200 meetings; brokering deals; launching strategic policy initiatives; acting as the spokesperson of the EU; representing the EU internationally; and managing activities in Pillars 2 (CFSP) and 3 (JHA). Some elements of the external role of the presidency, particularly representing the EU, will in future be shared with the new 'High Representative' (see Chapter 8).

The Committee of Permanent Representatives (COREPER, Comité des Représentants Permanents)

Preliminary negotiations preceding Council meetings are undertaken by COREPER. Under the terms of the TEU, COREPER is given the responsibility for preparing issues across all three pillars, as part of an attempt to ensure more consistency and coherence in decision-making. There are in fact two COREPERs. COREPER II consists of permanent representatives, the ambassadors of the member states who deal largely with external issues, and COREPER I, which is constituted by the deputy ambassadors and tends to have a more 'domestic' orientation. But they both operate similarly by identifying points of agreement ('A points') and trying to resolve points of disagreement. If points cannot be resolved, they go for resolution to the relevant Council meeting (as 'B points'). This sifting process is so successful that, in Dinan's estimation, possibly 80 per cent or more of EU decisions are taken at the level of COREPER or below (Dinan 1998: 69). 'Below' is a reference to the large number of committees and working groups (numbering approximately 250) that prepare the ground before issues are taken to the relevant COREPER meeting. These groups consist of middle-ranking civil servants from the national Brussels-based representation, domestic ministries and Commission officials.

The Council Secretariat

Administrative support for the presidency, the Councils, COREPER and working groups is provided by the General Secretariat, also located in Brussels. Consisting of approximately 2,300 officials, who are nationals of the 15 member states, the Secretariat also provides technical (including legal) expertise and an 'institutional memory'. It is divided into ten Directorate-Generals, with Directorate-General E covering external economic relations and CFSP. The Secretariat is headed by a Secretary-General and a Deputy Secretary-General, both of whom are appointed by the Council of Ministers.

The Political Committee (PoCo)

The Political Committee (PoCo) emerged from the process of EPC in the 1970s. It is composed of senior officials in the foreign ministries of member states, known as the Political Directors. Their role is to prepare the meetings of foreign ministers to discuss EPC and more recently CFSP issues. As such they are supported by a range of separate working groups, a dedicated communications system between foreign ministries (known as the COREU – *Correspondants Européens* network), with day-to-day liaison provided by more junior officials, known as the Political Correspondents. Since TEU, again in the interests of trying to ensure consistency across pillars and issues, this system has been brought to a greater or lesser extent into a common institutional structure (see Chapter 5).

The European Commission (Commission of the European Communities)

The Commission is perhaps the most controversial of all the EU institutions but it is very clearly at the centre of the EU policy process. It consists of the 'college of Commissioners' and, given the scope of its functions and responsibilities, a surprisingly small civil service based mainly in Brussels. The commission has approximately 21,000 employees of whom 17,000 work in Brussels. They are organized into 24 departments, known as Directorate-Generals (DGs) and a smaller number of other units. Each DG covers a range of policy areas. The 20 commissioners who are responsible for Commission activity across the different policy areas are, in Dinan's comprehensive formulation, 'nominated by the member states, appointed by the European Council, approved by the European Parliament and sworn in by the European Court of Justice' (Dinan 1998: 59). Each commissioner serves a five-year term.

Currently, the larger member states nominate two commissioners and the smaller members, one. One of the implications of the proposed enlargement of the Union, however, is that the continuation of this procedure will quickly lead to an unwieldy college where the established principle of collective responsibility will be difficult to maintain and, more importantly perhaps, there will not be enough significant portfolios to fill. It has been agreed (in a legally binding portfolio on enlargement attached to the Treaty of Amsterdam) that, in return for more weighted votes in the Council, the larger states will give up 'their' second commissioner. In theory, all commissioners are equal, but an informal hierarchy has emerged over time. In particular, the importance of the presidency of the Commission has grown. This has now been recognized in legal terms. The Treaty of Amsterdam states explicitly that 'the Commission shall work under the political direction of its President' (Art. 163). The president is selected by EU governments and has to be approved by the EP.

The Commission has a unique combination of administrative, executive, legislative and judicial roles in the EU policy process. First, it initiates legislation. The old phrase, 'the Commission proposes and the Council disposes' still has some accuracy but the EU law-making process has become rather more complex. The Commission still 'proposes' legislation, certainly with respect to Pillar 1 activities but, depending upon the issue, either the Council, or the Council and the EP jointly under co-decision procedures, 'disposes'. As we shall see in more detail in later chapters, the Commission has acquired a shared right to initiate policy (rather than legislation) with respect to CFSP. Second, the Commission executes or implements legislation in Pillar 1 areas of competence. To effect this, it issues some 5,000 Directives, Regulations and Decisions each year. But even in Pillar 1 areas of activity, the Commission does not have a free hand. Legislation is implemented through three types of committee: advisory, management and regulatory. These are chaired by the Commission but they are made up of civil servants from member states.

Third, the Commission has shared authority with respect to the Community budget. In particular, it prepares a draft budget each year that is sent to the Council and the EP for approval. It also has wide-ranging powers with respect to the administration of expenditure. For example, it administers huge amounts of money associated with the CAP, and also structural funds like the European Social Fund and external economic assistance in its various forms. Fourth, the Commission, in a very practical day-to-day sense, conducts external relations in the form of negotiating trade, aid and association agreements with third parties on behalf of the Union. In order to fulfil this role, the Commission has developed a very extensive network of overseas missions (in 124 countries). Finally, in at least a quasi-judicial role, the Commission acts as 'guardian of the treaties'. It has the right to bring member states and businesses to the European Court of Justice (ECJ) for alleged non-fulfilment of treaty obligations, but, it must be said, most disputes are resolved at an earlier stage.

The European Parliament

The EP is not a key player in external relations, but its role and significance is growing. The EP has the primary responsibility for exercising democratic scrutiny and control over EU decision-making. Since 1979, it has been directly elected and now comprises 625 members (MEPs) from the 15 member countries elected for five years. The proceedings of the EP are complicated by language, location and party organizational problems. It has no fewer than the 11 official EU languages in operation and three working locations. Its official 'seat' is in Strasbourg, France but MEPs spend on average only one week each month there in plenary session. Most of the committee meetings and an increasing number of plenary sessions are held in Brussels. Additionally, some two-thirds of EP staff are located in Luxembourg. The wide range of existing political parties across member states (more than 100) has also necessitated some creative coalition-building in the EP and most members are located within one of eight political groups that structure the work of the Parliament. There are currently 17 standing committees, including a Committee on Foreign Affairs, Human Rights, Common Security and Defence Policy.

The powers of the EP, some of which we have touched upon in earlier sections, are located within the areas of legislation, the budget, external agreements, and appointments. While the EP has no power to initiate, it has to be consulted on nearly all Community legislation and it is increasingly involved in legislative planning. But, as Dinan notes, it is the co-decision procedure adopted by the TEU (Art. 189b) that has given the EP most power to influence the law-making process across a widening range of issue areas. As one of the two arms of the EU budgetary authority (together with the Council) the EP also has considerable powers over the budgetary process, although these powers relate to expenditure rather than income/revenue. Within certain limits, the EP can increase or decrease expenditure, it can redistribute spending and, most significantly, it can reject the EU budget (Dinan 1998: 213).

Of particular interest in an external relations context is the requirement that the EP now has to give its assent to the enlargement of the EU (first used with respect to the accession of Sweden, Austria and Finland in 1995) as well as to association agreements with third parties. With respect to other international agreements such as trade agreements, however, the EP has no right of formal assent or even consultation, although its rights to information have gradually been extended. Finally, a significant extension of EP powers has taken place with respect to a growing range of EU appointments. The EP must now approve the choice of Commission president and it appoints individual commissioners on a vote of confidence. It is also consulted on appointments to a range of other EU institutions such as the European Central Bank and the Court of Auditors. To exercise these powers, the EP has developed confirmation hearings on nominees, not unlike those held by the US Congress. In more general terms, the EP also has other important powers of scrutiny and control, such as questioning other policy-makers in parliamentary committees, drawing up reports, holding public hearings and, on occasion, taking issues to the ECJ. Ultimately, and most dramatically perhaps, the EP has the power to dismiss the Commission as a whole by adopting a motion of censure. While no such motion has been adopted to date, in March 1999, following a report on the management of the Commission by a committee of independent experts mandated by the Parliament, the Commission under President Jacques Santer opted to resign en masse rather than face a formal censure motion.

The European Court of Justice

The ECJ located in Luxembourg is the court of, and the highest legal authority within, the EU. (It should not be confused with the European Court of Human Rights, an institution of the Council of Europe based in Strasbourg and concerned with cases brought under the European Convention on Human Rights.) The ECJ adjudicates on disputes arising from the interpretation or the application of the various European treaties or with legislation based upon them. It is composed of one judge from each member state who are selected by national governments to serve a six-year renewable term. The ECJ has three main functions. It helps to ensure that EU institutions do not exceed their authority. It helps to resolve disputes between EU institutions and member states and finally, it helps to ensure national compliance with EC laws (Dinan 1998: 192).

Like the EP, the ECJ is not a key player in external relations, although its role too is growing in certain areas particularly where competence is unclear. But it has no direct authority with respect to either Pillar 2 or Pillar 3 activities. In the early years of the EEC, indeed, the ECJ was not used extensively at all. Over time, however, ECJ decisions have developed into an important body of case law which has increasingly impacted upon the policy process as a whole. One example illustrates the general significance of case law. The important 1964 *Costa* v. *ENEL* (an Italian electricity company) decision helped to establish the doctrine of the supremacy of EC law, granting EC law primacy over the national law of member states when the two are in conflict. A more recent ruling shows that case law can also directly influence external policy-making. In November 1994, following the GATT Uruguay agreement, the ECJ ruled that only certain aspects of external trade in services and intellectual property come within exclusive Community competence. This ruling has effectively changed the balance of control of trade between the Commission and member states with implications that have still not been resolved (see Bretherton and Vogler 1999: 56–7).

What is 'Europe'?

Having reviewed the history of European integration and identified the key EU institutions associated with that process, we may still be unclear about who or what 'Europe' is – indeed the reader may initially

be more confused! Hence it is important to say a little more here about
the nature of 'Europe' as an international player or actor, both to seek
further clarification and to give us some clues about how we might
analyse its global role. We should also be aware that the 'what is
Europe?' question is not only a tantalizing problem for observers, it is
also a very practical problem for other international actors and, in
particular, for their policy-makers who want to negotiate with 'Europe'.
It was a problem that famously vexed US National Security Adviser
Henry Kissinger nearly 30 years ago when he sought to negotiate with
the 'Europeans' over the complex set of issues that emerged from what
he called the 'Year of Europe' initiative. Unfortunately for him, West
European governments failed to designate a single authoritative
decision-maker with whom he could consult and negotiate (see Allen
1998: 41). Just how serious this problem continues to be was brought
home to this author when he was invited in 1996 to lecture to the
Department of Foreign Affairs (DFA) in South Africa on 'Decision-
Making in the European Union' at a time when the DFA and other
departments in the South African Government had been engaged for
some time in trying to negotiate a complex trade deal with the EU. The
South Africans, like Kissinger before them, were still not entirely clear
exactly whom they should be talking to!

But the bad news is that there are no easy answers to the 'what is
Europe?' question or even to the apparently more focused and manage-
able question, 'what is the European Union?' And surprisingly perhaps
this question is no longer discussed extensively in the academic literature. In the 1960s and 70s, scholars did try to foresee the end result of
the European integration process, with the then EC treated variously as
a would-be supranational European state, a confederation of states or an
emerging federal union – the exact form depending upon the theoretical
perspective of the writer. But by the 1990s, in part because of the diffi-
culty of categorizing the EU, scholars had become less concerned with
characterizing the 'nature of the beast' than with analysing what it does
and how it does it (Caporaso 1996: 30). Nevertheless, there are two
familiar types of international actor, the state and the international
organization, with which the EU might fruitfully be compared.

The European Union as a state

Is the European Union a state that can be analysed in essentially the
same way that we might analyse the foreign policy behaviour of, say,

the USA or China? The notion that the EEC and later the EU might become a recognizable state with some sort of supranational structure of government has certainly been an aspiration of integrationists at least since Winston Churchill's famous call in 1946 for the creation of a 'United States of Europe'. More recently, the identification at Maastricht of a *Common* Foreign and Security Policy clearly denotes the collective aspiration of the EU to play a unified foreign and security policy role in world politics. As an expectation, the EU as would-be integrated state has informed at last one branch of integration theory, the neofunctionalists, who believed that the process of integration, if accompanied by sufficient political will, would eventually produce a new European political community (see, for example, Haas 1958). This expectation has also informed the perceptions of political leaders, for some a wholly negative prospect. The British Prime Minister Margaret Thatcher, for example, was convinced that what she liked to call the 'Brussels Empire' was a European 'superstate' in the making, which if not halted would destroy the sovereign independence of member states.

To compare the EU with a state, we need some idea of what constitutes a state. The conventional notion of a state encompasses the idea of an exclusive territorial entity, with a centralized hierarchical structure of authoritative decision-making (a government in other words), acting over a wide range of issues and, not least, enjoying external and internal sovereignty. Using these criteria of statehood, there are a couple of senses in which the EU is analogous to a state. But even here we must distinguish between the EU and the EC. The member states that signed up to the TEU in 1991 were not prepared to give the new Union legal status that would enable it to act legally on the world stage as a separate entity. This reflected continuing disputes about the degree to which member states were prepared to cede their sovereign rights. However, since 1957, Community law has given the EC a legal personality to act in a state-like way in certain contexts and with reference to certain issues. Where a common policy applies, as for example in negotiating an international fisheries agreement, the EC acts on behalf of the member states. In the WTO, to cite another illustration, the EC now sits alongside member states as a party in its own right. The EC/EU is also a territorial entity in the sense that it has established stringent rules that apply in relation to the flow of goods and peoples into 'its' territory (see Bretherton and Vogler 1999: 16–18, 31).

The extent to which the EC/EU has acquired state-like powers over time has led at least one analyst to argue that the USA's federal system of government has some relevance in terms of characterizing the nature of the EU. William Wallace argues that the EU system of government is analogous to the early union of (US) states – known as the 'Philadelphia system' – the loose federal structure under which the USA was governed between 1787 and 1860 (Wallace 1996: 445). But, even though the location of sovereignty remains disputed, the EU clearly lacks statehood in terms of having a centralized, hierarchical political structure independent of member states (a government in other words) that has exclusive control over territory and which can act authoritatively over a wide range of issues (Caporaso 1996: 33). So we can conclude that the EU is not like a conventional state even if it can act in limited state-like ways.

The European Union as an international organization

Is the EU alternatively an international organization (IO) that might more appropriately be analysed in much the same way that we might analyse the United Nations (UN) or NATO? The answer in legal terms is quite clear. In international law, the EC (as the legal actor) is formally an international organization that, like the UN, has the right to exercise certain agreed competencies, although not the full range that a state might exercise. The issue here is not whether the EU qualifies as an IO but whether it is overqualified. Nugent, for example, argues that:

> the EU is more than merely another international organization in which countries cooperate with each other on a voluntary basis for reasons of mutual benefit. Rather it is an organization in which states have voluntarily surrendered their right, across a broad range of important sectors, to be independent in the determination and application of public policy. (Nugent 1994: 207)

If the EU is an IO, he goes on to argue, it is unique in three ways. First, it has a much more developed and complex institutional structure that goes far beyond the permanent secretariats and attached delegations of other international organizations. Second, it has a far wider range of policy responsibilities than other IOs and finally:

> the EU has progressed far beyond the essentially intergovernmental nature of most international organizations and has incorporated many supranational characteristics into its structure and operation. (Nugent 1994: 430–1)

The EU as a unique international actor

If neither the conventional state nor the international organization
'models' seem adequate for different reasons to categorize the EU as
an international actor, some scholars have explored other analogies
that might provide guidance for the analyst but without, it must be
said, much more success in terms of finding an exact 'fit'. Nevertheless, we must note some of the useful insights about the nature of the
EU that have emerged from these efforts. Two related approaches in
particular have made a significant contribution to our understanding.
First, policy analysts have applied the idea of the 'policy network' to
characterize EU policy-making. Instead of the centralized, hierarchical
system of government familiar from conventional states, this approach
focuses on decentralized, non-hierarchical networks of different types
of actors who try collectively to solve common problems in different
issue areas (see Risse-Kappen 1996). Two important insights emerge
from this approach. First, it highlights the mix of actors – member
governments, EU institutions, non-governmental interest groups of
various kinds – that 'cluster' around different issue areas. Second, it
highlights the different types of policy-making processes that operate
in different issue areas. These include *intergovernmental* bargaining
(between member states), but also *transnational* (involving cross-
boundary, non-state actors like the European Commission), *transgovernmental* (involving subsets of different member governments like the
15 foreign ministries), *subnational* (involving, for example, interest
groups within member states) and, not least, *supranational* bargaining
(where binding decisions made by Community institutions such as the
ECJ are made).

   Characterizing the overall impact of different policy networks
operating across the EU has led international relations (IR) scholars to
suggest that the EU is analogous to an international regime, not unlike
regimes that have been identified in a variety of other international
policy arenas such as the environment or arms control (see, for
example, Rittberger 1993). A 'regime' in this context may be defined
as 'sets of implicit or explicit agreed-upon principles, norms, rules,
procedures and programmes that govern the interactions of actors in
specific issue areas' (Soetendorp 1999: 11). While this is a useful and
inventive way of characterizing particular structures and processes of
international decision-making that cannot be described in inter-state
or inter-organizational terms, again the point is made that the extent
of policy coordination in the EU, in particular, 'pooling decision-

making through arrangements for qualified majority voting and delegating authority over representation, formal agenda-setting and enforcement to semi-autonomous institutions', makes the EU qualitatively different from most if not all other international regimes (Moravcsik 1993: 514).

So we appear to be left with the rather intriguing idea that the EU, although exhibiting behaviour that is similar to other types of international actor, is not directly analogous to any one of them and may therefore be considered a unique type. With respect to different issues indeed, Europe, the EU or the EC may simply appear to be different entities. Piening illustrates this by looking at different areas of external relations. With respect to CFSP, this emerges very much as inter-state behaviour with essentially the member states acting jointly. Trade policy, on the other hand, is made by the EC acting collectively, with member states 'left with little more power than individual states in the Federal Republic of Germany, say, or the United States'. Development policy presents a different picture again; 'here the EU as entity acts in some ways like a distinct, sixteenth member, working with but alongside its member states' (Piening 1997: 193). But we still face the problem that, in terms of its global impact, the EU as international actor is clearly more than the sum of its parts and, as we illustrated at the beginning of this chapter, it is a key player in many areas of contemporary world politics. As such, we must try to make sense of its external behaviour. The question is, given that the EU is a unique type of actor, what approach should we take? We now turn to identify the approach taken in this book and to set out the ways in which the approach here is applied and developed in the chapters that follow.

The Approach and the Structure of the Book

Two related points can be underlined from the last section. The EU is unique although it has elements within it that are familiar from the behaviour of other international actors. Given the absence of a direct analogue, however, it follows that there are no obviously appropriate ways of analysing its international behaviour. Indeed, given the 'nature of the beast', a variety of different approaches can be justified and should be welcomed. This book has three objectives. First, it tries to understand Europe's relations with the rest of the world as illustrative of a relatively new area of foreign policy activity in contemporary world politics. This activity is labelled 'European foreign policy'

(EFP). The second related objective is to see whether, from this perspective, a common European foreign policy has emerged or is in the process of emerging. What is the nature and the status of European foreign policy at the beginning of the twenty-first century? The third objective is to test out the usefulness of applying a foreign policy analysis approach to the analysis of European foreign policy.

The approach taken here is to try to improve our understanding of European foreign policy by applying an analytical framework derived from the established sub-field of IR well known in Europe as Foreign Policy Analysis (FPA), better known perhaps in the United States as Comparative Foreign Policy (CFP). The analysis builds upon the idea of Europe as a unique but also non-unitary international actor. The working assumption here is that neither 'Europe' nor more narrowly the EU is a single actor but rather it is constituted for foreign policy purposes by three different types of policy, labelled 'Community foreign policy', 'Union foreign policy' and 'National (member state) foreign policy'. European foreign policy as a whole is conceived as an interacting foreign policy 'system' but these three types of policy are regarded as the 'sub-systems' that constitute and possibly dominate it. The core chapters of the book are devoted to applying an FPA framework to these three sub-systems of EFP, identifying differences between them but also charting over time the growing overlaps between these policy systems with a view to drawing conclusions about the current nature and status of European foreign policy as a whole.

Chapter 2 is primarily concerned to establish the approach and to spell out the FPA framework that is to be applied in turn to each type of European foreign policy. But the chapter begins with a brief critical review of two other major approaches to understanding Europe's global role. This provides an analytical context for a discussion of the potential utility of an FPA approach. However, it is recognized that to make sense of European foreign policy, FPA itself needs to be adapted from its traditional state-centred focus and there is some discussion about how this might be achieved. We are clearly dealing with a new type of foreign policy actor here that is not a state, certainly not a state of the conventional kind. Chapters 3 through 6 systematically apply a common analytical framework to each sub-system of European foreign policy in turn. Separate chapters cover Community foreign policy, Union foreign policy (there are two chapters on the related European Political Cooperation and the CFSP) followed by a chapter on British foreign policy which is used to test the extent to which the foreign policies of members states have been 'Europeanized'. Each chapter has the same structure and the analysis is framed by key elements of the framework: specifically, the context in which policy is made; the actors involved and the processes that characterize policy-making; the 'instruments' used to achieve policy objectives, and the action/outcomes that ensue from the policy process. Each chapter concludes with a detailed case study of a particular type of European foreign policy in action.

The remaining three chapters offer different sorts of reflection on the core chapters and, where necessary, update the analysis. Chapter 7 raises important questions about the comprehensiveness of our definition of European foreign policy. In particular, it deals with the frequently made argument that a European foreign policy worthy of the name must include a defence as well as a security dimension. While elements of what Christopher Hill has called 'the missing link' (Hill 1992: 136) can be contained within our characterization of European foreign policy – in both Union foreign policy (CFSP) and within national foreign policy sub-systems – there are grounds for arguing that the security/defence dimension has the potential at least to be regarded as a sub-system of European foreign policy in its own right. This chapter reviews conceptual issues surrounding the expanding notion of security, the debates about the relationship between a defence capability and the capacity to act, and reviews the substantive progress made to date towards a common defence policy in Europe.

What conclusions can be drawn from this study? Two different sets of conclusions, one substantive the other more theoretical, are located within the last two chapters of this book. While the main objective here is to improve our understanding of European foreign policy by applying a common framework to different forms of EFP, an FPA approach should also help to establish the extent to which the different forms of EFP have become interwoven. This will enable us to draw some conclusions about whether a common foreign policy currently exists at the European level and the prospects of such in the future. Chapter 8 brings the analysis up to the beginning of the twenty-first century by reviewing developments since Maastricht and incorporating the impact of the 1997 Amsterdam Treaty. Theoretical rather than substantive conclusions are located in Chapter 9, which reflects upon the theoretical implications of this study. How effective has an FPA approach been in unravelling the intricacies of European foreign policy? What are its strengths and weaknesses? Equally important from the perspective of the foreign policy analyst, what have we learned about FPA by adapting a traditional methodology to capture the dynamics of the relatively new phenomenon of European foreign policy? If applying FPA to European foreign policy demonstrates the continuing vitality of this sub-field of IR, what does the European application reveal about the overall status of this approach, continuing weaknesses as well as strengths. More ambitiously, what are the implications of this study for FPA studies in the future?

2

Making Sense of Europe's Global Role[1]

Chapter 1 highlighted the significance of Europe as a global player in contemporary world politics and the need to try to make sense of Europe's global role, even if we have learned that the problems start with identifying precisely who or what 'Europe' is! It also provided a useful historical context for understanding European integration and introduced the important institutions of the European Union. The purpose of this chapter is to establish the approach taken in this book. We start by providing an analytical context by reviewing two of the most popular ways of analysing Europe's role – the 'European Union-as-actor' and 'institutionalist' approaches. The limitations of both provide a justification for developing a rather different approach here derived from Foreign Policy Analysis (FPA). But before an FPA framework can be set up, two further sets of clarifications are needed which complete the subject matter of this chapter. First, we need to demonstrate that FPA can be adapted from its traditional focus on states which appears to be inappropriate in a European context. Second, we need to establish the alternative focus of the analysis here. Europe's global role will be analysed in foreign policy terms by reference to the controversial idea of 'European foreign policy' which needs some preliminary discussion.

Contending Approaches

The European Union as actor

There are two different approaches in the literature that dominate existing analyses of Europe's global role. The first, the 'European Union-as-actor' approach, starts from a position similar to that adopted in Chapter 1 in that it concentrates on the impact of Europe on world politics. Working backwards, as it were, from impact, scholars have tried to identify what sort of an 'actor' Europe is that has enabled it to be such an influential global player. Implicitly or explicitly, the working model has been the state, but increasingly scholars have moved beyond a state model to identify a distinctive non-state but nevertheless collective entity, with the EC and latterly the EU providing the 'actor' focus of the analysis. This approach has made a major contribution to our understanding of Europe's global role in both empirical and conceptual terms.

First, it has generated a wealth of useful empirical data about the capabilities that Europe can and does deploy on a global stage (see, for example, Whitman 1998; Bretherton and Vogler 1999). Quite simply we now have a comprehensive range of facts and figures at our disposal that illustrate a significant European global capability and global presence. We know, for example, that the EU is now the largest bloc of states in the world. Since the 1995 enlargement from 12 to 15 member states, the combined population of this bloc now exceeds 370 million people, a huge market by any standards. Enlargement also increased the Union's Gross National Product (GNP) to 5,909 ECU (European Currency Unit), 10 per cent higher than the United States and 64 per cent higher than Japan (figures cited in Hill 1998a: 25). For a direct comparison with the United States in trade terms, comparisons should be made between the European Economic Area (EEA) and the North American Free Trade Agreement (NAFTA) both of which came into force in 1994. By 1995, the EEA (EU15 plus Iceland and Norway) had become the world's largest free trade zone, accounting for 40 per cent of world trade, clearly exceeding NAFTA's share, its combined population and Gross Domestic Product (Whitman 1998: 59). Not only is the augmented EU the world's largest trading unit, it is the richest commercial bloc and (with its member states) the largest provider of development aid to the rest of the world.

But analysts have not simply gathered data. The evidently patchy record of the EC/EU in converting capabilities into usable power and influence – impressive in some areas of activity, much less so in others – has generated debates since the 1970s about how best to characterize this new international actor. One continuing debate has been on whether the EC/EU is best described as a 'civilian power' (Duchène 1972; Bull 1983; Hill 1990), denoting its strengths in the economic sphere and weaknesses in the military sphere, or, in less restricted terms, as a genuine 'superpower in the making' (Galtung 1973; Buchan 1993). The limits of that debate located within a realist framework led in the 1990s to different, less action-orientated ways of conceptualizing 'actorness', with the EC/EU characterized as an international 'presence' (Allen and Smith 1990) or as an 'international identity' (Whitman 1998). Most recently, Bretherton and Vogler have offered a different perspective again, seeing the various external roles of the EU as constructed from the 'interaction of external expectations and internal capability' (Bretherton and Vogler 1999: 13).

Important though this body of work has undoubtedly been in developing our understanding of Europe's global role, it can be argued that the EU-as-actor approach is limited in two particular respects. First, the focus is on outcomes rather than process. As Bretherton and Vogler admit, they are essentially concerned to assess 'the overall impact of the EC/EU' on world politics. They are much less concerned with analysing the processes through which the external policy of the EU is formulated. Indeed, they explicitly reject a policy analysis approach to understanding EU external policy (Bretherton and Vogler 1999: 2–3, 20). A different view is taken here and a different policy-orientated approach is offered in this book. The foreign policy analyst is less concerned with explaining and evaluating policy outcomes and more concerned to understand the policy process itself – how policy emerges, from whom and why. To the extent that 'actorness' or 'presence' characterizes the EU in world politics, the assumption here is that it is related to and emerges from elements of a policy system in action, such as the context in which policy is made, the nature of the policy process, the issue in question, and so on.

A second problem area with this approach is the persistent assumption that the EU can be appropriately analysed and evaluated as a single actor. The position taken here is that to conceive of the EU as *an* actor, a 'presence' or *an* 'international identity' – in short to adopt what is called an holistic approach to analysis that focuses on 'singleness' or 'unitariness' – is to misrepresent what Jorgensen calls the 'multiple realities' that constitute the EU (Jorgensen 1998: 12). Hence the assumption here is that the EU is more appropriately analysed as a non-unitary or disaggregated entity in world politics.

Institutionalist approaches

The other popular approach in the literature is very different from the first in terms of the perspective from which Europe is analysed. This approach can be located within an international relations (IR) theory called institutionalism, which, rather than focusing on actor-generated behaviour, provides an explanation of actor behaviour as a function of the international institutions or other structures within which actors are located. The essential focus is on structures rather than actors, hence variants of this approach have also been referred to a 'structuralist' approach (Hill 1996a: 6). Institutionalism emerged in IR as a reaction to the dominance of realist thinking which assumes that conflict between states is inherent in an international system characterized by anarchy (absence of government). For realists, the international system is the structure that determines the behaviour of the states within it (Waltz 1979). Institutionalists on the other hand, coming from a liberal tradition of political thinking, argue that institutions mitigate conflict and help to facilitate international cooperation and order. By the 1990s, it must be said, the differences between realists and institutionalists had become blurred. New versions of both theories brought them closer together (see Baldwin 1993; Kegley 1995). In particular, both now accept the anarchic nature of the international system and both regard states rather than other actors (highlighted in earlier institutionalist accounts) as the key actors within that system. While these theories remain divided by their concern to explain two very different international outcomes – conflict and cooperation – they are united by a common structuralist approach to explaining actor behaviour.

Although not initially developed in a European context, the relevance of institutionalist thinking to the increasingly institutionalized process of European cooperation and integration is evident. Indeed, institutionalist ideas have stimulated the integration process in Europe, and the EU is an important test case of institutionalist expectations about regional and international cooperation. The external relations of the EU have not been a major preoccupation for institutionalists but they too have made a significant contribution to our understanding of Europe's global role. First, as their label suggests, they have been fascinated by the growth of EC/EU institutions and the extent to which decision-making has become institutionalized. They have analysed the ways in which institutions such as the European Commission have constructed their own agenda and developed their own capabilities enabling them to act increasingly independently of states. Second, as indicated above, the new or neo-institutionalists have become increasingly interested in analysing member state behaviour, identifying ways in which states have adapted their behaviour as a result of operating within an EU institutional context. They have noted that the broadening agenda of European integration has tended to strengthen institutional and weaken governmental control. Third, institutionalists have been well placed to observe that the EU is not simply an intergovernmental system of states (as realists maintain) but is characterized by a wider range of policy processes including transnational, transgovernmental and supranational processes. Finally, the regional/global perspective of institutionalists has highlighted the relationship between Europe's global role and global processes such as interdependence and globalization. From this perspective, institutionalized European integration can be seen as a regional response to important global trends.

But structuralist approaches also have their limitations, stemming largely from the level at which they analyse the behaviour of states and other actors. What might be called the 'actor problem' is the first in a set of interrelated problems. The assumption that systemic imperatives (whether the system is conceived in global or regional terms) determine the behaviour of the actors within the system leaves little room to explain those occasions when the state or some other actor does not behave in accordance with the dictates of the system. Clearly, for those occasions at least, some other more actor-centred perspective is required that investigates the particularity of the actors. As Christopher Hill notes, this is an important illustration of the collective action problem that has concerned political theorists for many years. He suggests that states 'find it genuinely difficult both to reach agreement on group strategies and then to hold to these strategies once agreements are reached'. Significantly, he adds, 'solidarity is the exception rather than the rule... even in Western Europe' (Hill 1996a: 7). An analytical focus on states themselves (or other actors) is required to make sense of what may be called a predisposition to defect or 'free ride'. This is a major problem for structuralists who are concerned primarily to explain either international cooperation or conflict from a systemic perspective.

If structuralists are weak on agency, it follows that their conception of the foreign policy process within states and their understanding of the role of domestic factors in that process will also be underdeveloped or understated at best. Certainly a focus on structural imperatives leads to a simplified view of policy processes. If the behaviour of states and other actors is essentially determined by international structures, the assumed reaction of those actors will be limited to recognizing what they are required to do by the system and adapting their behaviour more or less effectively. While acknowledging important work by structural theorists that seeks to introduce domestic factors into their analyses (see, for example, Moravcsik 1991; Buzan et al. 1993), what has emerged is a reintroduction of the 'rational actor model' of state behaviour described in the next section. The resulting picture of an integrated political elite in one state bargaining with similar elites in other states by manipulating the interests or 'preferences' of the state according to rationalist principles may capture important elements of the foreign policy process but, as Hill argues, this focus offers 'a somewhat impoverished view of politics in general and the domestic environment in particular' (Hill 1997: 11).

There is a problem relating the imperatives of structuralist approaches to an understanding of Europe's global role and there is arguably a need to complement the 'macro' approach of institutionalism-structuralism with some form or forms of 'micro', actor-centred analysis but which, unlike the EU-as-actor approach, do not make inappropriate assumptions about single 'actorness'. The central question is whether FPA can be adapted to fill this role in a European context.

The Adaptability of Foreign Policy Analysis

One of the main arguments of critics of FPA is that despite the transformed nature of contemporary world politics, FPA is outdated because it is still locked into 'state-centric realism' with, as Michael Smith puts it, 'the state and governmental power' still providing the 'central conceptual building block of the field' (Smith, M. 1994: 22). Marjorie Lister's recent study of the EU illustrates a view that FPA is unable to throw any light on the EU's external relations. Not only does the EU not have a foreign policy, in Lister's view, but 'the tools of traditional foreign policy analysis add relatively little to our understanding of the EU. The EU is best understood as a unique type of institution rather than an embryonic state' (Lister 1997: 6).

A response to these criticisms requires some understanding of the development of FPA as a field of study. Many years ago, the American political scientist Jo Nye labelled the traditional foreign policy analysis approach, 'state-centric realism' (Nye 1975: 36). Three assumptions underpin this approach. First, **state-centricity**, as the phrase suggests, captures the assumption that states are the most important actors in the international system, consequently, it is their foreign policy behaviour rather than any other actors that interests foreign policy analysts. Second, the idea of the **state-as-actor** denotes the assumption that states act in the international arena as unitary, rational actors (Allison 1971; Allison and Zelikow 1999). State behaviour, in other words, is assumed to be analogous to that of a rational individual. Third, reference to realism in this context denotes the idea that assumptions about the state are in turn linked to realist assumptions about the nature of the international system. In particular, given assumptions about the anarchic nature of that system, states are assumed to be preoccupied in their foreign policy behaviour with military-security and with issues and instruments associated with security. From this perspective, **security politics** conceived in military terms defines the essence of state behaviour and, indeed, of world politics.

The development of FPA as a field of study can be seen as a response to challenges to these traditional assumptions (see Clarke and White 1989: Chapter 1). The first major challenge came in the 1950s with the introduction of a decision-making approach, which led to foreign policy behaviour being analysed less as a response to a hostile, anarchic international environment and more as a process essentially internal to the state. Building upon the work of Graham Allison and others in the 1970s, analysts developed a solid body of knowledge about the way foreign policy processes work and the relationships between process and output. A behavioural approach with a focus on trying to explain the behaviour of decision-makers rather than the abstract 'state' appeared to constitute a major attack on realist assumptions (White 1978/1994).

With hindsight, however, we may argue that the decision-making approach offered a limited critique only of traditional assumptions. While both the idea of the unitary, rational 'state' and realist assumptions were undermined, the state-centric focus of FPA was left relatively unscathed. Indeed, critics of FPA argued that the decision-making approach was leading foreign policy analysts into an excessive preoccupation with the domestic context of foreign policy-making within states and, consequently, predisposing them to take insufficient account of important changes in the international environment (Light 1994). While foreign policy analysts were indeed focusing on domestic policy processes, fundamental changes in the international environment were being analysed by other IR scholars.

The cumulative impact of these changes was to undermine all the traditional assumptions of FPA including, critically, the assumption that states and governments remain the only important actors in world politics. In broad terms, these changes conveniently organized here in terms of actors, processes and issues challenged traditional FPA assumptions as follows:

■ **State-centricity** has been challenged by an evident increase in the forms and variety of states in the international system, the changing roles and functions of developed states in particular, and the emergence of a range of non-state actors operating at different levels of activity. What has been characterized as a more complex 'mixed actor' international system (Young 1972) raises fundamental questions about the nature of statehood and poses a major challenge to foreign policy analysts. State-centricity is further challenged by related processes such as interdependence and transnationalism which directly challenge the autonomy of states and their ability to control outcomes (see Keohane and Nye 1988).

■ Interestingly, both **state-centricity** and the **state-as-actor** assumptions have been undermined by what Keohane and Nye refer to as transgovernmentalism (Keohane and Nye 1974). This denotes the predisposition of subunits of governments to form international coalitions across national boundaries and to operate on the basis of shared interests that might undermine the operation of 'national interests' in policy-making processes.

■ **Security politics** assumptions, derived from a traditional realist account of IR, have been directly challenged by the new agenda of world politics, an agenda that is itself a product of both the changing role and function of the state – in particular the growing welfare functions of the modern state – and a changing international environment. This agenda consists of a far wider range of issues than military-security; indeed, as we shall see in Chapter 7, security itself has been defined in much broader terms that go beyond the military-defence arena (Buzan 1983). One of the defining features of newer processes such as interdependence and integration is that they are less conflict orientated and more geared to achieve cooperation between states and other actors.

If we consider the overall challenge to FPA that these changes represent, we might reach one of two conclusions. One conclusion is to accept the view of critics that these changes fundamentally undermine FPA to such an extent that it is no longer a helpful way of understanding world politics. Many IR scholars have indeed concluded either implicitly or explicitly that states and the governments that represent them no longer constitute a useful level of analysis from which to make sense of world politics. The structuralist assumption, as we noted above, is that the structure of the international system effectively determines the behaviour of its constituent units, therefore the international system itself is the appropriate level from which to analyse the workings of the system. Hence, various types of structuralist accounts of IR have predominated in recent years to the partial exclusion at least of explanations like FPA.

The other less radical conclusion advanced here rejects the idea that FPA is anachronistic but recognizes that FPA must be further adapted to take account of a transformed international system. The importance of the European context here is that the global changes outlined above are more clearly illustrated in Europe than in any other region in world politics. It might be argued, therefore, that if foreign policy analysts can use their analytical techniques to make sense of European foreign policy, this will not only throw light on an important new area of foreign policy activity but will also make a major contribution to the development of FPA itself (a possibility discussed in the final chapter of this book).

Clearly, much hinges on the extent to which FPA is still wedded to 'state-centric realism'. Looking first at state-centricity, there appears to be no obvious reason why the perspective of and the analytical techniques associated with FPA cannot be transferred from the state to other significant international actors or, indeed, mixed actor systems (see Hill 1974). After all, FPA emerged as a major field in IR during the early post-war period when there were no serious challengers to the state and it was logical to base a 'micro' analysis of international relations upon the state, evidently the principal actor within the international system. But, arguably, it was always the actor perspective rather than a specific actor or actors that was important to the foreign policy analyst.

If replacing 'state' with 'actor' appears to do no fundamental damage to an FPA perspective, what of the associated focus on government and governmental power? Clearly, the emergence of what Stephen Krasner has called 'authority structures that are not coterminous with geographic borders' whether territorially or regionally based (such as the EU) or issue-based (such as the regimes discussed in Chapter 1) has to a greater or lesser extent posed problems for all political scientists (Krasner 1995/1996: 116). The solution elsewhere has been to substitute the term' government' with the term 'governance' to facilitate a study of government-like activities. As with replacing state by actor, it does not obviously damage the essence of an FPA approach to replace government with governance. Indeed, if governance is taken to subsume government, it can provide a framework for analysing policy-making and policy outcomes that emerge from a political system such as the EU which is constituted by interactions between traditional 'authority structures' (that is, states and governments) and newer forms of non-state authority (see Rosenau 1992: 3–6). The focus on policy at the international level is arguably what is important to the foreign policy analyst rather than whether the actor is a conventional government or not.

Finally, what of the relationship between FPA and realism? The brief overview of the development of the field presented here suggests that there is no necessary connection. Certainly, foreign policy analysts have not been content to accept uncritically the idea of the state as a unitary, rational actor struggling to survive in an anarchic international environment or the associated simplicities of a traditional power analysis of state behaviour. Stimulated by the introduction of a decision-making approach, analysts have persistently looked within the 'billiard ball' state to identify key decision-makers and to unravel the domestic processes of foreign policy decision-making. While the now conventional attempts, following the pioneering work of Graham Allison, to disaggregate the state-as-actor and to 'domesticate' foreign policy have attracted criticism for understating the extent to which state behaviour is constrained by the international system, it would be difficult to maintain that FPA at the beginning of the twenty-first century is hopelessly tied either to state-centricity or to a realist agenda.

What is European Foreign Policy?

Having made a case for the adaptability of FPA as an approach but before taking a look at how an FPA framework might be developed in a European context, it is important at this point to clarify exactly what we mean by 'European foreign policy', the putative focus of the analysis here. Why 'European' rather than 'EU' foreign policy? Problems with the holistic EU-as-actor approach have already been discussed. Another reason for staying with 'Europe' rather than 'EU' as the qualifying adjective is to capture more effectively developments in Europe since the end of the cold war. Prior to the 1990s, as we saw in the first chapter, the process of integration in Europe was limited by ideological East–West divisions to Western Europe. The end of the cold war has opened up the prospect of including the states of what was formerly Eastern Europe in the integration process. Whether or not all these states eventually join the EU, a Europe-wide foreign policy is at least a theoretical possibility that should not be ruled out by unnecessarily restrictive language.

But we do need to recognize that the notion of a *European* foreign policy is a controversial idea subject both to sharp intellectual debate and the same passions and emotions that the whole process of European integration evokes, especially in Europe (Hill 1992: 109–10). Any discussion of European foreign policy, in short, is part of the wider debate about European integration and, as such, is a very live political issue. Intellectuals, politicians, journalists and the 'attentive public' in Europe and elsewhere take at least three different views on the possibility and the desirability of a European foreign policy:

■ One view is that European foreign policy already exists although that term may not be used. From this perspective, it is an integral part of the process of European integration that increasingly – particularly since the Single European Act and the Treaty on European Union – has a foreign, security and defence dimension to it.

■ A second view is that a European foreign policy does not yet exist but it should. Problems illustrated by the inadequate collective European performance in the succession of crises in the Balkans are taken as a clear indication that a common or even a 'single' European foreign policy is needed to deal effectively with such issues.

■ A third view is that European foreign policy does not exist, it never will and, moreover, it never should! Proponents of this view are wedded to the idea that the ability to control foreign and defence policy is a fundamental, defining characteristic of the nation-state. Accepting both the concept and the reality of a European foreign policy would mean nothing less than member states giving up both independence and sovereignty and must lead inexorably to the early demise of the nation-state.

This last view, it should be noted, is linked theoretically to a 'state-centric realist' perspective which maintains that foreign policy is essentially the preserve of states and governments. If EU member states wish to retain national foreign policies they cannot also be a party to something called European foreign policy. The latter is a contradiction in terms at best and a myth at worst. David Allen, for example, argues that 'the determination to preserve national foreign policies is ultimately at odds with the ambition to create a *European* foreign policy' (Allen 1998: 42; see also Allen 1996). Quite simply, the EU is not a state – it may well never be – and therefore it does not qualify as a foreign policy actor. Indeed, from this perspective, the very concept of a 'European foreign policy' is an intrinsic part of an ideological, federalist vision of Europe and the logical corollary is that a 'European foreign policy worthy of the name' must await a federal European state (Hill 1993: 316).

What might constitute European foreign policy from a broadly state-centric realist perspective is the sum of member states' foreign policies studied as a limited set of cases in an exercise (implicit or explicit) in comparative foreign policy analysis (see, for example, Hill 1983, 1996b; Stavridis and Hill 1996). At first sight, Roy Ginsberg's influential work on foreign policy actions in the EC looks like a useful model to build upon, foreign policy being defined there as 'the process of integrating policies and actions of the member states' (Ginsberg 1989: 1). That definition and the ensuing analysis make it clear, however, that Ginsberg's apparent state-centric approach is essentially locked into a structuralist perspective. He looks first to integration theory and global interdependence to explain foreign policy, invoking what he calls 'self-styled logic' (internal decision-making and political dynamic) only when actions are not taken in response to outside pressures (Ginsberg 1989: 4).

Ginsberg is unusual, nevertheless, in including *all* the external relations of the Community within his analysis of 'foreign policy actions'. Much more typically from a institutionalist perspective, as Hazel Smith points out, European foreign policy has been rather narrowly defined both in scope and level by the way 'foreign policy' is defined at the level of the European institutions themselves (Smith, H. 1998: 154–7). Thus European foreign policy viewed through the lens of the standard institutionalist literature is synonymous (since 1993) with EU foreign policy. It refers to the process of foreign policy coordination known as European Political Cooperation (EPC), which began in the 1970s and was upgraded by the Maastricht Treaty into a Common Foreign and Security Policy (CFSP) in 1993 (see, for example, Allen et al. 1982; Ifestos 1987; Nuttall 1992; Regelsberger et al. 1997).

From an institutionalist perspective, moreover, ECP/CFSP is 'real' European foreign policy (despite the resistance to actually using the words 'foreign and 'policy' until 1993) that can be contrasted with the external powers or 'competences' originally established by the Treaty of Rome, which are generally labelled 'external relations' (Laffan 1992: 150). If this narrows the scope of European foreign policy to the processes and the outcomes of ECP/CFSP with significant political implications, the contribution of individual member states' foreign policies to European foreign policy is either downgraded by the institutionalists, with their focus on cooperative, integrative behaviour at the European level, or passed over almost entirely by adherents of the 'EU as actor' approach.

The foreign policy analyst, on the other hand, concerned both to track and to analyse actor-directed policy at the international level, can and arguably should offer a less restrictive definition of European foreign policy. The position taken here is that to be useful for analytical purposes, the concept has to encompass the fragmented nature of agency at the European level and the variety of forms of action. Observation of foreign policy activity in Europe, reflecting what Hill calls 'the sum of what the EU *and* its member states do in international relations' (Hill 1998a: 18, my italics), should lead us to conclude that defining European foreign policy as 'member states' foreign policy' or as 'EU foreign policy' or, indeed, as 'EC foreign policy' (see Smith, M. 1998: Chapter 5) is too restrictive. European governance in the foreign policy field appears to take all three forms, which can be differentiated for analytical purposes, although, it should be stressed, a key research task that the foreign policy analyst can undertake is to establish the extent to which these types have become interwoven over time (see Peterson 1998: 15). Clearly, the more extensive the interrelationships between them, the more justified we are in using the label European foreign policy.

An FPA Framework of Analysis

We have argued so far that existing approaches to understanding Europe's global role are limited. Institutionalist analyses of European foreign policy in particular are limited by a set of weaknesses, the most serious of which are the absence of a developed view of state/actor behaviour, a simplified view of policy-making processes and, as highlighted in the last section, a restrictive definition of foreign policy in a European context. The possibility of FPA providing an approach that fills those gaps is dependent upon the adaptability of traditional FPA. If FPA remains tied to state-centric realism, its value is clearly limited, although this should not to be taken to imply that states are not important actors in European foreign policy. The argument here is that FPA is not necessarily tied to state-centricity nor is it dependent upon a realist paradigm. To summarize the rest of the argument, the essence of FPA is that it offers an actor rather than a state perspective and, equally important, it provides a policy focus at the international level. Building upon these premisses, this section outlines and develops an analytical framework that will be used in this study.

A starting point is provided by posing six standard FPA questions:

1. Who makes European foreign policy?
2. What is the nature of the European foreign policy process?
3. What issues constitute the European foreign policy agenda?
4. What instruments are deployed by European foreign policy?
5. What is the context within which policy is made?
6. What are the outputs generated by the policy process?

It is assumed that the elements of this framework – actors, processes, issues, instruments, context and outputs – are interrelated and constitute a foreign policy system in action. Thus, the nature of the policy process is affected by the identity of the actors involved, the issues being dealt with, the policy instruments available and, not least, the context within which policy is made. These interrelationships in turn generate the outputs from the system (see Clarke and White 1989).

Before the elements of the analytical framework can be further specified, however, we need to underline the conceptual analysis in the last section by clearly identifying the different types of European foreign policy:

■ **Community foreign policy** refers to the foreign policy of the EC that emerged as a direct consequence of the establishment of the original European Communities in 1957. These powers established by the Treaties of Rome codify the external consequences of the Common Commercial Policy and cover principally trade and development relations with third parties. From an FPA perspective, this form of policy-making is uncontentiously foreign policy and can be regarded as constituting the foreign economic policy dimension of European foreign policy.

■ **Union foreign policy** refers to the more overtly political dimensions of European foreign policy and consists of the coordination of the foreign policies of member states in a process that, until the Single European Act of 1986, was pursued outside the legal framework of the Community. As described in Chapter 1, this type of policy was established in the early 1970s as an intergovernmental process known as European Political Cooperation (EPC). The Treaty on European Union (TEU) upgraded this process and replaced EPC with a commitment under the terms of TEU to establish a Common Foreign and Security Policy (CFSP). CFSP was established as a separate 'pillar' of the EU, hence the label adopted here despite its prescriptive, federalist connotations (see Smith 1996: 257ff.).

■ **National foreign policy** refers to the separate foreign policies of member states that have continued to exist and indeed to thrive in the 1990s. What is important in the context of establishing the parameters of a European system of foreign policy, however, is the extent to which the foreign policies of member states have been transformed by the process of operating within the EU institutional context. Hill and Wallace offer an initial description of the transformed context in which member states operate. 'Habits of cooperation, accepted advantages of shared information, responses to common threats, cost saving through increased collaboration, have all significantly altered patterns of national policy-making' (Hill and Wallace 1996: 12).

Their conclusion offers a useful but, from an FPA perspective, limited characterization of the relationship between the three types of European foreign policy. 'This is an intensive system of external relations in which the cooperating actors which constitute the system intertwine' (Hill and Wallace 1996: 12). While the problem with the term 'external relations' has already been noted, if the various elements of a European foreign policy system are interrelated we must assume that the system includes but extends beyond the 'cooperating actors'. Having identified different types of 'governance' in this field, we can begin to explore the extent to which each type attracts a different cluster of actors, is characterized by a different policy process, operates within a distinctive context and across a specific agenda, utilizes different sorts of policy instruments, and generates different outputs.

Actors and policy-making

The first and possibly the most important element in our integrated FPA framework attempts to relate actors to policy-making by a sustained focus on the nature and dynamics of the policy process or, more accurately, policy processes, given the different types of European policy identified here. For analytical purposes, this element naturally subdivides into studying the different stages of the policy process from policy-making/formulation through to policy implementation via policy instruments. We can assume that the nature of the policy process – and the identity of the key actors involved – depends upon the type of European foreign policy being analysed. If foreign policy in this context is defined in political terms as Union policy, then European foreign policy can be described and analysed as essentially an intergovernmental process. This suggests that the governments of the member states effectively control a process in which unanimity is the rule.

The problem with this model of policy-making is that the notion of intergovernmentalism also implies that member states remain the 'classical sovereign states of realist theory', independent and autonomous in the defence of their respective national interests (Hill and Wallace 1996: 11). But, for many institutionalists like Wessels and Edwards, this understates the degree to which member states are locked into a 'complex network of institutions and procedures' at the European level. Constant interaction within that network serves to limit the autonomy of any member state, even the most powerful (Wessels 1991; Edwards 1996: 127–47). This point is again neatly summarized by Hill and Wallace: 'Intergovernmentalism in theory does not erode sovereignty; in practice, over time, it too has ties that bind' (Hill and Wallace 1996: 11).

While the nature of the Union policy process can and will be debated in later chapters, other types of policy appear to show even more clearly the limits of state power. If European foreign policy is defined as Community policy, the process of policy-making, as this label suggests, is assumed to be more akin to the Community model of decision-making, with the European Commission in theory at least playing the role of principal actor at the European level. Once again, however, a simple characterization of the policy-making process is likely to be deceptive with respect to establishing who controls what. As Michael Smith notes, some areas of foreign economic policy, such as monetary policy and investment, have never been subject to a community-level policy-making process (Smith 1996: 249). And even in areas such as trade policy, where in theory the Commission has exclusive competence, a careful reading of the relevant Articles of the Treaty of Rome shows that there is a division of powers between the Commission and the Council of Ministers.

Capabilities and instruments

The critical link in the foreign policy literature between the policy process and output is the existence or otherwise of capabilities, resources that can be converted into usable policy instruments. Reflecting and to some extent defining its limited actor status, the EU as a whole appears to have an incomplete set of policy instruments of varying effectiveness. While a powerful set of economic and financial instruments has been developed over time in Community policy, policy instruments deployed in Union policy are either much weaker or non-existent. With respect to diplomacy, as we shall see, a growing dissatisfaction with the effectiveness of diplomatic statements led to the adoption of 'common positions' and 'joint actions' mechanisms in the TEU. That treaty also finally addressed the significant absence of a military capability/set of instruments at the European level. The replacement of EPC by a commitment to a CFSP signals a determination at least to move forward on that front via the mechanism of the Western European Union. We need to explore whether aspirations have been converted into a genuine European military capability.

The effectiveness of policy instruments may well reflect the issue being addressed. Two related analytical concerns have dominated the FPA literature on issues, and both are equally relevant to a discussion of issues and policy areas in a European foreign policy context. The first relates to the range of issues that constitute the foreign policy agenda and how different issues attract different sets of actors and are handled by different policy processes. The central point in that literature is that for a variety of reasons the agenda, particularly for 'modernized' states, has dramatically expanded. This raises questions about the effectiveness of what might be called systems of policy management. A related focus is the extent to which an expanded agenda of issues creates 'boundary' problems. These boundaries are of two types, broadly between economic and political issues – or, as Edward Morse described it – between 'high' and low' policy issues and second, issues that cross the 'boundary' between domestic and international politics (Morse 1970). The boundary problem dimension also raises questions about policy management but it also introduces problems relating to the political sensitivities of member states.

The European foreign policy agenda has clearly expanded, particularly in recent years as a result of the end of the cold war. Since 1989, the 'new Europe' has been confronted by a host of new issues and old issues in a new form that raise broadly the same analytical questions as those familiar to foreign policy analysts. Maintaining coherence across an expanding agenda and dealing with boundary problems demands, for the EU as for developed states, a constant search for new instruments and new institutional mechanisms to manage policy. One example of the former is the Europe Agreements reached with Central and East European countries, while the creation in 1993 of DG1A in the European Commission illustrates a continuing attempt at a European institutional level to manage more effectively both the growing politicization of EU activities and the ever more blurred boundary between economic and political issues.

Policy context

An important set of variables used in foreign policy system models relates to the context within which policy is made, sometimes referred to in that literature as the 'setting' or 'environment' of policy-making. These variables are generally conceived from this perspective as constituting important 'inputs' into the foreign policy system helping to define the parameters within which the system can operate. If context is subdivided into internal and external elements, this aspect of the analytical framework can be further elucidated. The 'internal' setting though is more complex in a multi-level European policy context than in a state. Account has to be taken of intra-EU factors as well as the traditional 'domestic' intra-state setting to the extent that they impact upon European foreign policy.

At the EU 'internal' level, analysts might focus on, for example, the constitutional context – broadly who is given what powers or competences to do what in foreign policy-making. Like many other contextual elements, constitutional provisions are a dynamic, changing element in the policy process. Not only have we seen a series of treaties refine and expand the constitutional provisions established in the 1957 Rome Treaties but, as illustrated in Chapter 1, European Court of Justice interpretations can also change the context of foreign policy-making in the broadly defined sense in which the term is being used here. Another dynamic element of the internal environment is the development of a burgeoning diplomatic machinery controlled by the Commission. This extends to a permanent network of representation abroad together with a growing number of diplomatic missions accredited to the Community. This element links to the multi-level nature of the decision-making process, which not only helps to shape the policy process(es) but should also be regarded as part of the context within which policy-making takes place. As summarized by William Wallace, multi-level governance denotes *inter alia* 'complexity and the contested character of policy-making' which in turn 'makes for dispersed and disjointed decisions, and for incomplete implementation' (Wallace 1996: 445).

From an external perspective, similarly, different factors can be identified and built into the analysis. The obvious example, which has been dealt with at length in the literature, although not necessarily from this analytical perspective, is the impact of the end of the cold war on the foreign policy process in the new Europe. As Michael Smith notes, underlining the interrelationship between the elements of our analytical framework, the transformations in Europe have dramatically 'reshaped both the context and the agenda' of what he calls 'the EC's external relations'. One important element within this transformed policy environment, although ostensibly part of the internal policy agenda, has been the establishment of the Single Market which has major ramifications for European foreign policy (Smith 1997: 280ff.).

It should not be forgotten at this point that FPA can also provide a framework for analysing member states' foreign policy as well as the other sub-systems of European foreign policy. The 'Europeanized' context within which national foreign policy is made and implemented is a particularly important element within that framework. While there is a need for more comparative research here on foreign policy, the indications are that this dynamic policy context poses major problems for national governments in terms of constructing an effective machinery for coordinating policy at different levels of activity (Wright 1996: 148–69; see also Meny et al. 1996). On the other hand, there is some evidence with respect to smaller member states that operating through EPC/CFSP has, in Ben Tonra's conclusion, 'improved the effectiveness, broadened the range and increased the capabilities of foreign policy-making' (Tonra 1997: 197).

If the above is taken as a preliminary effort to 'flesh out' an FPA framework, it might be useful to conclude this chapter with a brief comment on how this framework might be applied and specifically to what. Two possible applications are suggested by the FPA literature, the use of case studies and the issue area approach. With respect to the former, there are numerous studies that offer an in-depth analysis of particular cases of foreign policy decision-making. Although the focus has often been on major 'turning point' or crisis decisions rather than on more routine decision-making, these studies provide a model for applying an FPA framework to cases of European foreign policy-making. The objective crudely would be to discover who did what to whom, when and how. While the cases selected might cover different types of policy-making, foreign economic policy, more overtly political or security cases, for example, another approach would be to try to compare policy-making more explicitly across a range of issue areas on the assumption that the nature of the issue as an independent variable determines the range of actors, the type of policy process and the other elements of the analytical framework.

Stimulated by the work of Theodore Lowi and James Rosenau in the 1960s, the 'issue areas' approach attracted a number of FPA adherents who endeavoured to construct a framework around this notion (Lowi 1964; Rosenau 1967). It became clear by the 1980s, however, that this approach was problematic. The absence of agreement on how to define issue areas and other methodological difficulties led to the effective abandonment of this approach by foreign policy analysts. Similar problems are likely to face any attempt to operationalize this approach in a European foreign policy context (Potter 1980; for a more optimistic view, see Collinson 1999). If the issue areas approach looks unpromising, it might be argued that the case study approach lacks specificity given the different types of European foreign policy that we have identified. In this context, the old question would clearly emerge – case studies of what?

The preference here is for a third focus, to take the different types of governance in European foreign policy and to analyse each of them comparatively using FPA techniques and the common analytical framework outlined above. Case studies would, of course, be a useful element in research and they are used extensively in this study, but they are tied to a specific type of governance. This application offers a promising, systematic way of establishing the differences between sub-systems of European foreign policy while also revealing the extent of overlap and interweaving between them. Application of the framework begins in the next chapter with Community foreign policy.

Note

1. Some sections of this chapter draw extensively upon White, B. (1999) The European Challenge to Foreign Policy Analysis. *European Journal of International Relations*, **5**(1): 37–66.

3

External Relations: Community Foreign Policy

This is the first of four chapters that look at each of the three types of European foreign policy identified in Chapter 2. An analysis of Community foreign policy here is followed in succeeding chapters by Union policy in the form of the Common Foreign and Security Policy (CFSP).This is prefaced by a discussion of its predecessor, European Political Cooperation (EPC). Finally, what has been called the 'Europeanization' of EU member states' foreign policy is tested by reference to a case study chapter on British foreign policy.

The analysis of each type of policy is framed by the common analytical framework that was also discussed in Chapter 2. Four interrelated elements will constitute that framework: **policy context**, the internal and external context within which policy is made; **actors and policy-making**, in which the nature of the policy process and the roles of the key actors in the policy process are established; **capabilities and instruments**, which analyses the instruments available to implement policy and to facilitate action, and finally **action** itself. This final element of the framework assumes that the policy process has outputs in the form of action that flow from the operation of the policy system as a whole. The strengths and weaknesses of each sub-system of European foreign policy in action are discussed at the end of each chapter by reference to an illustrative case study.

Context

An important insight into the historical and political context in which Community foreign policy has been made can be gleaned from a preliminary clarification of terminology. While 'Community foreign policy' rather than 'external relations' is the preferred label here, the latter also appears in the title of this chapter because it is so frequently used in the institutionalist literature to characterize the foreign economic policy arena. But two important and related points need to be made at the outset. First, from an FPA perspective, there is a possibility of confusion here because 'external relations' is also used in the foreign policy literature to refer to the totality of policies and relations between a unit (usually a state) and other units, *including* foreign and defence policy. References to Britain's external relations, for example, would denote a wide range of external activities and relationships that Britain maintains with other states and international organizations – foreign policy, defence, foreign economic policy and a host of 'new' issue areas including technology, environment, agriculture, and so on.

In the case of the EC, however, the use of the term 'external relations' in this sense would be problematic because the foreign and particularly the defence policy dimensions of external relations have always been politically sensitive because of their linkage to state sovereignty. From the establishment of the European Economic Community (EEC) in 1958, it was apparent that member states were resistant to giving the Community competence over these areas because, as they saw it, this would seriously compromise their sovereignty. What member states were prepared to concede was that the Community could and – in the case of commercial and trade policy – must be given competence over some aspects at least of what was regarded as the less politically sensitive area of external economic relations. This is the area often labelled 'low policy' to contrast with the politically sensitive 'high policy' areas of diplomacy and military security (Morgan 1973; Morse 1976).

Second, although international economic relations and economic issues as a whole have become increasingly politicized over time, the use in a Community context of the term 'external relations' rather than, say, '*foreign economic policy*' has served as a useful euphemism to avoid political embarrassment. In the next chapter, we will note that the rather awkward label 'European Political Cooperation' also served a similar euphemistic function masking (or possibly revealing) political sensitivities in a potent linguistic form. But observers of EU politics are under no obligation to follow the linguistic conventions of those whose behaviour they are attempting to understand or indeed the language of other scholars in the field. The argument here is that the use of the term 'external relations' in an EU context amounts to nothing less than an admission that this area of policy is not 'real' foreign policy at all and is 'by definition', as it were, less important as an object of study for the foreign policy analyst than EFP/CFSP. Hence we shall refer to Community foreign policy in this chapter.

If linguistic clarification can provide significant insights into the historical and political context of Community foreign policy, arguably the legal context is even more crucial to an understanding of this policy area. As Piening puts it, 'the key to understanding how and why the Community became an international actor lies in the 1957 Treaty of Rome, which set up the European Economic Community' (Piening 1997: 15–16). If member states were prepared to concede some aspects of foreign economic relations to the Community, they were determined to contain and constrain these competences within a very tight legal structure. 'The European Economic Community', Piening explains, 'was created to facilitate trade between its six member states through the establishment of a common market. Within its borders, trade in goods was to be free: there would be no tariffs, no restrictions, and no quotas' (Piening 1997: 13). But in order to establish an *internal* 'common market' for trade (in reality a customs union until the establishment of a genuine single market in the 1990s), it was necessary to create a common *external* frontier for trade. Otherwise, incoming goods could simply exploit differential tariffs within the various member states. A common trade or commercial policy (CCP), therefore, together with a Common External Tariff (CET) was also established by the Rome Treaty.

Without overwhelming the reader with legal details, an understanding of some key articles of the Rome Treaty is necessary here. The reader should also note, however, that many of these articles have been updated and often confusingly renumbered in later treaty revisions but, to avoid confusion, we will stick to the Rome article numbers where possible. Article 110 extends the common market principle to external trade with an additional commitment to the progressive liberalization of world trade. The important Article 113 spells out how the common trade policy process will operate in general terms with respect to goods, and Article 228 provides the basis for negotiating specific trade and economic cooperation agreements with third parties. Article 238 is the fourth key article in the area of trade and economic cooperation policy, which provides the legal basis for concluding what are called association agreements, the closest form of relationship with the Community. These typically include preferential access to EC markets, economic and technical cooperation, financial aid and possibly eventual membership.

[handwritten annotation: Treaty of Rome. legal grounding for cooperation.]

Development cooperation, the second major area of Community foreign policy, is only partly ceded to the Community but, like trade policy, it is also tightly constrained by a legal structure contained within the Rome Treaty. Part Four of the Treaty – Articles 131–6 – was originally established to provide for largely duty-free access to the EEC market for products originating in the overseas colonies and dependencies of the member states. These arrangements were carried over into special provisions for economic relations with those territories after independence. Initially restricted to former French colonies under the Yaoundé Conventions in the 1960s, these arrangements were extended to a much larger group of African, Caribbean and Pacific (ACP) countries in various Lomé Conventions from the mid-1970s. The main provisions of the Lomé Conventions are trade concessions but they also provide for a package of aid and other measures.

Actors and Policy-making

Each area of Community foreign policy can be characterized by different sets of key actors and more or less distinctive policy processes. If we start by focusing upon trade policy in goods, we can get a clear sense of who the key actors are and the nature of the policy-making process, which may not be replicated in other areas. The point about trade policy is that this is the area of foreign policy in which the Community acts most clearly in a collective manner and we see the European Commission playing perhaps its most significant international role acting on behalf of member states in an apparently supranational way.

From the beginnings of the Community, the Commission was entrusted with implementing common policies and with proposing new ways of carrying forward the Community endeavour. And, as Hill notes, 'each of these tasks has an external face' (Hill 1992: 118). More specifically, under Article 113 of the Rome Treaty, the Commission represents and negotiates on behalf of member states in both bilateral and multilateral international economic fora. One very high profile example of this, noted in Chapter 1, is the role of the Commission in the various rounds of the General Agreement on Trade and Tariffs (GATT) – most famously perhaps in the tortuous negotiations in the Uruguay Round (UR) which were ultimately concluded in December 1993 after a deal was negotiated between Community Trade Commissioner Leon Brittan and US Special Trade Representative Mickey Kantor.

Even in the area of trade policy, however, other actors – specifically the Council of Ministers, member governments and their representatives in Brussels – play a much more significant role in the process and exercise far more control over the process than is immediately apparent. This will become clearer if we look at the stages in the policy-making process. As laid down under Article 113, the negotiating procedure for a 'simple' trade agreement has several key stages (see Nugent 1994: 388–9):

■ The Commission makes a recommendation to the Council of Ministers (usually the General Affairs Council in this context) about a trade agreement with a third country or organization.

■ The recommendation is discussed with COREPER (the Committee of Permanent Representatives) who may modify the recommendation.

■ The Council decides to proceed (or not). If the decision is positive, possibly made by a qualified majority vote, the Council will give the Commission directives to follow in the negotiations. This Council mandate, as it is usually known, 'spells out in some detail the framework of an agreement, including its objectives and the areas it is to cover' (Piening 1997: 26). Significantly, the mandate may reflect a compromise between member states and may well, therefore, be tightly drawn.

■ The Commission negotiates with the party(ies), with DG1 (the Directorate responsible for external economic relations) traditionally taking the lead. Throughout the period of negotiations, the Commission will remain in touch with the '113 Committee' of the Council – consisting of the Permanent Representatives or senior national trade officials – who meet regularly as the 'guardian of the mandate' to review and consult about ongoing negotiations (Smith, M. 1997: 271). In difficult negotiations the Commission may report back to the Council to get guidelines clarified or even amended.

■ The Commission reports back to the Council with an agreed, initialled agreement.

■ The Council and only the Council has the authority to sign an agreement on behalf of the Community. The decision may be made by a qualified majority vote.

If a review of the formal process of decision-making with respect to trade agreements reveals less Community control through the Commission than is immediately apparent, other areas of Community foreign policy-making show a more evident set of mixed competences across a wider range of key actors including, significantly, the European Parliament (EP). Article 228, used as the basis for economic cooperation and assistance agreements, requires the Commission and the Council to receive an opinion from the EP. The provisions for association agreements under Article 238 are more precise, requiring unanimity among Council members and EP agreement on the basis of a majority vote. Indeed, the consultative role of the EP in negotiating international agreements is even more pervasive than these legal provisions suggest. As Piening notes:

> since the 1983 Stuttgart 'Solemn Declaration', Parliament has been consulted on all important international agreements, regardless of the legal basis on which they are to be concluded. It is also kept informed by the Commission and the Council, both before and during the negotiations, under the so-called Luns-Westerterp procedure. (Piening 1997: 27)

With respect to development policy, the policy-making process is also characterized by mixed competences with extensive control of the process retained by member states. Although this area of policy is framed legally by Part 4 of the Rome Treaty, specific actions in the development field are usually taken under the various articles we have discussed – trade agreements under Article 113, and so on – with the appropriate policy-making conditions applying. The various Lomé Conventions have gone beyond these provisions, however, by establishing a rather different policy-making structure involving a distinctive set of actors. Three sets of actors are involved, the ACP–EC Council of Ministers, the Committee of Ambassadors and the Joint Assembly. The Council, with EC Council, Commission and ACP representation, takes the major policy decisions while the Ambassadors, with the same representation, advise the Council, monitor progress and supervise the many committees set up under the Convention. The Joint Assembly, on the other hand, with MEP and ACP representation, acts as a general advisory and deliberating body (Nugent 1994: 408).

Clearly then, the Commission has exclusive competence only where development policy involves trade policy. Aid policy-making in particular is shared with member states. Multilateral EC financial aid, administered largely through the European Development Fund (EDF), relies upon national allocations that have to be negotiated with the Commission on a regular basis. These allocations in turn represent only about 15 per cent of total EU aid (the Community together with combined efforts of member states). The great majority of EU financial aid is bilateral, negotiated between member states and other recipient parties (Nugent 1994: 407).

For the sake of completeness here and to underline further the central point about mixed competences, we should note that there are other areas of Community policy-making that have foreign policy dimensions and other areas of foreign economic policy that do not enter the realm of Community competence. Many areas of common policy – such as agriculture and fisheries – clearly have international dimensions that at the very least complicate the making of trade policy and the forging of trade agreements (Smith, M. 1997: 272). On the other hand, it should not be forgotten that there are important areas of foreign economic policy that are not subject to decision-making at a Community level at all. Member states retain the right, for example, to conclude their own treaties of economic cooperation with third parties that may cut across undertakings made at Community level. Monetary policy and investment decisions are cited by Michael Smith as examples of foreign economic policy taken exclusively at a national level. Even the European Monetary System (EMS), he argues, is effectively operated by the central banks of member states (Smith, M. 1996: 248, 1997: 272).

Capabilities and Instruments

Reference to the operation of EMS reminds us that any policy process has implementation as well as policy-making dimensions that link to this section on capabilities and instruments. Implementation, a crucial final stage of the policy process, is concerned with how decisions are translated into behaviour and action – crudely, with how effectively things get done. We can assume that all aspects of European foreign policy pose implementation problems and Community foreign policy is no exception. As a general comment, we can start by noting with Allen and Byrne that policy implementation at the European level poses the same problems as those faced at the national level – 'ambiguous goals, imperfect procedures and instruments, bureaucratic resistance and inadequate control mechanisms'. But also, 'the context of multilateral decision-making introduces new complications – the interplay between national and European interests, the lack of a clear central authority, doubts about the competence and commitment of partners and working within a relatively inflexible ideological framework' (Allen and Byrne 1985: 140–1).

With respect to Community foreign policy, two sets of implementation issues emerge, one particular and the other more general. First, where the Commission has more or less exclusive competence to implement and to monitor policy on behalf of the EC, does it have the resources, the coherence, and the capability generally to fulfil this role effectively? Second, where no institution has the prime responsibility for implementation, how do a series of agencies with different competences and different interests fulfil this role and what are the overall effects on policy? We shall pursue the first set of issues here in more detail.

In order to perform the implementation and monitoring role authorized by the Treaty of Rome, the Commission has developed substantial capabilities over time in the form of a growing network of international representation, an extensive if small bureaucracy and a powerful set of trade or trade-related instruments. The permanent diplomatic machinery established by the Commission has been matched by a growing number of diplomatic missions accredited to the Community in Brussels. Given that both policy-making and implementation is a two-way process, this network is important both to the Commission and to non-member states and other international organizations. For the Commission, it facilitates its role as both negotiator and regulator of agreements. For third parties, the network provides lines of communication and access to a policy process that can often seem to them complex, confusing and difficult to penetrate (Piening 1997: 23; see also Chapter 1).

Largely through the effective deployment of these capabilities, the Commission, acting on behalf of the Community, has had some considerable success in influencing foreign economic relations and trade, in particular with third parties – a level of success in implementation terms that member states individually could scarcely have achieved. Even in an area of mixed competence such as development policy, it has been argued that the Commission has been a successful implementer in the area it controls. This is a result largely of the establishment and allocation of funds to the EDF. Given EDF financial resources to distribute and treaty powers to set the terms of trade with less developed countries, Allen and Byrne argue that the EC 'could not fail to develop and implement a "European" policy'. They cite the Lomé Convention as a particular example of a foreign policy that 'works at the European level because there are (for the Europeans) no major resource problems' (Allen and Byrne 1985: 132).

But as the role of the Commission has expanded to encompass more and more policy areas, questions have been asked about whether it has enough resources, human and financial, to play an effective implementation role. As Smith notes, 'the Commission can often find itself negotiating on a wide range of fronts at any given time, thereby increasing the strain on its limited resources and diffusing its attention with potentially dangerous results' (Smith, M. 1997: 274). In his writings on the subject, Smith has developed the useful notion of the 'negotiated order' to characterize the complex, multi-levelled, highly political nature of both the Community foreign policy-making and policy implementation environment that places particular strains on the Commission's resources – particularly outside the 'core' area of trade policy in goods where its competence is established. Not only is the Commission frequently negotiating with other parties to extend the scope of its competence to act but it is also almost permanently negotiating with other parties in arenas where those parties also have rights to represent and to act – in the World Trade Organization (WTO) and the Organization for Economic Cooperation and Development (OECD), for example, where both the Commission and member states are represented. The location of the Commission 'at the intersection of several types of policy network', Smith adds, 'has generated its own distinctive brand of "bureaucratic politics"' (Smith, M. 1996: 259–60, 1997: 173–4).

With respect to coherence, another dimension of bureaucratic politics emerges that will be familiar to foreign policy analysts. It has been the case for many years that different parts of the Commission are involved in different areas and often the same areas of Community foreign policy. This raises at least the potential for conflict. It should certainly not be assumed that the Commission acts as a monolithic unitary actor. Until the structural reorganizations in the 1990s, it was the role of DG1 to coordinate foreign economic policy but this became increasingly difficult with the growing linkages between 'internal' and 'external' policy concerns. Analogies have been drawn between DG1 and the US Trade Representative in Washington with both 'trying to coordinate and moderate the needs and interests of powerful internal baronies without possessing a great deal of coercive power' (Destler 1992; Smith, M. 1997: 270). While, as we shall see, 'turf wars' have been a particular feature of reorganizations of the Commission in 1990s, there were indications of bureaucratic politics much earlier. For many years, the Commission was criticized for 'a lack of internal coordination with individual commissioners jealously guarding their own spheres of interest and knowing or caring little about those of their colleagues' (Allen and Byrne 1985: 129). Hill notes the history of disputes between DG1 and DG8, the latter having been given the responsibility for administering development policy. Particularly under Claude Cheysson as Commissioner, DG8 became a significant source of influence and ideas in its own right in the 1970s and 80s and this led to disputes (Hill 1992: 119).

To the extent that policy instruments can be separated analytically from capabilities in a Community context, it can be argued that three types of economic instrument or economic diplomacy constitute the 'sharp end', as it were, of Community foreign policy. For analytical purposes, they will be referred to here as **framework**, **regulatory** and **coercive** instruments, although these are not wholly distinctive categories. **Framework** instruments denote the growing range of cooperation, association and partnership agreements that provide, as the label suggests, a set of frameworks through which the Community can respond positively through aid, economic concessions and privileged relationships of different sorts, first, to those states and organizations whose partnership is valued by the Community and second, to the growing number of 'supplicants' who want access to the European market and a share of European wealth (Hill 1992: 128). The third group of states that Hill identifies graphically as targets of EC economic diplomacy are the 'delinquents' – those states whose behaviour can be punished only by **coercion** in the form of the removal of economic favours in the absence of 'harder' forms of coercion at Community level.

Regulatory instruments refer to a powerful set of trade policy instruments developed by the Commission to take action to stop unfair trading with third parties. The Commission is charged under Article 113 and other articles with monitoring trade agreements and coping with the commercial disputes that inevitably arise, and a variety of instruments such as anti-dumping regulations and rules of origin 'operationalize' this role (Smith, M. 1997: 269). By the 1980s, a period quickly dubbed by outsiders as the 'new protectionism', non-tariff barriers as a way of regulating trade had become much more significant than the tariff barriers contained within the Common External Tariff. These included instruments such as 'voluntary' export quotas, 'orderly marketing arrangements', tariff quotas and agreements from an earlier period such as the Multi-Fibre Agreement. With the adoption of the New Community Trade Instrument in 1984, anti-dumping duties became formalized and extensively used – particularly against Eastern Europe and China – although, following the conclusion of the Uruguay Round, this was replaced by a new Trade Barriers Regulation (see Whitman 1998: 56–7).

Of the three types of instrument described here, arguably the framework type has been most successful and certainly the least controversial. Although, as Hill argues, 'the resources available for inducements have always been limited', as the EU has become an increasingly powerful economic bloc, the prospect of membership for third parties has perhaps been the single most important policy instrument of all. As *The Economist* (18 July 1998) has argued:

> the EU has long practised one of the world's most successful foreign policies... By manipulating a single instrument, the prospect of membership, it has brought the once-marginal countries of the Mediterranean securely into the West European fold. It has cast a similar spell over most of Central and Eastern Europe.

Certainly, giving economic concessions and privileged relationships as a 'carrot' in the context of encouragingly regular rounds of enlargement has posed fewer implementation problems than the 'stick' of restrictions, particularly at the more punitive end of the spectrum. As Hill confirms, all the cases of sanctions in the 1980s 'posed major problems of implementation and consensus-building' (Hill 1992: 133, 135).

We shall return to the sanctions cases outlined here – particularly those targeted against apartheid South Africa – in the next chapter on European Political Cooperation. But it is important to note here that sanctions were adopted more or less successfully although not uncontroversially under the legal authority of Article 113 and other articles of the Treaty of Rome. Hence they are categorized here first as Community instruments and as an important dimension analytically of Community foreign policy. In terms of effectiveness, sanctions taken against the Soviet Union and Iran at the beginning of the 1980s can be easily dismissed. The Community delayed joining US sanctions against the Soviet Union following the imposition of martial law on Poland in 1981, agreeing eventually 'only to impose derisory sanctions on a short list of luxury goods' under the authority of Article 113 (Hill 1992: 134). Sanctions under Article 113 and also Article 223 were to have been deployed against Iran following the seizure of American hostages in Teheran. But, by the time agreement had been reached – the delay in part caused by concern over the proper legal basis for sanctions – the Carter Administration had opted for the abortive military option.

The response to the British request for sanctions against Argentina in 1982, following the invasion of the Falklands Islands, was much speedier and initially more consensual. With both Articles 113 and 224 cited for authorization, a one-month ban on Argentinian exports and an open-ended ban on arms deliveries were quickly agreed. Within two months, however, that unity had evaporated, largely although not exclusively as a consequence of the British use of military force to resolve the Falklands crisis. Both Ireland and Italy backed away from the agreed measures when they came up for renewal. Disunity and delay also characterized the process of agreeing upon sanctions against South Africa, certainly until 1986. As early as 1977, it was agreed that a Code of Conduct would regulate the operations of EC companies in South Africa, although the implementation of this Code remained primarily a national responsibility. More substantial EC actions were agreed in 1985 including tightening up the UN arms embargo, stopping oil exports and prohibiting nuclear cooperation. The British Government, however, issued a 'footnote' opting out of this agreement. It was not until 1986 that, in Martin Holland's view, 'the Community at last demonstrated recognizable actor-capability' (Holland 1991: 187). Unanimity was restored and maintained for a period, and agreement was reached on an admittedly modest series of measures including a ban on new investment and bans on the import of iron and steel – although not on the more significant area of coal imports. The first breach of this collective policy came in February 1990 when the Thatcher Government unilaterally withdrew from the ban on new investment. Nevertheless, in terms of impact, sanctions against South Africa were arguably more effective than the other cases described here to the extent that sanctions 'represented an important form of pressure on the apartheid regime' (Hill 1992: 135. See also the case study in Chapter 5).

Community Foreign Policy in Action: The Community and the GATT

This chapter concludes by looking at a case study of Community foreign policy in action in order to illustrate in more detail the characteristics of this sub-system of European foreign policy and, in particular, its strengths and weaknesses. In this context, the case study virtually selects itself. Community policy with respect to the GATT illustrates the importance of the context within which policy is made,

the complexities of the policy-making process with its mixed competences, the problems associated with both the making and the implementation of policy, and the complex nature of particular issues which
are the substance of Community policy that defy any simple catego-
rization such as 'high'/'low' or 'domestic'/'foreign'. As we shall be
focusing on the most recent UR of GATT (1986–93), this case study
also gives us an early look at some of the factors that impacted upon
the development of European foreign policy after the Single European
Act. The weaknesses revealed by this case study include tension and
overt conflict, particularly over agriculture, between the different actors
involved – between member states, between the Commission and the
Council, and within the Commission itself. The strengths focus on the
ability of the Community to play a shaping role in the final outcome of
the Round.

Context

The GATT was originally established in 1947 when 23 countries signed
an agreement to facilitate international trade by lowering trade barriers.
The GATT was originally intended to be only an interim arrangement
pending the establishment of a more comprehensive International Trade
Organization (ITO). In 1950, however, the United States Senate failed
to ratify the Havana Charter and the proposed ITO collapsed. Thereafter the GATT became the key international trade organization 'by
default', as it were, with a secretariat established in Geneva and with
growing numbers of states joining the GATT through a series of negotiating Rounds (Dinan 1998: 248). At the conclusion of the UR, 119
states signed the Final Act in April 1994. The following year, under the
terms of the Final Act, the GATT Secretariat was replaced by a new
international organization, the WTO.

Relations between the Community and the GATT and the principles
of representation predate the establishment of the EEC in 1957. The
European Coal and Steel Community (ECSC) was created within the
existing framework of trade rules established by the GATT. The six
members of ECSC became signatories to the GATT and were bound by
its principle of equality of treatment and the extension of 'Most
Favoured Nation' (MFN) status to all members. As a preferential
trading arrangement, however, the ECSC had to seek exemption from
MFN treatment. This exemption was granted by the GATT in
November 1952 and, at the same meeting, it was agreed that both

member states and the High Authority of ECSC (as joint representative of member states) would have rights of representation in the GATT – although member states formally remained the 'contracting parties' to GATT. From 1956 onwards, the High Authority negotiated in the GATT on behalf of, although still instructed by, member states. The institutions of the ECSC were formally merged with those of the EEC in 1967 and the role of the High Authority was replaced institutionally by the European Commission, but the essential principles and indeed the practices of the relationship between the Community and the GATT remained the same thereafter (Whitman 1998: 36).

Throughout the various negotiating Rounds within the GATT (Dillon, Kennedy, Tokyo, Uruguay), which progressively reduced tariffs and other barriers to free trade, the objectives of the EC were twofold: to promote the general liberalization of trade but also to try to ensure that the consequences of that liberalization were not damaging to Community or member states interests (Nugent 1994: 387). While there were difficulties at each stage in 'squaring' that particular 'circle', for a variety of reasons the most recent UR provided easily the most difficult and complex negotiating context. As Desmond Dinan argues, the UR was unique in terms of the number of participants involved, the scope of the agenda, and the dynamic international context within which UR was negotiated (Dinan 1994: 439–41). UR began with 92 'contracting parties' and increased beyond 100 after the demise of the Soviet bloc and the Soviet Union itself. Also, given more assertive parties than in previous Rounds, achieving a unanimous agreement was always going to be tough, particularly in the relatively short time frame established at the outset of UR (agreement by December 1990).

While earlier Rounds had been restricted to trade in manufactured goods, UR also covered agriculture, trade-related aspects of intellectual property rights and services, and finally trade in textiles, which was regulated by agreements outside the GATT framework. With respect to such a broad agenda, different parties naturally had different objectives and priorities and that also complicated the reaching of a consensus. From a Community policy perspective, the range of issues on the agenda raised major questions of competence and control, which, as we shall see, complicated the policy process. Some issues such as agriculture fell 'exclusively' within Community competence whereas other issues such as services and intellectual property rights were mixed. This of itself led to repeated tensions between the Commission and the Council of Ministers and to disputes about who was in control of the process. The range of issues also blurred the 'boundary' between domestic and foreign policy in that a much wider range of actors was involved in policy-making. The 'externalization' in a UR context of domestic policy issues such as agriculture and audiovisual policy was a significant complicating factor in the negotiating process.

The new agenda in UR was partly a product of the Single European Market (SEM), which was itself a response to the increasing globalization of the world economy with attendant interdependence and the politicization of economic activity. But globalization was not the only factor within the dynamic international context that framed negotiations in UR. While the Round began towards the end of the cold war period, it intersected with the end of the cold war. This dramatically changed the dynamics of the policy context in at least two related ways. First, it further politicized commercial policy. As Woolcock and Hodges explain: 'After the cold war, Europe's security interests had less to do with the deterrence of a potential military aggressor and more to do with promoting economic prosperity and social stability in neighbouring countries. In this battle commercial policy plays a crucial role' (1996: 304). Second, the end of the cold war, and in particular the demise of the Soviet Union, changed the nature of the relationship between Western Europe and the United States. It removed both a central plank of Western cooperation and automatic US pre-eminence in GATT (Dinan 1994: 440–1).

Process

The nature of the policy process with respect to trade policy has been described in general terms earlier in this chapter. Under the terms of the Common Commercial Policy, the Commission, as the external trade representative, negotiates in the GATT on behalf of member states, but there are control mechanisms built into the process at every stage. A case study of the UR of GATT offers an excellent opportunity to see how complex that process can become given the context of the UR detailed above. One way of characterizing and analysing the process that is consistent with our FPA approach is to regard the Commission as ostensibly the key actor in the process, engaged in a variety of bargaining games at different levels of activity with, in particular, member states, the Council of Ministers and indeed within the Commission itself, as well as 'simply' negotiating at the international level with third parties (see Putnam 1988; Devuyst 1995). If this provides a useful framework for analysis, the dynamics of the process through the different phases of UR can most effectively be illustrated by a convenient subdivision of the history of UR. These 'games' as analytical themes will be explored here through three phases of UR: from 1986 to the collapse of the Brussels talks at the scheduled deadline in December 1990; from May 1992 when the Community agreed to reform the Common Agricultural Policy (CAP) to December 1992; and finally the breakthrough in the talks in the second half of 1993 culminating in the signing of the Final Act in April 1994.

1986–90

The eighth Round of GATT negotiations was launched at Punta del Este, Uruguay in September 1986. The driving force was undoubtedly United States' concerns about the trade consequences of the EC both 'deepening' (with the Single European Act promising to deepen the process of European integration) and 'widening' with the admission of Spain and Portugal to the Community (Dinan 1994: 249). The initial phase of negotiations saw the establishment of 15 working groups. Most of the talks were held at GATT headquarters in Geneva with GATT Director-General Arthur Dunkel playing a leading role. As far as the key players and the dominant issues in the international negotiations were concerned, all soon became clear. By 1989 if not before, 'it was obvious not only that agriculture was the linchpin of the UR but that Washington and Brussels were monopolizing the agenda' (Dinan 1994: 442). A sustained conflict between the main parties had been assured much earlier with the 1987 US demand for an elimination of all trade distorting measures within ten years. With respect to agriculture, this was formulated more specifically into a demand from the US and the Australia-led 'Cairns' group of 14 farm exporting countries that the Community cut internal farm subsidies by 75 per cent and export subsidies by 90 per cent over a ten-year period.

The ability of the Community to respond adequately to this demand in the first phase of the negotiations was complicated by two problems within the Council of Ministers, one structural and the other contextual. The absence of a formal Council of Trade Ministers and the preoccupation of the foreign ministers with other issues meant that the Community position on agriculture was determined essentially by the Council of Agriculture Ministers who, in effect, were given a veto on policy. An adequate response to demands on agriculture would have necessitated a reform of the CAP, which the agriculture ministers implacably opposed. As Woolcock and Hodges explain, 'the agriculture ministers developed a coherent but restricted position in the – what proved to be mistaken – belief that the US would, as in previous rounds, accept the conclusion of a round without agriculture' (Woolcock and Hodges 1996: 312).

A lead on this issue arguably should have been taken by the foreign ministers in the General Affairs Council. Their ability to represent a wider Community interest on this issue was limited, however, not only by a flood of issues emerging from the end of the cold war but also by the preparations for the upcoming launch of the twin IGCs on Economic and Monetary Union (EMU) and Political Union. The issue was addressed in depth by foreign ministers and heads of government at the Group of 7 (G7) summit in Houston in July 1990 and the results appeared to be promising. There was a clear commitment at the highest levels to reduce agricultural support and protection. But translating the 'Spirit of Houston' into progress in Brussels in terms of substantially reducing agricultural subsidies proved to be extremely difficult. An early indication that the Commission itself was less than united on this issue had already been given by Agriculture Commissioner Ray MacSharry who felt compelled to state publicly in June that he, not Trade Commissioner Frans Andriessen, was 'in charge of agriculture negotiations' (Nugent 1994: 390). But, intra-Commission problems notwithstanding, by the autumn the Commission as a whole, not for the first (or the last) time, was being accused of exceeding its mandate.

In order to meet an agreed deadline of mid-October for tabling negotiating positions, the Commission proposed a compromise of a 30 per cent cut backdated to 1986. But this was blocked by France, Germany and Ireland in the Council. It took a series of Council meetings and 'a marathon joint session of Agriculture and Trade ministers' before a negotiating brief was agreed for the Commission in early November. The 30 per cent figure was maintained but was hedged around with all sorts of clauses to protect European farmers in other ways (see Nugent 1994: 378). While other contextual factors – a focus elsewhere on the SEM, on developments in Eastern Europe as well as the forthcoming IGCs – reduced the significance of GATT on the Community agenda at that time, the collapse of the talks in Brussels in mutual recriminations was mainly due to the Community position on agriculture.

May–December 1992

The UR resumed in 1991 but, despite heroic rhetoric on both sides of the Atlantic that suggested the possibility of an agreement in the near future, there could be no breakthrough until the CAP was reformed. After 18 months of discussion and another marathon four-day meeting of agriculture ministers, agreement on CAP reform was finally agreed in May 1992. The basis of the agreement was outlined in the 1991 Commission paper called *The Development and Future of the CAP*. This envisaged the principle of substituting to a greater or lesser extent price support for direct income support for farmers, although the Commission proposals were substantially watered down in the ensuing negotiations (see Nugent 1994: 371).

Agreement on the 'domestic' politics of CAP reform enabled the multilateral process of negotiations to continue, in effect it 'resuscitated the stalled Uruguay Round' (Dinan 1994: 444). This more flexible position on agriculture, however, needs some explanation, which again illustrates the complexities of the Community policy process. Two developments were crucial here. First, the essentially negative influence of the agriculture ministers in the GATT negotiations began to be counterbalanced by the attempts of successive presidencies of the Council through 1991–92 to increase, at least on an informal basis, the involvement of trade ministers in the decision-making process. From an analytical perspective, this introduces the Council presidency as another significant actor and illustrates the ability of the presidency to influence the policy-making process. Second, a growing concern 'to ensure continued market access for German manufactured products' led to a shift in Germany's position on agriculture towards the end of 1991. A new willingness in Bonn to make concessions on agriculture in order to complete the Round removed a potential blocking minority in the Council (together with France and Ireland) against concessions (see Woolcock and Hodges 1996: 315).

The result of the agreement to reform Community agriculture was to give the Commission greater flexibility in negotiations and to avoid the isolation that had been evident in Brussels. The problem that was to 'dog' the remainder of this phase of the negotiations, however, was that France was now becoming clearly isolated. The text on the table in Geneva was the Draft Final Act, or the Dunkel Text as it was known after the GATT Director-General. This, as Woolcock and Hodges note, was 'a draft agreement... but not an agreed text' (Woolcock and Hodges 1996: 316). The Commission, supported by Germany and

Britain, took the position in March that the Dunkel Text provided a basis for a final agreement. This helped to restart negotiations but the cost was further disunity within the Community when the French Government again accused the Commission of exceeding its mandate.

In fact little progress was made over the next few months as other differences emerged in the GATT negotiations and both the process of ratifying the Maastricht Treaty and forthcoming national elections diverted attention in Europe and complicated negotiating positions. By the autumn of 1992, attention was focused on the bilateral negotiations between the United States and the Community. Domestic politics was intervening again, this time in the form of the US presidential election. The 'carrot and stick' approach of the outgoing Bush Administration – making concessions on some issues but taking a tough line on others including, for no obvious reason, retaliation against the export of subsidized Community oilseeds – was followed by a bilateral meeting in Chicago just before the election. This focused on trying to resolve both agriculture and the oilseeds issue. But, not only did these negotiations fail, they revealed in a rather dramatic way further disunity within the Commission itself. This did not take the form on this occasion of a split between commissioners. Both Ray MacSharry and Frans Andriessen were keen to accept the deal on the table but their boss, Commission President Jaques Delors, argued that the deal would not be acceptable to all member states (France in particular). This was regarded by MacSharry as excessive interference and he went so far as to resign, albeit temporarily, from his position (Nugent 1994: 390; Woolcock and Hodges 1996: 317).

It was not long, however, before US and Community negotiators were meeting again. The breakdown of the Chicago talks led the US to announce punitive tariffs on a range of EC agricultural exports to come into operation within a month. This, together with the election of a new US President, Bill Clinton, who was expected to take a much tougher line on European subsidies, persuaded the Commission, supported by the British presidency, to return to bilateral talks. This time, in late November, an agreement was reached at Blair House in Washington on both the oilseeds issue and wider agricultural issues (see Dinan 1994: 444). The 'breakthrough' at Blair House, however, could not serve as a pre-agreement that might conclude the UR while France objected to its terms and even threatened to veto it if brought to a vote. With French intransigence underpinned by a general election in France pending in March 1993, the second phase of the negotiations came to an unsatisfactory conclusion. The main lesson to be learned from this phase with respect to the policy process was apparent. As Woolcock and Hodges conclude, 'the experience of this 1991–92 phase of the Round... shows there are clear limits to the ability of the European Commission, even with backing from some member states, to press ahead in critical negotiations without a consensus of the member states' (Woolcock and Hodges 1996: 315).

1993–94

The prospects for a settlement looked equally unpromising at the beginning of 1993. The expectation that the new Clinton Administration would take a tough line on GATT appeared to be realized; a number of hostile trade actions – against European steel exports in particular – matched by equally hostile speeches from Washington, seemed to suggest a determination to reopen parts of the Dunkel Text. Statements issued from the Commission also suggested a less than conciliatory approach (Dinan 1994: 445). Nevertheless, the negotiating context was about to change, dramatically increasing the possibilities of, although certainly not guaranteeing, a final settlement. In Woolcock and Hodges' words:

> By spring 1993 the political and economic climate had improved; Europe was following the US out of recession, the Maastricht ratification process was coming to an end, and [after the French election] there were no general elections pending in any of the major member states. (Woolcock and Hodges 1996: 318)

The Clinton Administration also gave notice that it was seeking a twelve-month extension of 'fast-track' negotiating authority from Congress, clearly indicating a resolve to reach a settlement, in effect by the end of 1993.

If the negotiating context was improving, the Community policy process also changed in ways that (certainly with the benefit of hindsight) can be seen to have facilitated a settlement. Two developments should be noted here, both of which remind us of the importance of actors in the policy process who can make crucial decisions despite structural constraints, if the context is permissive. First, new negotiators in key positions enter the scene in 1993. Sir Leon Brittan became the new Community Trade Commissioner and immediately established links with his opposite number Mickey Kantor, the new US Trade

Representative. Brittan took a tough line from the outset, asserting that it was Commission policy to stick as closely as possible both to the Dunkel Text and to the Blair House pre-agreement. This line was intended to head off potential problems in the Community as well as in the United States (Woolcock and Hodges 1996: 318).

The second development highlights again the proactive, agenda-setting role that the Council presidency can play. In the summer, the new Belgian presidency, following consultations, established the principle that agreement on the final UR package would be by consensus rather than by qualified majority vote (QMV). This was a key element in a cohesion-building strategy that had two objectives: to ensure that France was 'on board' with respect to the final settlement and to improve the flow of communication between the Commission and member states. The Blair House agreement had been negotiated by the Commission largely in secret and this had clearly damaged relations, precipitating a serious crisis of confidence between the Commission and certain member states. Both objectives were eventually advanced by a so-called 'Jumbo Council' meeting of foreign, agriculture and trade ministers on 20 September. Youri Devuyst offers a useful summary of what was achieved:

> In the end, the Jumbo Council proved to be the first step in the Community's cohesion exercise leading to the successful conclusion of the Round. Indeed, the negotiations on the Jumbo Council's conclusions created a positive Franco-German dynamic on Uruguay Round matters, which was actively supported by the Presidency because it helped to bridge the gap between the more protectionist and more free-trade orientated members, while preventing France's isolation. (Devuyst 1995: 453–4)

This Council meeting also ensured that the Council was fully involved in the last three months of the negotiations. Thereafter, the Council endorsed various aspects of the Commission's negotiating mandate, agreeing the final negotiating tactics at the beginning of December. This legitimization process, together with an agreement with the US on agriculture, enabled the Commission to play a more 'aggressive' role in the final stages of the multilateral negotiations in Geneva, securing important concessions on a number of issues (see Woolcock and Hodges 1996: 320).

Before the Council approved the Final Act by consensus on 15 December, however, a number of important issues had to be resolved both within the Community and in the multilateral negotiations. With respect to the latter, the most intransigent issue to be resolved after agriculture was the negotiation on audiovisual services. While the Community, at French insistence, remained opposed to including audiovisual services in the proposed GATS (General Agreement on Trade in Services), which would have led to the progressive liberalization of this sector, one of the prime objectives of the United States in the UR was to gain access to the lucrative Community audiovisual market. Ultimately, an 'agreement to disagree' was the only solution. The cultural sector as a whole was included in the GATS but was not made subject to any obligations (see Devuyst 1995: 457–9). Desmond Dinan is less charitable to the Community, seeing this episode as a crucial last minute concession by the US, effectively letting 'the Community off the hook' of what he calls 'French obstructionism' (Dinan 1994: 445).

Success on the audiovisual issue, however, was not enough to secure French compliance. They insisted on and to some extent secured a deal that the agricultural commitments under GATT would not exceed the agreed terms of the 1992 reform of the CAP. Certainly, French farmers were 'bought off' in advance of the GATT deadline by a considerable amount of financial compensation for the reformed CAP, largely financed by the Community. French demands with respect to improving the effectiveness of the Community's instruments to combat unfair trade practices by third countries were also conceded at the last minute. The other member state threatening to reject the Final Act at the last minute was Portugal, on the grounds that it was bearing a disproportionate burden of the costs associated with the proposed GATT agreement on textiles. A special Community action of 400 million ECU was sanctioned by the GAC to 'buy off' the Portuguese textile industry and maintain a consensus (Devuyst 1995: 456–9).

Even after the signing of the Final Act, a serious implementation problem emerged in the shape of whether or not the agreement would be ratified. The main problem here was a dispute over competence between the Commission and the Council. The member states took the view that the UR Final Act was a mixed agreement containing both Community and member state competences. The Commission, on the other hand, argued that the Act should be seen as a package to be ratified as a whole by the Community. Without prejudice to resolving this issue in legal terms, the Greek Council Presidency, Trade Commissioner Leon Brittan, and representatives of each member state all signed the Final Act in Marrakesh in April 1994.

In order to resolve the question of competence, the Commission requested the binding opinion of the European Court of Justice under Article 228(6). The Court's opinion in November 1994, however, did not support an extension of EC and by implication Commission competence. While it confirmed Community competence to conclude agreements on trade in goods, it opined that member states and the Community were jointly competent to deal with both GATS and TRIPs (Trade-Related Aspects of Intellectual Property Rights). While the Court underlined the obligation on all parties to ensure close cooperation in areas of mixed competence in future negotiations, this judgement scarcely resolved the competence issue (Devuyst 1995: 460–2; Woolcock and Hodges 1996: 320–1; see also Chapter 1).

Conclusion

This detailed case study has revealed important aspects of Community foreign policy and important conclusions that can be drawn from it. From a general analytical perspective, it has demonstrated the usefulness of an analytical framework that enables us to track the interrelationships between context, actors and policy process that are particularly complex when dealing with a set of issues as politically sensitive as those dealt with in the UR. All elements of the policy system interacted with each other and clearly impacted upon the ability of the Community to act in the form of engaging in multilateral economic diplomacy. Both the international and the domestic context in which policy was made clearly affected policy output. Through the late 1980s and early part of the 1990s, a dynamic context operated as a constraint upon policy and helped to prevent a successful outcome to the negotiations. By mid-1993, however, contextual factors had become much more permissive, constituting one set of factors that enabled the policy process to operate more effectively as well as contributing to the eventual signing of the Final Act.

As expected, the policy-making process in the Community revealed tensions between and among the key actors, given the range of issues and the mixed competences involved. Structural as well as contextual factors resulted in the agriculture ministers playing a dominant and, from the perspective of the negotiations, an essentially negative role, certainly up to 1991–92. What was less expected from our earlier review of the process, however, was the important role that the presidency of the Council of Ministers can play in shaping the policy agenda and changing the operation of the process. The presidency intervened at two crucial points in the negotiations: to alter the 'balance of power' within the Council, bringing the trade ministers more into the process and, later, establishing the principle that agreement on the final UR negotiating package would be by consensus rather than by QMV.

Working towards a consensus was particularly important for both internal and external reasons. By December 1993, as Woolcock and Hodges note, 'national ministers felt no need to disown the negotiations or to blame the EC or the Commission for failure. Unlike in Chicago or Blair House, all member states were associated with the final package' (Woolcock and Hodges 1996: 320). Having achieved a 'domestic' consensus, which not only required bringing all member governments 'on board' but also 'buying off' certain domestic interest groups, this then strengthened the hand of the Commission in the multilateral negotiations and significantly enhanced the ability of the Community to play a proactive role in the final stages of the UR and to deploy effectively its principal policy instrument in this context – economic diplomacy (Devuyst 1995: 463; Woolcock and Hodges 1996: 323ff.).

4

European Political Cooperation

The demand for an explicitly political dimension to the external relations of the EC eventually produced a commitment to a Common Foreign and Security Policy (CFSP) in the 1993 Treaty on European Union. We shall be analysing the CFSP in the next chapter. This outcome, however, emerged from an incremental process of change over many years. It is necessary, therefore, to preface a discussion of Union foreign policy by applying our analytical framework here to the predecessor of CFSP known as European Political Cooperation (EPC), which began life in 1970 and was replaced by CFSP in 1993.

Context

European Political Cooperation can be defined as 'the procedures used from 1970 to allow member states of the European Community to discuss and coordinate their positions on foreign affairs and, where appropriate, act in concert' (Bainbridge 1998: 244–5). But if this was foreign policy-making at the European level in all but name, the language used to describe it is a clear indicator of the sensitive political context within which EPC emerged. For member states, the formal adoption in 1974 of the euphemism 'European Political Cooperation' (rather like 'external relations' discussed in the last chapter) was a way of avoiding the political embarrassment of appearing to concede foreign policy in any sense – and by implication, national sovereignty – to Community competence. Indeed, there was a resistance to references even to 'policy' as such in this context. References, as above, to EPC as 'procedures', or as 'process(es)' or 'mechanisms', and to action as collective only 'where appropriate', also suggest the very limited nature of the enterprise being undertaken. As indicated by the language of the Luxembourg Report, which produced EPC, the process was envisaged as being limited to 'regular exchanges of information and consultations', working towards a 'harmonization' of 'views' and a 'coordination' of 'positions', but acting jointly only where feasible or desirable (Luxembourg Report, Part 2:1, 1970: 24–32).

There are other important contextual factors that help to explain how EPC emerged and, equally importantly, why it developed in the way it did. We start with the situational factors, the particular blend of internal and external factors that help to explain the emergence of EPC in 1970. Internal factors include fears that the proposed enlargement of the Community would obstruct further European integration (this concern had led directly to the Luxembourg Report) and the wish of the West German government to 'legitimize' its policy of Ostpolitik (seeking cooperation with the Soviet Union and its allies in Eastern Europe) by locating it within a European political framework. Important external factors included European concerns about the reliability of the United States as an ally following Vietnam and a desire to play a more effective role in the Middle East following the crisis generated by the 1967 Arab-Israeli war.

Situational factors in turn can be placed within a wider context and across a longer time frame. With respect to internal factors, EPC should be understood in the context of the dynamic of European integration. Integral to the original integration ideal was the notion that economic integration was only a stage en route to political union. The goal was always a European union that would not only define a 'European identity' but would enable Europe to play an active role in world affairs, acting as a single unit, 'speaking with one voice'. Even before the establishment of the EEC, as we noted in Chapter 1, explicitly political and security arguments were used to justify the development of European institutions. The Schuman Plan of 1950, for example, talked about establishing a European Coal and Steel Community (ECSC) in order to make 'any war between France and Germany... not only unthinkable but materially impossible' (quoted in Hallstein 1962: 10). ECSC in turn, it will be recalled, was followed by the abortive attempt to establish a European Defence Community which, if successful, would have been followed by a European Political Community.

The establishment and the success of the EEC revived aspirations to give an overtly political dimension to Community discussions about external relations. De Gaulle had the idea of regular meetings of heads of government to coordinate foreign policy. This inspired the Fouchet talks in 1961–62, which ultimately failed to produce an agreed outcome although they did help to establish an intergovernmental approach to foreign policy cooperation. As external relations developed in a restricted sphere of activity through the 1960s, it became increasingly apparent that it was difficult in practice to separate external economic activity from a political context. It was clearly difficult, for example, to be discussing aid policy in the context of the Lomé negotiations without securing agreement on the broader political context within which aid was to be given. This problem became even more apparent in the early 1970s when growing interdependence between states (between European states and the Organization of Petroleum Exporting Countries (OPEC), for example) made economic relationships highly sensitive and political in the broadest sense. The changing international context within which the Community operated served only to underline the practical utility of establishing some system of coordinating foreign policy rather than simply relying on bilateral relations between member and non-member states.

Once established, it became apparent that EPC was galvanized by external imperatives, either in the form of crises or other sorts of demand emanating from the international environment. Simon Nuttall has constructed a history of EPC in four parts, all of which are characterized to a greater or lesser extent by interaction with contextual factors. The initial flurry of EPC activity up to the mid-1970s can clearly be linked to two external crises: the crisis in transatlantic relations centred upon the 'Year of Europe' in 1973 and, in the same year, the war in the Middle East. The 'revival of activity' in the early 1980s, following the 'dismal time' of the late 1970s, was very much underpinned by external developments (Nuttall 1997a).

Following the Soviet invasion of Afghanistan in 1979, it was 'European dismay at the drift of US policy towards confrontation with the USSR' that fuelled a demand that European security policy be coordinated, an issue first addressed in the 1981 London Report (Forster and Wallace 1996: 415). Thereafter, it was the pressure of outside events – martial law in Poland, the Argentinian invasion of the Falklands, the Israeli invasion of Lebanon – that stimulated more effective EPC action by increasing the 'readiness of the member states to make use of Community instruments to enforce their foreign policy decisions' (Nuttall 1997a: 21). Finally, it was the dramatic changes in the whole post-war architecture of world politics from 1989 that finally overwhelmed the whole EPC machinery and opened the way for CFSP.

If the pressure of external events impacted upon the development of EPC, external demands also included the reaction of other international actors. Almost as soon as EPC was established, third parties began to exert a persistent demand that the Community act in an increasingly unified way. An early example of this was the arrival of a delegation of foreign ministers from Arab states at the European summit meeting in December 1973. As Whitman comments, this indicated that the Community was already being 'treated as a substantive entity' and was being placed 'under direct and immediate pressure to respond directly to outside actors'. The result was a commitment by the nine member states to initiate what became the Euro-Arab dialogue (Whitman 1998: 83).

The legal context within which EPC developed is the final contextual element considered here. Until the 1986 Single European Act (SEA), EPC operated without any legal basis at all, being guided only by various Reports, Declarations and procedures that are reviewed in the next section. The principal aim of the SEA was to revise the Treaty of Rome by incorporating new policy areas within it and to launch the SEM programme. Title 3 of SEA, however, also established a separate legal basis for EPC activity. Two articles in this treaty are important to the analysis here. First, Article 30.1 commits the parties to 'endeavour jointly to formulate and implement a *European foreign policy*' (my italics). Given the powerful symbolism of language in this context, this was a highly significant statement to be given legal form, if only in aspirational terms. Second, under Article 30.5, the parties agree that 'the external policies of the European Community and the policies agreed in European Political Cooperation must be consistent'. Nevertheless, EPC remained separate from, if parallel to, the Community framework of institutions and obligations on member states. In Trevor Salmon's words, 'despite having been incorporated into the SEA, EPC still entailed political obligations, not legally binding ones and foreign policy cooperation remained strictly intergovernmental' (Salmon 1998: 218). Precisely how 'strictly intergovernmental' the EPC process was, however, needs to be addressed by a more detailed look at the actors and the policy process involved.

Actors and Policy-making

The key elements of the EPC process were originally laid down in the 1970 Luxembourg Report of foreign ministers. Thereafter they were developed and codified in the Copenhagen (1973) and London (1981) Reports, the Stuttgart 'Solemn Declaration on European Union' of 1983 and finally the Single European Act (1986). The key actors involved were the rotating presidency, the European Council, the

General Affairs Council (GAC), the Political Committee of Political Directors and a more junior group of national foreign office diplomats known as the European Correspondents. Ostensibly, the European Commission was not a significant actor in the EPC process, and the European Parliament, until the SEA, had no role in the process at all other than to receive irregular reports from the foreign ministers.

Intergovernmental principles were clearly established at the outset in the sense that decisions were to be made by consensus; no votes were to be taken and any member state was at liberty to disassociate itself from collective positions. As Michael Smith notes, states 'retained the right to pursue purely national foreign policies at the same time as participating in the EPC mechanism' (Smith 1996: 249). The rotating presidency was responsible for initiating periodic meetings of foreign ministers who met formally 'in the margins' of Council meetings or informally. Acting through the GAC, the presidency also provided for EPC 'the dynamism which is given by the Treaties to the Commission within the Community: taking initiatives, convening meetings, setting the agenda, building a consensus; acting as the spokesman for the [member states], managing and conducting consultations with third countries, and as far as necessary implementing decisions taken' (Wallace 1983: 3).

Additional institutionalized support for the process at the highest levels was provided by the creation in 1974 of the European Council. Preparation work for foreign ministers' meetings was done by a Political Committee formed by Directors of Political Affairs (or simply Political Directors) who were senior officials in member state foreign offices. The Political Directors were empowered to form working parties consisting of foreign ministry officials for special tasks. Day-to-day management of the process was entrusted to the European Correspondents, a group of junior national officials who communicated with each other through a secure communications network known as COREU, which linked foreign ministries in member states for the exclusive conduct of EPC business. Administrative support for EPC was provided initially by the country holding the presidency, although this was extended under the 'Troika' system to include officials seconded from the previous and the following presidencies. Not until the SEA was a full-time secretariat established to aid the presidency.

If this was formally an intergovernmental process, there were important dimensions of the process as it developed that call into question the 'strictly intergovernmental' interpretation offered by Salmon. First, there were growing links with Community institutions that over time moved the EPC policy process progressively closer to what might be termed 'normal' Community decision-making, although this movement was politically highly contentious. This can be seen most clearly in the growing involvement of the European Commission in EPC activities. The Luxembourg Report had stated that the Commission would be consulted only if Community activities were affected by EPC. Almost immediately, however, an incremental process of increasing involvement began. As Forster and Wallace observe, the Commission 'crept slowly into working group after working group, from its first invitation to join the discussions on those economic aspects of the Conference on Security and Cooperation in Europe (CSCE) negotiations which fell within Community competence in April 1971' (Forster and Wallace 1996: 417). The launch of the Euro–Arab dialogue in December 1973 also involved direct linkage between political and economic relations and necessitated limited Commission involvement.

By the beginning of the 1980s, de facto Commission involvement in EPC had been recognized, although it remained highly contentious for certain member states. It was agreed in the 1981 London Report that the Commission would thereafter be 'fully associated with Political Cooperation at all levels'. The following year, this linkage enabled sanctions to be applied to the Soviet Union by Council Regulation (that is, by an EC legislative instrument). As Nuttall comments:

> this proved to be an extremely important precedent. The ice was broken; the rigid separation between EPC and the Community was relaxed and, in the future, Community instruments could be employed for the implementation of foreign policy goals. (Nuttall 1997a: 32)

The Commission was also searching for a more overtly political role in areas of 'high' rather 'low' politics. Hill gives two examples: in 1983, it was the Commission rather than member states who expressed regret at the US invasion of Grenada; three years later, it was the Commission again that condemned the South African invasion of the 'front line' states of Botswana, Zambia and Zimbabwe (Hill 1992: 119). Under the terms of the SEA, the role of the Commission in EPC was increased in two significant ways. First, it confirmed in legal terms the 'fully associated' status of the Commission with EPC. Second, and more importantly, it made the Commission together with the presidency jointly responsible for consistency between external relations and EPC. Moreover, as Cameron notes, the SEA 'commitment to intensify cooperation between member states, diplomatic missions to third countries, and international organizations' had the effect of drawing the Commission's external delegations into the EPC framework (Cameron 1997: 99; Nuttall 1997b: 309).

But, more than anything else perhaps, it was the evolving agenda of EPC that finally brought the Commission centre stage in the EPC process, illustrating an important linkage between the contextual, agenda and process elements of the policy system. After 1989, following the collapse of communism in Eastern Europe, 'low policy' issues in the shape of financial and economic diplomacy, technical and, to some extent, humanitarian assistance came to dominate the EPC agenda. These were precisely the sorts of issue that played to the strengths of the Commission. This was clearly recognized outside the Community when the G7 countries, at their 1989 summit, gave the Commission the task of coordinating assistance, initially to Poland and Hungary and later to all the countries in Central and Eastern Europe. The Commission also took the leading role in negotiating the Europe Agreements with those same countries (Cameron 1997: 99). With respect to this whole set of issues, as Nuttall comments, 'it was the Commission that held the levers of power, whether through its control of the implementation of the Community budget, its coordination of the international aid effort on behalf of the countries of East and Central Europe or its mastery of the process of negotiating agreements on behalf of the Community' (Nuttall 1997b: 310; see also Nuttall 1996: 142–3). The Europe Agreements are analysed under instruments in the next section.

If a clear line between intergovernmentalism and the Community method of decision-making was blurred by the growing involvement of Community institutions in EPC (which included the EP after the SEA stated that in future it too should be 'closely associated' with EPC), a 'strictly' intergovernmentalist approach was also modified by the nature of the EPC machinery that evolved and by the growing impact of EPC on governmental behaviour over time. It may be helpful here to clarify what exactly is meant by intergovernmental in this context and to compare it with other ways of characterizing the policy process. A straightforward definition of 'intergovernmental' would be 'the supremacy of national governments in the integration process over supranational and other actors' (Dinan 1998: 297). From this state-centric realist perspective, EPC simply represented the interplay between separate national interests, those interests being defined by member states and constituted outside the EPC policy process.

But the term 'intergovernmentalism', as Helen Wallace has argued, is 'too rigid' to characterize 'the engagement of policy elites from the member states in the process and the structuring of dialogue that was achieved'. Drawing upon neo-functionalist rather than realist approaches, Wallace describes a 'process of *engrenage* or locking in' of member states in which 'the costs of defection were significant, even if the scope for penalizing defectors was less than in the classical Community framework' (Wallace, H. 1996: 51). As for the pursuit of separate national interests, Wallace argues that the representatives of member states may 'use the vocabulary of national interest' but 'they frequently articulate more narrowly based interests' whether they be partisan, sectional or domestic. With respect to the substance of decisions taken in EPC, consensus did not necessarily emerge either around the lowest common denominator or some aggregation of national interests, as realists might have predicted. In fact, as Geoffrey Edwards notes, a 'consensus tended to form around the median line between the two extremes' (Edwards 1996: 133).

The critical point here is that interests were in part at least a function of the policy process itself, that is, they were internal to the policy process rather than simply externally constituted. The very process of interaction itself between member states in EPC helped to modify both state interests and strategies. The social pressures of working together in what Nuttall revealingly calls a 'club atmosphere' produced what was being referred to as early as the 1973 Copenhagen Report as a 'coordination reflex'. A critical part of the socialization process was a collective albeit implicit agreement to reach an agreement. That was the 'bottom line'. Nuttall talks about a culture in which diplomats were predisposed 'to regard a failure to agree as the worst of outcomes' (Nuttall 1992: 314).

Two comments may be helpful here. First, it may well be that different analytical perspectives are helpful, but in explaining different things. As Ginsberg suggests, a realist, intergovernmentalist analysis may help to explain either the breakdown of common action or untried attempts at common action. But it may well be less helpful in explaining what actually triggers common action (Ginsberg 1989: 18). The second point is to say that, from a perspective familiar to foreign policy analysts, intergovernmentalism remains a fundamentally flawed explanation here, to the extent that it is tied to a monolithic conception of 'government'. As Carole Webb perceptively commented many years ago, 'as long as [intergovernmentalism] is associated with the "billiard ball" image in which monolithic governments are seen as preserving their hard shell against external penetration by international negotiating forums like the EC, it cannot be a complete answer' (Webb 1983: 27). Webb goes on to argue that two related dimensions of the policy process are 'inadequately accommodated' within this approach.

First, intergovernmentalism underestimates the degree of *intra*governmental 'negotiation and coordination – made necessary by the content of community issues and the political context in which they are mediated'. Intergovernmentalism also diverts attention away from the degree to which bureaucratic politics have been 'externalized' in negotiating forums such as the Community. This is the process called *trans*-governmentalism, which describes the 'intensive and continuous consultation process' across subsets of national governments (see also Keohane and Nye 1974). Thus, Webb suggests, transgovernmentalism may be a more appropriate label for describing political processes 'at the nexus of Community and national politics', to the extent that the term 'capture[s] the potentially centrifugal and cross-cutting interests inherent in bureaucratic negotiations within the European Community' (Webb 1983: 27).

However, there remains the problem that this term continues to focus attention exclusively on the *governmental* dimension of policy-making in a mixed actor policy system, which, as Webb notes, under-plays the role of domestic politics in Community politics. Equally importantly, we may add, it ignores the role of non-governmental actors in the policy process. This suggests that the label 'transnational' activity – defined by Webb as 'the external representation and mobi-lization of non-governmental *and* intragovernmental interests' – is a more inclusive and perhaps more appropriate label to describe the policy process (Webb 1983: 34, my italics).

Hopefully, this rather extended discussion of the nature of policy processes within the EC has usefully clarified some key terms and perspectives. While we will revisit these ideas again in the context of the transition from EPC to CFSP in Chapter 5, it enables us to draw two conclusions here about the nature of the EPC process. First, it is diffi-cult to sustain the argument that the EPC policy process was essentially or 'strictly' intergovernmentalist. Second, we may conclude that any simple characterization of the process does an injustice to the growing coordination of national and community machinery both in Brussels and in third countries that developed from EPC, which arguably contained elements of intergovernmentalism, but also growing elements of transgovernmentalism, supranationalism and transnation-alism (see Hill 1992: 120–1).

Capabilities and Instruments

A simple typology of policy instruments associated with EPC would include three types – political diplomacy, economic diplomacy and a mix of political *and* economic diplomacy. Political diplomacy contains two instruments, Declarations and dialogue. The economic diplomacy category contains a set of measures that we reviewed in a different context in Chapter 3. The final category looks at a mix of instruments across the political/economic 'divide' and is illustrated here by looking at the Europe Agreements signed with Central and East European countries (CEECs) after 1989. This section analyses the types of instrument not discussed earlier, introduces, where appropriate, problems relating to capabilities and implementation, and concludes with a brief discussion of the strengths and weaknesses of EPC in action as a preface to a detailed case study on South Africa in the final section.

The most characteristic and most overtly political form of EPC action was political diplomacy consisting of Declarations and more or less structured dialogues with third parties. (In typological terms, dialogues can also be located with the category of framework instruments discussed in Chapter 3.) Declarations that emerged from common positions taken at Council meetings constitute a much-debated category of action or perhaps 'action' given that, for many observers, they epitomize all that was wrong with EPC. 'In few cases', Peterson and Bomberg comment bluntly, 'did the EPC facilitate any kind of "action". Decision-making usually focused on common declarations of one kind or other' (Peterson and Bomberg 1999: 229). In similar vein, Holland talks disparagingly about 'a declaratory diplomacy that lacks effective instruments and recognizable actor-capabilities' (Holland 1991: 196). At best, Declarations lacking in any legal force had a functional utility that had more to do with avoiding divisions between member states than contributing to the achievement of external objectives.

For other analysts, however, Declarations that required minimal capabilities and per se posed no implementation problems – strictly speaking they had only to be stated to be implemented – had a role to play as one of a set of policy instruments. Taking a more positive view, Nuttall argues that EPC Declarations could constitute action and, moreover, could on occasion be 'effective tools and substantial diplomatic events' (Nuttall 1992: 13). As illustrations of this, he cites the December 1980 Venice Declaration on the Middle East and EPC Declarations on Central America in 1983 and 1984. Hill also cites the

Venice Declaration as the centrepiece of EPC diplomacy on the Middle East during this period, which, he argues, broke new ground by pushing for a more 'even-handed' policy that 'balanced Israel's right to exist in conditions of security with the need to acknowledge the suffering of the Palestinian people and their "legitimate rights", particularly to "self-determination"'. This Declaration was followed up by an intensive round of diplomatic contacts over the next 12 months or so and helped to set the agenda on Middle East negotiations thereafter (Hill 1992: 122–5; for a more sceptical review of the impact of the Venice Declaration, see Gomez 1998: 136–7).

If EPC declaratory diplomacy attracted controversy, dialogues or 'structured political consultations' (Hill 1998a: 33) with third parties were much less controversial and arguably more effective. Dialogues emerged for two reasons. First, structured consultations with other parties provided valuable opportunities for the Community collectively to shape and influence international relations in different ways. To this end, the London Report of 1981 specifically invited 'more or less regular contacts', although later Community communications differentiated between ad hoc contacts and 'institutionalized' relationships with other parties (Monar 1997a: 263). But the initiative for dialogues also came increasingly from third parties themselves, who came to regard political consultations with the EC as valuable in themselves and as a way of facilitating other benefits from the relationship. What started as a 'trickle' of requests for dialogue became a 'flood' after the London Report and produced a 'confusing patchwork' of relationships, with many different patterns emerging (Nuttall 1992: 282–3).

For the Community, as Monar has argued, the dialogue instrument offered several benefits. First, it facilitated the pursuit of particular strategies such as the promotion of regional stability and cooperation. Many of the dialogues were held with regional groups beginning with the Euro–Arab dialogue in the 1970s and continuing with groups such as the Association of South-East Asian Nations (ASEAN), the Rio Group and the Gulf Cooperation Council in the 1980s. Second, dialogues played a useful 'conveyor role' – informing third parties of Community positions on particular issues and soliciting their support for them, and in return getting a clearer picture of third party positions, Third, dialogues were a useful mechanism for articulating and affirming a 'collective identity vis-à-vis the dialogue partners'. Finally, and perhaps most usefully, dialogues were a very flexible policy instrument. Without necessarily incurring substantial political obligations, bilateral or multilateral dialogues could be established at a variety of different levels of contact denoting the importance attached to the relationship and could be upgraded or downgraded relatively easily depending upon any changes in the status of the relationship (Monar 1997a: 266–7).

Success in terms of the number of dialogues established, however, also brought problems in terms of the limited intergovernmental capabilities of the EPC process. Maintaining dialogues placed a heavy burden on the presidency – in particular on the foreign minister, the Political Director and the Political Correspondent of the presidency representing the various levels at which dialogues were held. This was relieved to some extent by involving the Troika (past and future presidencies) in the dialogue process and, after 1983, allowing limited Commission involvement in dialogue meetings (Regelsberger 1991: 164–70). Nevertheless, demands from more and more third parties for more and more meetings at the highest possible levels had led by the end of EPC's life to decisions to restrict dialogue commitments in a number of pragmatic ways (see Monar 1997a: 271–3).

As noted at the beginning of this section, economic diplomacy instruments deployed by EPC were reviewed in Chapter 3 in the context of Community foreign policy. It is unnecessary, therefore, to introduce them again, although they are discussed in detail in the case study on South Africa. But it is important to review here a third category of EPC instrument that offers a mix of political and economic instruments. This type is illustrated by looking at the Europe Agreements signed with the CEECs after 1989.

A special meeting of the European Council in April 1990 agreed to 'create a new type of association agreement as a part of the new pattern of relationships in Europe' (Sedelmeier and Wallace 1996: 367). This was an explicit reference to the dramatically transformed international context in which EPC was now operating and the wide ranging content of these agreements with the former East European bloc also reflected the new 'domestic' context of European foreign policy-making in which the SEA now demanded consistency between EPC and the Community's 'external relations'.

Beginning with Poland and Hungary in December 1991 (with other agreements extending into the CFSP period), Europe Agreements contained a comprehensive political partnership including an institutionalized political dialogue, an improved trade-based agreement, technical and financial assistance (for details, see Sedelmeier and Wallace 1996: 368–9, Box 14.4). These were clearly mixed agreements negotiated by the Commission under Article 238 but covering areas of both

Community and national competence. As such they were signed both by the Community and by member states and required the approval of the Council of Ministers, the EP and the parliaments of both member states and associated countries. One significant procedural innovation, given the overload problem discussed above, is that the Commission was formally involved in sharing the burden of maintaining the political dialogues with the CEECs (Nuttall 1992: 293).

Having identified and discussed EPC instruments, we conclude this section with a tentative summary of the strengths and weaknesses of EPC that might be tested in the detailed case study on South Africa in the next section. First, whatever problems surrounded EPC, it did provide a distinct international identity – a 'foreign policy personality' in Nuttall's phrase – for the Community which differentiated it from other international actors such as the United States (Nuttall 1997a: 22). Whatever the problems of securing agreement among member states on substantive rather than merely symbolic action, some common actor capability was evident and the Community was clearly capable of having an impact on international developments.

A case study illustration we might have chosen for detailed appraisal is the role of the Community through EPC in the Conference on Security and Cooperation in Europe (CSCE) in the 1970s. According to Nuttall, the Community 'set the agenda for the CSCE and largely contributed to its success' (Nuttall 1997a: 23). Forster and Wallace contrast the role of the Community with that played by the United States. The Community, in their view, 'played a more active role in CSCE than the United States in shaping the agenda and in negotiating the complex package of the Helsinki Declaration' (Forster and Wallace 1996: 414).

Second, although revealing the weakness of the intergovernmental capabilities at its disposal, EPC did provide a concrete response to the SEA aspiration to create a European foreign policy by linking together political and economic instruments in a reasonably 'consistent' manner. Indeed, as noted in Chapter 3, the 1982 decision to follow up an EPC Declaration against martial law in Poland by adopting economic sanctions against the Soviet Union through Community mechanisms provided the important breakthrough in linking EPC and EC instruments. This action predated the SEA.

But, whatever the positive contribution of EPC, as the 1980s closed, commentators were emphasizing the weaknesses rather than the strengths of the process. While it was possible to note the impact of EPC on specific issues such as CSCE, there was more scepticism about the wider impact of EPC on key problem areas in international relations and the usefulness more generally of the process. Forster and Wallace (1996: 420), for example, argue that:

> there was little evidence that EPC had exerted any direct influence on Arab-Israeli relations... or on events in sub-Saharan Africa or the Persian/Arabian Gulf. These were procedures without policy, activity without output, while American arms and American diplomacy still determined the course of western interests throughout the regions to Europe's immediate south.

European Political Cooperation in Action: The Community and South Africa

Having reviewed the policy instruments associated with EPC, we move on to analyse EPC in action by looking in detail at a case study. The case chosen – South Africa – is both interesting and relevant here. First, it is controversial – it certainly divided member states – and the longer-term impact of EPC policy has also attracted controversy. There is much debate about how effective the EC contribution was in helping the transition from an apartheid regime to a democratic government in South Africa. Second, the case study not only spans historic changes in South Africa but also in the EC. The case was an important issue through most of the period of EPC.

South Africa was also one of the first 'joint actions' selected as subjects (or possibly objects) of the new CFSP in 1993. South African policy later evolved outside CFSP in the second half of the 1990s into a bilateral cooperation agreement encompassing trade, development and human rights (Holland 1998: 428). Although we are not considering CFSP per se until the next chapter, there are important continuities in the transition from EPC to CFSP and beyond which South African policy illustrates, so the case will be updated here beyond 1993 even if some of the analysis must wait its turn! Third and not least, this case study can be fitted neatly into our analytical framework. It illustrates the interaction between the key actors and the linkages between different elements of the policy process. It demonstrates both the scope of European foreign policy during this period and a range of EPC policy instruments in action. Not least, as discussed in the first section, it shows the importance of context in framing policy.

Context

The development of European policy towards South Africa has passed through at least three different phases since the 1970s; this gives a convenient structure to the analysis in the next section. An important part of any explanation of both the substance and the changing nature of that policy, however, lies in a series of events, both external and internal to the Community, that impacted upon policy over time. Two sets of external events provided an initial stimulus. First a Community interest in Southern Africa as a whole followed the breakup of the Portuguese colonial empire and a consequent fear that the Soviet Union might expand its influence in the region (Nuttall 1992: 6). Second, the growth of an international movement through the 1970s and 80s, which condemned an increasingly violent apartheid regime in South Africa, clearly served as both a context and a stimulus to the Community to take an overt stance through EPC, if only at the declaratory level. The 1976 Soweto uprisings and the repressive South African Government response to them was a turning point here. Rather more specifically, the expansion of the EEC to include Britain in 1973 brought into the Community the former colonial master of South Africa and the Western country that had continued to have most deal-ings with South Africa after independence. This of itself helped to focus the attention of the Community on this issue. Significantly, in the light of EPC action, it was also the British Government in 1974 that first established a Code of Practice with respect to businesses operating in South Africa.

The immediate context that provided the stimulus for the first phase of EPC policy was the perceived need for the Nine to agree a common position at the forthcoming UN Conference on Apartheid at Lagos in August 1977. As Nuttall comments, the very fact that there was an expectation that the Nine would and should agree a common position shows how far the political cooperation process had already gone at that stage (Nuttall 1997a: 35). If the policy outcome was limited to a Code of Conduct, the consensus on even this limited measure was seriously challenged by further developments in South Africa itself. In particular, the growth of civil unrest and political violence in 1984, to which the South African Government responded by declaring a state of emergency in July 1985, increased worldwide condemnation of the apartheid regime and increased pressure upon the Community to take a tougher stance. But there was strong resistance from member states to change. Martin Holland suggests that context was crucial here and it was only 'the political necessity to be seen to be doing something in response to the mounting international anti-apartheid pressure [that] provoked the Community into reforming and extending its South African foreign policy' (Holland 1995b: 39; see also Nuttall 1992: 231).

The eventual release of Nelson Mandela in February 1990 brought to an end the rather uneasy period of Community sanctions against South Africa, behind which an awkward consensus among member states had nevertheless prevailed. Mandela's release and the consequent moves towards democracy in South Africa frame the last phase of EPC policy in which sanctions were progressively relaxed and finally removed in November 1993. As Holland puts it, the Community now faced 'the difficult process of redirecting its foreign policy from sanctions toward the creation of normal bilateral relations' (Holland 1998: 428). The last important contextual factor that helps to explain European foreign policy towards South Africa was essentially internal, the signing and eventual ratification of the Treaty on European Union in 1993. This Treaty not only replaced EPC with CFSP but introduced the concept of 'joint actions', a programme of specific actions designed to elicit a higher level of commitment from member states. South Africa was chosen as one of the first five joint actions undertaken under CFSP, underlining its central importance as an issue in European foreign policy.

Actors and Policy-making

In the early years of EPC, South Africa continued to be regarded as a bilateral issue on which the national positions of those member states with special interests in the region predominated. It was not until March 1974 that the Political Committee decided that the purview of EPC might be usefully expanded to include the region and a Working Group on Africa was established (Nuttall 1992: 127). Even then, there was an unwillingness to allow South Africa to feature seriously on the policy agenda and 'action' was restricted to rhetorical statements. The first EPC statement on South Africa came in February 1976 when the Belgian presidency on behalf of the Community issued a 'condemnation of the policy of apartheid in South Africa' (Foreign Ministers, 1976).

1977–84

Given the worsening situation in South Africa and the need to agree a common position at the UN Conference in Lagos, however, rhetoric was clearly not enough. But the problem was to agree a course of action that went beyond Declarations. The solution brokered by David Owen and Hans-Dietrich Genscher, the British and West German Foreign Secretaries respectively, was to adapt the British Code of Practice to all Community firms with subsidiaries operating in South Africa. This was adopted at the GAC meeting in September 1977. The only significant change from the British Code was the decision that firms should publish annual reports on the application of the Code (Nuttall 1992: 132–5).

But there was no further concession from the larger member states on implementation. Despite pressure from the Dutch, the Danes and the Irish for mandatory implementation, the Code would be both voluntary and a national responsibility without any Community competences invoked. Firms would report annually to member governments who in turn would report annually to the presidency on implementation. In terms of analysing the EPC process here, the adoption of the Code clearly represented an intergovernmental consensus based on the lowest common denominator of national interests. The states with significant commercial interests in South Africa simply would not agree to anything beyond the Code. Moreover, it quickly became apparent that, for those states, the adoption of the Code was a way of avoiding any further action that might damage their interests. As Nuttall puts it, the Code 'acted for many years as a lightning rod against the need to take additional action' (Nuttall 1997a: 36).

This assessment complicates any evaluation of the implementation of the Code. If the objective was simply to maintain a consensus and protect member's commercial interests in South Africa, then the Code can be judged a success certainly up to the mid-1980s. If, however, the Code was intended as a serious policy instrument that would actively promote change in South Africa, then no such easy judgement is possible. We should note that at the same time as the Code was adopted, a 'twin-track' strategy for EPC action in the region was also enunciated. The policy objectives were to facilitate the economic liberation of the black states of Southern Africa and to abolish apartheid in South Africa. The Code did nothing to further the first objective and a limited amount only towards the achievement of the second. Holland notes that a consensus on the Code did not extend to making it a coherent and cohesive policy. Indeed, there was no 'uniform and vigorous application of the Code'. While it was intended to improve the working conditions of black workers, 'its impact was modest given that at its peak fewer than 200,000 workers were covered by its provisions, which many employers were reluctant to implement fully' (Holland 1991: 186; see also Holland 1998: 428; for a slightly more positive assessment, see Nuttall 1997a: 35–6).

1985–90

Significantly, the next phase of EPC policy was characterized by a rather different policy process and a wider range of policy instruments, although similar question marks remain about effectiveness. If the larger member states could have maintained the status quo with respect to South African policy through the 1980s, there can be little doubt that would have been their preferred position. But this became increasingly untenable as the domestic situation in South Africa worsened through 1985–86 and other member states became more determined to toughen Community policy. Even so it took 'two bites at the cherry' for the Community to come up with an agreed policy. A package of essentially voluntary embargo measures agreed in September 1985 was expanded to embrace a limited package of sanctions in September 1986. The latter included a ban on the import of certain iron and steel products; a prohibition on the import of krugerrands (gold coins) into the Community and a ban on new Community investment in South Africa. A package of restrictions on trade with South Africa, however, was explicitly linked to a set of 'positive measures' that took two forms: more extensive deployment of regional funds to promote the economic independence of Southern Africa; and the launch of Special Programs for the Victims of Apartheid (Holland 1991: 188, 1998: 428). Significantly, both types of positive action were managed and administered by the Commission on behalf of the Community.

In order to explain this new policy we have already noted the importance of context, but the impact of the EPC process itself on national decision-making is also significant. South African policy after 1986 clearly illustrates a median position rather than the lowest common denominator of member states' national interests. Bolstered undoubtedly by the new SEA commitment to 'endeavour jointly to formulate and implement a European foreign policy', all member states sought to maintain a consensus *and* were prepared to a greater or lesser extent to compromise their national interests in order to do so. The result was a policy that was 'less advanced than the Dutch, for example, would have wished, but more so than the British or the Germans ever intended'. Despite huge differences between the positions of member states over sanctions in particular, 'the process of consultation and coordination made consensus possible' (Nuttall 1992: 237; Holland 1995b: 219).

It is interesting in this context to compare and contrast the positions of the two incoming presidencies in 1986, the Netherlands and Britain. The Dutch, as Nuttall notes, took over the presidency in January 1986 'anxious to achieve a toughening in the policy of the Twelve' (Nuttall 1992: 234). They were replaced by the British in the second half of that year who were equally determined to prevent a tougher policy emerging. While the presidency, as we noted earlier, had considerable powers under EPC procedures to set the agenda, this was constrained by the requirement to find and maintain a consensus. Both the Dutch and the British from their different perspectives were similarly empowered but also similarly constrained. The British in particular were unable to prevent a sanctions policy albeit one limited in scope from emerging under the auspices of a UK presidency.

Paul Taylor notes that even the British Prime Minister, Margaret Thatcher, appeared to be sensitive to 'an extension of the level of mutual commitment' following the SEA.

> She was entirely opposed to any tightening of the sanctions against South Africa by the European Community, and succeeded in heading off the more ambitious proposals. She boasted about the small scale of the agreed sanctions, but it was striking that she had nevertheless felt obliged to concede these, when she would have preferred to concede nothing. (Taylor 1996: 117)

If this was at best a very qualified form of intergovernmental decision-making in action after 1986, the overt involvement of the Commission and the machinery of the Community in South African policy now made the whole process appear much closer to the 'normal' Community method of decision-making. As noted above, the Commission set up and administered a new programme of aid to black South Africans, although responsibility for the programme was shared by the Community and member states bilaterally. Ten million ECU in aid was initially provided and the money was distributed through four non-governmental channels in South Africa. The Commission also expanded the deployment of regional funds to promote the economic independence of the front line states and this focus, Holland suggests, became 'the major theme of Community policy from early 1987' (Holland 1991: 188). But the involvement of the Commission in EPC policy remained controversial. Certain member states objected to the way in which the special funds were dispensed. The Commission itself, despite pressure from the EP to take a more proactive role on South Africa, was sensitive to the need to avoid moving ahead of the consensus position of member states (Nuttall 1996: 138–9).

Nevertheless the Community was at last demonstrating through EPC a capacity to act or, in Holland's phrase, a 'recognizable actor-capability' (Holland 1991: 187), but how effective was this new combination of limited sanctions and positive action at the implementation stage? An evaluation of instruments again depends upon the criteria adopted: whether action is evaluated in symbolic terms or whether policy is regarded as a substantive attempt to achieve the 'twin-track' objectives. Holland broadly supports the first position arguing that sanctions against South Africa were symbolic rather than substantive.

First, they rested upon different legal instruments, which enabled them to be 'implemented neither simultaneously nor comprehensively by all member states, in spite of their obligation to do so' (Holland 1998: 416). Second, the economic impact of sanctions was modest at best. In particular, the exclusion of coal from the list of sanctions meant that only 3.5 per cent of total South African exports were targeted and, indeed, trade overall increased. The record on positive measures was only slightly more favourable (Holland 1991: 187–91, 1995b: 44–6, 1998). Simon Nuttall, on the other hand, offers a rather more upbeat assessment. He argues that the Code of Conduct did make some contribution to bringing about change in South Africa. Sanctions too were important in the sense of the Community adding its not inconsiderable collective weight to a global anti-apartheid effort and, he argues, both sanctions and the positive measures developed by the Community provided a model for other states, such as Japan, to follow. Ultimately, however, even he concedes that 'the changes that came about in South Africa can be attributed, if at all, only to the cumulative effect of the disapproval of the world community as a whole' (Nuttall 1997a: 35–6).

1990–99

The consensus on policy, such as it was, lasted until the beginning of 1990. The main catalyst for change was again contextual. This time, the dramatic release of Nelson Mandela from prison on 11 February produced an immediate crisis. On 20 February, British Foreign Secretary Douglas Hurd informed the EPC meeting in Dublin that the UK intended to withdraw from the Community embargo on new investments in South Africa. As Hill comments, this revealed the Thatcher Government's notional commitment, at best, to the prevailing consensus on sanctions (Hill 1996c: 73). From a policy process perspective, the unilateral British 'opt-out' also clearly exposed weaknesses in the legal basis of measures adopted against South Africa. Developing an earlier point, of all the measures adopted, only the import of kruggerands was enacted through an EC Council Regulation. The ban on iron and steel was enacted through ECSC regulations (with member states responsible for implementation) and 'the remaining decisions [all took] the weaker form of community decisions or EPC statements' (Holland 1991: 189). In particular, the British Government could exploit the 'loopholes' surrounding the ban on new investments. First, 'new investments' were defined in very narrow terms to facilitate compromise. Second, despite a Commission preference for using Article 235, the new investment ban in October 1986 was introduced as a Council 'decision' that lacked legal compulsion or penalties for non-compliance (see Holland 1991: 189–91). In short, there was little to stop a determined British Government from opting out.

Nevertheless, a consensus was re-established by the end of 1990 and sanctions were progressively lifted over the next three years, although, as Holland notes, there were divisions between member states over 'the appropriate speed of doing so' (Holland 1998: 428). Despite continuing problems with sanctions through the early 1990s, however, there was a high level of consensus on the continuation of positive measures towards South Africa. This made it appropriate to select South Africa as one of the first 'joint actions' under the new CFSP in November 1993. Thus a continuity in policy was maintained and developed. Indeed, the core elements of the joint action – monitoring the election process in South Africa, the negotiation of a new bilateral economic framework and extending development assistance – were outlined by the Danish presidency as early as June 1993 (Holland 1995a: 562).

After the 1994 elections in South Africa, the focus of the joint action and beyond was the economic framework and a development strategy. The latter was the less problematic and again illustrated continuity. A new programme known as the European Program for Reconstruction and Development in South Africa (EPRD) built upon the existing Special Program for the Victims of Apartheid and by 1999 at the end of its five-year period was channelling 900 million rand into a number of different development projects in South Africa. In June 1995, negotiations began to develop a longer-term framework for cooperation. The EU proposed a two-pronged approach offering qualified membership of the Lomé Convention (agreed April 1997) combined with a bilateral agreement that would, as it were, 'plug the gaps' in the limited Lomé arrangement. After a lengthy negotiating process, and with some elements of the deal still to be settled, a bilateral trade, development and cooperation agreement was agreed in March and finally signed in Pretoria in October 1999. It was envisaged in this agreement that bilateral trade would continue to be liberalized over the following 12 years with ultimately a free trade area established between the parties (http://europa.eu.int/comm/dg08/SouthAfrica/index).

Conclusion

This concluding section tries to bring together the key elements of the analysis of South African policy in order to evaluate the strengths and weaknesses of EPC as a whole. But first it is worth underlining again the utility of the analytical framework here, which has effectively highlighted the interaction between contextual factors, actors, policy process, capabilities/instruments and action. Interestingly, a detailed analysis of the policy process with respect to South Africa reveals an intergovernmental process in form but scarcely in substance. Moreover, the extent to which policy was in fact coordinated and even a consensus maintained, despite the radically different positions of member states on this issue, is testimony to the robustness of the EPC process and the commitment of the parties to making it work.

Was EPC a success in South Africa? As indicated above, this has been hotly disputed. While policy outputs were disappointing to many observers, it can be argued that European foreign policy made a contribution to creating the economic conditions that were a precondition for political change in South Africa. Despite the criticism that EPC as a whole was all 'procedures without policy, activity without output' (Forster and Wallace 1996: 420), policy on South Africa does demonstrate that the Community had developed a genuine capacity to act by the mid-1980s. The case study also shows the broadening scope of European foreign policy in two senses. First, EPC did effectively bridge the gap between the economic and the political areas of foreign policy. Second, South African policy illustrates the range and the flexibility of instruments available to EPC (for a comprehensive description of all instruments used in South Africa, see Holland 1991: 191–4, 1995a: 560).

If EPC had undoubted strengths, South African policy also highlights the weaknesses of EPC, particularly at the level of policy implementation. The inadequacy of the state-level Code of Conduct and the need to seek Community-level instruments against the apartheid regime shows the limitations of the intergovernmental capabilities available. But the limited use of genuine Community instruments particularly in the restrictive measures also gave rise to serious problems of implementation. The unilateral UK withdrawal from the agreed package of sanctions dramatically illustrates the weakness of instruments deployed essentially on the authority of national governments. The result was a package of measures that was strong on symbolism but relatively weak on substantive impact. The continuing search for a more effective foreign policy grounded upon Community authority and deploying genuine Community instruments fuelled the debate about what became CFSP, to which we turn in the next chapter.

5

From EPC to CFSP: Union Foreign Policy

The replacement of European Political Cooperation (EPC) by a Common Foreign and Security Policy (CFSP) under the terms of the 1993 Treaty on European Union (TEU) promised to create a much more effective European foreign policy within the context of a new commitment to external policy as a whole, including for the first time security and defence policy. Under TEU, it will be recalled that the EC was transformed into an EU constructed upon three 'pillars', the second of which contained CFSP. Thus CFSP immediately became one of the new Union activities and may appropriately be labelled Union foreign policy. An intergovernmental approach to foreign policy was reinforced by the pillar structure, but it was envisaged that CFSP would be integrated into other Union activities in ways that appeared to resolve continuing debates between integrationists and intergovernmentalists.

This chapter analyses the nature and effectiveness of Union foreign policy by reviewing the context in which CFSP emerged and developed, identifying the key actors and processes involved, looking at the policy instruments available, the implementation of policy, and finally evaluating action itself. The strengths and weaknesses of this sub-system of European foreign policy are discussed by reference to an illustrative case study. The case study chosen for detailed inspection here, policy towards the former Yugoslavia – like the South African case discussed in the last chapter – spans the EPC and CFSP eras. This helps to underline the continuity between the two modes of Union policy.

Context

Problems with CFSP in action detailed in later sections can at least partly be explained in terms of the context within which it emerged and developed. We can identify a potent combination of internal and external factors that helped to frame CFSP in important ways. The international context was particularly significant here. Not only was it transformed by the end of the cold war but European policy-makers had also to contend at the same time with related issues emerging from the reunification of Germany and crises in the Gulf and the former Yugoslavia. All these developments in different ways served to underline the inadequacy of EPC and the consequent need for a new structure of foreign policy-making, and they clearly indicated what form the new framework should take. They also demanded that a new structure be in place as soon as possible.

The end of the cold war in Europe gave a huge boost to the idea of a common foreign policy. As Piening notes:

> there could be no question of exclusively bilateral foreign policy approaches by the EC's individual member states to the countries of Eastern and Central Europe, not least because it was immediately clear that the thrust of policy towards the new democracies would have to be in the economic field. (Piening 1997: 38)

In a wider context, the end of the cold war raised fundamental questions about the stability of the new international environment, the role of the United States and the future of NATO. Almost overnight it became apparent that Europeans would have to be prepared to take much greater responsibility for their own security rather than rely on the United States. The Gulf War of 1990–91 provided a timely illustration of the woeful absence of an integrated European approach both to foreign and to security policy (see Eliassen 1998: 5; Salmon 1992). It was certainly evident that security could no longer be left off the new European foreign policy agenda. Nevertheless, the Community had already responded quickly and effectively to the call to organize and provide assistance to the countries of Eastern and Central Europe (CEECs) and there were powerful international expectations that the Community could and would expand its international role and become a much more significant international player 'across the board' of external activities.

But changes in the international environment, however dramatic, could not be addressed in isolation. The process of European integration continued to evolve and, as outlined in Chapter 1, the Community was already embroiled in major internal debates, and these debates perhaps inevitably coloured the way the Community responded to these external transformations. The European Council had decided in 1989 to hold an intergovernmental conference (IGC) to prepare for the establishment of Economic and Monetary Union (EMU). This sparked a debate about whether an effective EMU also required a Political Union including a genuinely 'communitized' foreign policy. By mid-1990, it had been decided to hold a parallel IGC on Political Union the following year. But this decision was 'grafted' onto the existing EMU agenda and the proposals for a CFSP which emerged from the IGC discussions were hastily put together, certainly in comparison with the provisions for EMU, which had been 'much more carefully and extensively conceived' over a much longer period (Ginsberg 1997: 23).

If CFSP was conceived in haste, it emerged with all the hallmarks of major political disputes scarcely resolved. The TEU as a whole may have been 'a marvel of complexity born of the need to compromise' (Piening 1997: 39), but the inventive pillar structure served only to obscure the deals done. In Holland's summary 'the CFSP was the result of intergovernmental bargaining and compromise. In places, the text is intentionally, if frustratingly, vague and existing practices were either confirmed or complicated unnecessarily by the creation of the second pillar' (Holland 1997a: 7). Parts of the text indeed reveal where deals simply could not be done in the timescale available. The imperative to include a security/defence dimension in CFSP, for example, clearly emerged without reconciling 'deep differences between Franco-German proposals for a new EU "defence identity" and a more circumspect UK-Italian plan' (Peterson and Bomberg 1999: 233). What appears in the Treaty is a bland statement that CFSP would include the '*eventual* framing of a common defence policy, which *might* in time lead to a common defence' (Article J.4, my italics).

Nevertheless, in terms of language, already highlighted in earlier chapters as an important indicator of political context, CFSP was a model of clarity compared to its predecessors, deploying all the words in a legal document that had hitherto been politically unacceptable – not only referring explicitly for the first time to 'foreign' and 'policy' but also to 'security' and 'common' in the same context. As Piening comments, 'gone are the terminological somersaults needed to explain European foreign policy-making' (Piening 1997: 39). But the very clarity of the language used served to raise expectations that CFSP would significantly increase the commitment of member states to common action and produce a more effective European foreign policy. The following sections consider whether these expectations have been realized. Was CFSP an improvement on EPC in terms of establishing a more efficient policy process, providing more useful instruments that went beyond 'declaratory diplomacy' and most importantly, producing more effective action?

Actors and Policy-making

There was an intention that CFSP would be more firmly integrated into external policy-making than EPC had been. While in essence the EPC machinery was retained, it was adapted for CFSP in ways that raised the profile of Community institutions in the policy-making process. Different policy domains within the new EU were located in different pillars but they were to be managed within a 'single institutional frame-work'. Significantly, the TEU appointed Community institutions, the Council of Foreign Ministers (now renamed the 'Council of the Union'), COREPER (the Committee of Permanent Representatives) and the Commission to be jointly responsible for decisions emerging from both Pillar 1 (Community competence) *and* Pillar 2 (CFSP) 'with a view to encouraging more coherence in EU external policy' (Peterson 1998: 7).

While, as for EPC, the European Council remained responsible for providing overall direction and guidelines for CFSP, the Council of Ministers was placed explicitly at the heart of the new process. The intergovernmentalist fiction that the Council acted on foreign policy matters only when designated as 'the foreign ministers meeting in the framework of political cooperation' (when it was the same group of people involved) was removed, and the Council, with the revolving presidency representing its deliberations, was to be the key decision-maker. At lower levels of the policy machinery, important changes were made again in the name of coherence and consistency. Under EPC, the Political Committee of national Political Directors (PoCo) had been responsible for preparing and coordinating the work of foreign ministers and for the separate intergovernmental working groups established to serve EPC. For the management of CFSP, the TEU introduced the COREPER into the institutional hierarchy, located it above the PoCo and reorganized the operation of the working groups. COREPER was given the responsibility for coordinating these groups and for reconciling the aims of CFSP with the means provided by the first pillar. EPC working groups were moved to Brussels (rather than presidency capitals) and were gradually to be merged with Community working groups.

But the growing role played by the Commission in EPC activities was also reinforced by TEU. The Commission was given a co-equal right of initiative with member states in CFSP and was now legitimately involved in all stages of CFSP activity from initiation to implementation of policy. Its representational role was also enhanced. Not only did it represent all areas of Pillar 1 competence but, together with state diplomatic missions, it was now responsible for consistency in all external actions, and it was involved through the Troika at ambassadorial level in advocacy and coordination of CFSP policy 'on the ground'. This made it, as David Spence notes, 'the only permanent element in the changing constellations of external representation through the Presidency of the Council of the EU'. Given its enhanced representational role and greater visibility generally, it is not surprising, as Spence adds, that other international actors were increasingly seeing the Commission 'as the prime focus of the European input into international affairs' (Spence 1999: 259–61. For a comparison of Commission and member state networks of representation, see Table 14.1, 261).

In order to increase the Commission's control of the operational side of European foreign policy, its President, Jacques Delors, tried in 1993 to shift the institutional balance in favour of the Commission and away from the Council Secretariat (now combined with the EPC secretariat) by reforming the bureaucratic machinery. He split DG1 (responsible for external economic relations) into DG1 and DG1A (responsible for external political relations) with a special commissioner responsible for it. Although this was rather undermined two years later when his successor Jacques Santer, in part to accommodate three new commissioners, divided the external portfolios into four, organized on a regional rather than a functional basis (Soetendorp 1999: 74–5).

The relationship between policy process and policy output also reflected a desire to integrate CFSP more firmly into the Union. Not only is the CFSP label 'more *communautaire*-sounding' than EPC (Holland 1997a: 5) but it was soon agreed that any declarations made under CFSP would be made not 'on behalf of the EU and its member states' but on behalf of the 'EU only' (see Spence 1999: 266). This has more than linguistic significance and can be regarded as an important step towards creating a more integrated actor identity in foreign policy. The distinctively new policy instrument created for CFSP, 'joint actions' (reviewed in the next section), also went beyond the intergovernmental controls that had characterized EPC instruments. Although the decision-making process associated with joint actions is complex, there are provisions under the TEU to implement a joint action on the basis of a vote rather than on the strict unanimity principle.

The really striking attempt to differentiate CFSP from EPC was the inclusion of security in the domain of the new Union. Article J.4 of the TEU spells out this aspiration in blunt terms. CFSP 'shall include all questions related to the security of the Union'. This was a highly significant development given that EPC had at most been allowed (by member states) to deal only with the political and economic aspects of security rather than defence per se. In process terms, as Piening notes, 'the role of elaborating and implementing decisions and actions of the Union that have defence implications' are handed over to the Western European Union (WEU). In institutional terms, this led to the transfer of the WEU's secretariat to Brussels and to the establishment of 'close cooperation' and the sharing of information between WEU and EU institutions. But the political compromises in the TEU are again evident in the 'hedging in' of WEU. It may have become the defence arm of the Union but it cannot undermine member state commitments to NATO or interfere with bilateral defence relations (Piening 1997: 42; see also Chapter 7).

Despite efforts to integrate CFSP into wider Union activities, the process of policy-making under CFSP has not in practice differed dramatically from EPC policy-making. With respect to joint actions, despite the (albeit complex) provision for voting on implementation, decisions have continued to be made essentially on a consensus basis, with significant implications for the effectiveness of CFSP. As Spence and Spence argue, 'the universal application of the unanimity rule is still a major impediment to the development of CFSP and a reason for member states to act unilaterally or to seek international coalition partners outside the EU' (Spence and Spence 1998: 49). As we shall illustrate in our case study at the end of this chapter, the process of financing joint actions has also served to divide rather than to integrate policy-makers. Finance and budgetary mechanisms for CFSP were left unresolved by the TEU but quickly became a divisive issue once particular joint actions were implemented.

In general terms, the 'turf' battles between Community and national institutions in the policy-making process did not end, indeed some argue that they worsened under CFSP, and the battles have not necessarily been resolved in favour of Community institutions. The PoCo has remained a key actor in the shaping of CFSP – preparing the discussions and drafting the common positions and joint actions taken by the foreign ministers – despite its ostensibly subordinate position in the new hierarchy and the practice has evolved that COREPER will not normally change proposals forwarded by PoCo particularly if they relate exclusively to Pillar 2 activities. Although, it must be added, more and more external activities involve a mix of CFSP and Community competences and instruments and here COREPER, in the name of consistency, has 'the final word' (see Soetendorp 1999: 73; Allen 1998: 53). One other important reason for PoCo's continuing importance in the policy process, however, is that the 'EU Political Directors are based in national capitals, have direct lines to their Foreign Ministers, and thus usually have ample opportunity to circumvent COREPER' (Peterson 1998: 8).

But if attempts to integrate CFSP more firmly into Union activities have been less than successful, is it appropriate to describe the 'new' process as essentially or 'strictly' intergovernmental? At this point, we return to the debate about intergovernmentalism detailed in Chapter 4. Having briefly reviewed the CFSP policy process here and noted the continuing importance of national actors and national institutions, can we conclude that attempts to 'communitize' Union foreign policy have failed and that intergovernmentalism has (again) triumphed? The argument here is that such an analysis is too simple. Communitization of foreign policy may have failed but several commentators, including those of a 'state-centric realist' persuasion, have noted a growing 'Brusselization' of the policy process since Maastricht – meaning that Brussels-based actors and institutions are increasingly dominating both foreign policy-making and policy implementation.

With hindsight, this development can be dated from the Single European Act in 1986. A concern with consistency saw the legitimization of an enhanced role for the Commission, the establishment in Brussels of an EPC Secretariat and also the moving of EPC working groups to Brussels. Thereafter, the pillar structure of the TEU may have 'helped preserve the appearance of unfettered national sovereignty over foreign policy' but what David Allen calls 'the subversive seeds of a Brussels-based foreign policy had been sown'. There was now an evident 'awareness that a European foreign policy required more consistency and thus more Brussels-based activity' (Allen 1998: 50). As we have noted, the role of the Commission was further enhanced, the EPC Secretariat was merged with the Council Secretariat and EPC working groups were merged to a greater or lesser extent with Council working groups (Peterson and Bomberg 1999: 246). After Maastricht, moreover, member states transferred 'progressively more authority and expertise in Pillar 2 questions' from their national foreign ministries to their Permanent Representation in Brussels. Of significance, both institutionally and politically, has been the establishment of a new group of CFSP Counsellors who meet weekly in Brussels (see Peterson and Bomberg 1999: 246–7).

An important analytical dimension of 'Brusselization' is the extent to which this changing focus and associated institutional shifts has reinforced policy networks at the working group level (see Chapter 1). This is the level that John Peterson has called the 'sub-systemic' or the 'policy shaping' level of decision-making (see Peterson 1995). Peterson and Bomberg claim that 'CFSP has induced policy networks, generally very loose and sometimes only nascent during EPC, to become more cohesive'. While networks should in theory provide incentives for collective action, which should in turn impact on higher levels of decision-making, they argue that, for a variety of reasons, CFSP networks to date have been dominated by national actors and national orientations (see Peterson and Bomberg 1999: 246–8). Nevertheless, to the extent that more cohesive policy networks extend and deepen the process of socialization of those involved, we see again the limits of a 'strict' intergovernmentalist analysis of the policy process. As Peterson and Bomberg put it, 'the continued interaction of national experts at the working group level means that, to a considerable extent, national preferences are formed more endogenously, or within a context of intergovernmental bargaining than ever before in the history of EPC/CFSP' (Peterson and Bomberg 1999: 248).

Although this interesting assertion requires more research to support it, one possible illustration of this process in action is the French role in the 1994 EU joint action to extend the Nuclear Non-Proliferation Treaty (NPT). Long opposed to an international nuclear non-proliferation regime from a core 'national interest' perspective, France finally joined the NPT in 1991 and by 1995 was taking a leading role in 'selling' the Treaty to reluctant non-nuclear states. Crucially, after a number of years of 'exposure' to the bargaining process, French opposition 'appeared to shift under the influence of a [transnational] epistemic community of national experts that supported the Treaty's extension' (Peterson and Bomberg 1999: 248; Muller and Van Dassen 1997: 68–9). Peterson and Bomberg conclude that 'at the very least, national preferences on many CFSP matters are shaped by interactions between specialists at the sub-systemic level'. As for the impact of specialist groups on decision-making at higher levels, they are more circumspect. It is 'elevated', they argue, 'when they can reach agreements and recommend truly joint positions to the Political Committee and their political masters' (Peterson and Bomberg 1999: 249).

Capabilities and Instruments

Reference to apparent 'policy shaping' associated with one of the 'joint actions' taken under CFSP links us neatly to this section, which offers a more general review of capabilities and instruments. The key question here is whether or not CFSP has provided enhanced capabilities and more effective instruments compared to EPC. The most optimistic reading of the TEU again reveals a real attempt to improve upon EPC, particularly at the policy implementation stage. The distinction between 'joint actions' and 'common positions' – the 'new' instruments associated with CFSP – was intended to encourage a higher level of commitment to a more specific (if narrower) range of issue areas in which common interests might produce genuinely common policies. The language adopted clearly implied 'action' in a limited number of areas – connoting *inter alia* the deployment of resources beyond simply issuing declarations – and more systematic cooperation between member states although not necessarily 'action' in others.

TEU also promised more effective coordination between Community and Union sub-systems of European foreign policy. As Hill notes, the TEU explicitly refers for the first time to the necessity for consistency between development policy and foreign policy, and the use of Community funding in September 1992 to protect humanitarian convoys in Somalia made it apparent that the pillar structure of Maastricht need not preclude effective coordination between instruments and resources located in different pillars. More tangibly the TEU introduced a new Article (228A) linked to common positions that has provided, for the first time, a cross-pillar legal basis for the use of sanctions against third parties, the absence of which had caused many disputes in the 1980s (see Hill 1998a: 26–7).

Much consideration was given from the outset to the selection of joint actions and the criteria upon which they were to be selected. The objective, Soetendorp suggests, was 'to reach consensus among member states on objectives in a particular area and to facilitate rapid and coherent reaction to events when they occur' (Soetendorp 1999: 81). In advance of the TEU coming into force, the so-called 'Lisbon goals' (June 1992) identified three criteria for deciding which areas or issues would be subject to joint action: geographical proximity; the extent to which the Union had an important interest in the political and economic stability of a country/region; and the existence or otherwise of threats to the security interests of the Union.

Between November 1993 and May 1995, eight 'joint actions' were taken and they are detailed here to illustrate the wide range of issue areas involved, including actions in the security field broadly defined. The first five actions involved observing elections in Russia and South Africa, supporting measures to enhance stability and peace in the CEECs and the Middle East, and providing humanitarian aid to Bosnia. Interestingly, the next three joint actions were established in areas that in different ways were explicitly related to security interests – certainly to the political and economic aspects if not directly to the military/defence dimension of security. These were actions to promote the indefinite extension of the NPT, to control the export of so-called 'dual-use' (civil and military) goods and finally an action to strengthen the review process of the 1980 Convention which prohibits anti-personnel landmines. During the same period, 14 'common positions' were also adopted, mostly under the new Article 228A as they concerned various levels of economic sanctions against a number of third parties (for comprehensive lists and useful commentaries on each of the joint actions, see Ginsberg 1997: 18–22).

In advance of our case study on the former Yugoslavia, it will be useful to provide an overview of the strengths and weaknesses of joint actions specifically and CFSP generally. Summarizing here from a number of analyses of particular joint actions, commentators would broadly agree that joint actions were more likely to be successful – although criteria of success/failure are not easy to establish – if the following conditions were met:

■ Intervention at an early rather than a later stage of a (potential) conflict. Preventive diplomacy scores over crisis diplomacy (see, for example, measures to stabilize the CEECs).

■ Success was much more likely if the action did not mobilize strongly divergent 'national interests' (CEECs, South Africa).

■ An important precondition for success was effective planning and efficient implementation across the pillars (Russia, CEECs).

■ Success was more likely if implementation did not pose major financial or budgetary problems.

■ Success was far more likely to follow if the action required the deployment of 'soft' (that is, non-military) rather than 'hard' (military) power.

Clearly, the absence of these conditions has posed problems as we shall note shortly. But, in general terms, it can be argued that CFSP actions across the range of instruments have built upon the strengths noted with respect to EPC. One of the key objectives of the new Union is 'to assert its identity on the international scene' (TEU, Title 1, Common Provisions, Article B). Problems with particular actions notwithstanding, CFSP has helped to further that objective by raising the international visibility of the Union. Action is now more likely to be proactive rather merely reactive and the EU is involved in different phases of crisis management. The Union has demonstrated the ability to act (actor capability) and to have an impact upon international events across a wider range of issue areas than had been the case under EPC. In some areas at least, the ability to link actors and action across instruments and pillar responsibilities has been impressive.

Piening cites the Russian election joint action as a good example of the 'genuinely "Union" dimension of a foreign policy activity' and he is worth quoting at greater length on this action:

> The Commission's delegation in Moscow played the central role in coordinating the Community's own contribution (in human resources, money, and equipment) and the contributions of the individual member states and acted as the nerve center during the deployment of EU observers to electoral districts around the country, working with member states' embassies to ensure that national teams were integrated into the overall Union effort. Meanwhile, the Belgian embassy [Belgium being the country holding the presidency at the time] cooperated with its troika partners in arranging political briefings for all the incoming teams of observers. (Piening 1997: 41–2)

Despite these positive comments, other commentators have stressed the weaknesses of joint actions and problems with CFSP as a whole. Several of these problems (as we shall see in Chapter 8) were discussed although not necessarily resolved at the 1996 Intergovernmental Conference to review Maastricht and in the 1997 Amsterdam Treaty that followed. The first problem that emerged with CFSP in action was definitional. Joint actions were insufficiently specified in the legislation, largely because of a lack of consensus among member states. The distinction (albeit vague) between joint actions and common positions, as the Commission noted in its report for the Reflection Group on the 1996 IGC, 'was not followed in practice. The result is confusion about the role of different instruments. "Positions" can extend to cover both fundamental orientations and concrete actions. "Actions" can be limited to ad hoc or administrative measures' (European Commission 1995: 64). This served to undermine the higher level of commitment states were expected to give to joint actions in particular and therefore undermined the distinctiveness of CFSP as a whole.

A second problem that beset CFSP was financial. The question of who pays for action had not emerged with EPC because it was assumed that, in the spirit of intergovernmentalism, member governments would pay. With respect to CFSP, however – to be managed within a 'single institutional framework' – the TEU created possibly the worst of all worlds. On the one hand, Title V did not create a budget for CFSP but, under Article J.11, it did propose a cross-pillar, mixed system of funding without apparently realizing the consequences that would follow. As Ginsberg notes, this article 'stipulates that the administrative costs of CFSP joint actions may be charged to the EC budget and that the Council shall decide whether or not to charge the EC budget or the member governments for operational expenditures associated with joint actions'. Almost inevitably, this resulted in procedural battles about who pays for what and on what criteria every time significant financial obligations followed the decision to act, which dramatically slowed reaction time to international crises (Ginsberg 1997: 24; Monar 1997b). Financial/budgetary problems illustrate and underline more general procedural problems associated with trying to act across pillars together with the limits of inter- and intra-pillar cooperation. Our case study will reveal other process problems such as the absence of an independent planning capability.

Third, at the operational stage of decision-making, commentators have highlighted the narrow focus and the limited range of policy instruments deployed and have been disappointed by the apparent inability of the EU to have a major impact on the international issues selected for attention – although, it has to be said, this outcome was not the result of inactivity. As Spence and Spence comment, the level of foreign policy activity since Maastricht, measured in terms of meetings, exchanges of information and views through COREU, has 'exploded'. 'But', they argue, 'despite this enhanced activity, it remains the case that the policy output of CFSP is not fundamentally different from EPC. Policy declarations are the still the main vehicle. Joint actions have only exceptionally taken the form of major policy initiatives' (Spence and Spence 1998: 51, 56). The continuing absence of a military capability, despite the promise of the Maastricht treaty, has attracted most adverse comment largely because of the widely perceived failure of EU policy in the former Yugoslavia. As this case illustrates the range of procedural and operational problems that we have touched upon in this chapter, it is appropriate that we now turn to a detailed analysis of this case in the final section.

CFSP in Action: The EU and the Former Yugoslavia

No other area of international activity to date has attracted more adverse publicity for either the Community or the EU than the attempt to contain and resolve the set of interrelated conflicts – in Slovenia, Croatia, Bosnia-Herzegovina and, most recently, in Kosovo – that emerged from the disintegration of the federal state of Yugoslavia. No other single issue has been more damaging, not only to the prospects of a genuine CFSP but also to public confidence in the EU, and indeed to hopes that the international community might be able to establish a 'New World Order' following the end of the cold war. The widely perceived failure of the EU in the Balkans, however, needs to be set in context, the procedural problems detailed and the full range of instruments and actions evaluated. The analysis here will focus on the period from 1991 to the Dayton Accord of November 1995.

By way of a further introductory comment, it would be difficult to imagine a more complex, intractable issue to serve as the first serious test of CFSP – and with hindsight it was clearly foolish of various political leaders in Europe to play up this aspect at the beginning of the crisis. It was soon apparent that it would test the most sensitive aspect of the fledgling CFSP, namely the ability of member states to agree on the use of military force. It would expose, therefore, the most serious and divergent interests of member states; and, given the significance of the issue, it would require the EU to work harmoniously and effectively with a growing list of other international actors who were 'sucked into' the expanding Balkan crisis, including the UN, NATO, the United States and Russia. Of the preconditions for successful action tentatively listed in the last section, this case met few if any of them. Nevertheless, we will try to evaluate the strengths as well as the weaknesses of CFSP in action by looking first at the context in which policy in this area emerged and developed.

Context

A mix of contextual factors helps to explain the initial involvement of the Community in the disintegrating Yugoslavia but also served to condition the nature of that involvement. We will focus here on factors that were particularly relevant to understanding the first few months of the crisis but it is important to note that a dynamic context was a characteristic feature of this issue certainly through to the Dayton 'settlement' at the end of 1995. Starting with external factors, we have already noted the general impact on CFSP of a rapidly changing international environment. The end of the cold war in Europe was followed in quick succession by the Gulf War and then by the determined Yugoslav/Serbian military action to maintain an integrated Yugoslavia following the Slovenian and Croatian declarations of independence in June 1991. With two member states sharing borders with Yugoslavia, the threat to national frontiers and territorial stability that this issue posed was a particular concern to the Community because of the danger that ethno-nationalist problems would spread to Eastern and Central Europe. Thus, as Edwards comments, there was 'a strong sense that the EC/Twelve could not simply stand aside and allow the situation to deteriorate but had, at some point, to step in to contain and neutralize the conflict as much as possible' (Edwards 1997: 174).

Precisely what to do and how to do it, however, was seriously complicated by the ongoing internal debates about political and economic union. The outlines of a CFSP were being hotly debated at this time and, as Forster and Wallace note, 'when the Yugoslav crisis broke... many of the most sensitive issues remained unresolved' (Forster and Wallace 1996: 423). A preoccupation with internal debates extended through 1991 and, even after the TEU was signed, 1992 was dominated by the 'domestic' concern to prevent Maastricht from being derailed by the ratification process in member countries. But if the Community and member states could scarcely devote their whole attention to the escalating crisis in the Balkans, there was nevertheless a determination to respond as promptly and as effectively as possible. As several commentators have noted, there was a perceptible mood of confidence in the Community at this time. This was partly a result of the unprecedented acceleration of integration since the mid-1980s, capped by the commitments undertaken at Maastricht, and partly a result of being seen to be playing a key role in the transformation of Central and Eastern Europe. Stimulated by that role, there was certainly a determination to improve upon the dismal collective performance in the Gulf War (Peterson and Sjursen 1998: 171; Soetendorp 1999: 128).

If the Gulf was seen as essentially an 'American show', with Europe playing at best a rather incoherent secondary role, a crisis in the Balkans – in Europe – could be seen as an opportunity for Europe to 'grab' the limelight and demonstrate its ability to play a leading role in resolving the crisis. The Gulf War notwithstanding, there were many, both inside and outside the Community, who believed that the Community's status as a 'civilian power' in what was regarded as a new post-cold-war world 'made it perfectly suited to take the lead in an environment where military force now suddenly seemed irrelevant' (Hill 1998a: 21). It is not surprising that in this climate of expectations the Community should believe that it could deploy an appropriate blend of political and economic instruments to resolve the Balkan crisis.

This belief was reinforced by what appeared to be evidence of success in deploying these instruments at an early stage of the crisis. Diplomatic mediation and an agreement in July 1991 to send observers to monitor a ceasefire turned confidence into what soon became wildly over-optimistic predictions of early success for the Community's intervention, combined with rather disparaging comments about the ability of the United States to achieve the same outcome. The most famous and damaging comment, although not the only one in similar vein, came from Jacques Poos, Foreign Minister of Luxembourg, then acting as President of the Council. 'This is the hour of Europe', he announced to the world, 'not the hour of the Americans' (cited in Kintis 1997: 148). 'If one problem can be solved by the Europeans, it's the Yugoslav problem. This is a European country and it is not up to the Americans and not up to anybody else' (cited in Gow 1997: 50).

If this was a classic case of hubris, the 'fall' was not long in coming. It was the potential use of one of the available political instruments – diplomatic recognition – that soon sparked a series of developments that were crucial not only in a contextual sense but also in terms of illustrating the procedural problems created by the perceived need to maintain a consensus at all costs and the propensity of individual member states to pursue their own interests rather than a common policy on this issue. By the autumn of 1991, the worsening situation in the Balkans prompted a discussion of action beyond diplomatic mediation, including the question of whether or not to recognize the two breakaway Republics, Slovenia and Croatia. Largely for domestic political reasons, Germany took a strong lead on this issue and sought to persuade other member states to agree to recognition. In December, in order to maintain agreement, a compromise was reached whereby an arbitration commission would suggest guidelines for recognition. Before the commission even had a chance to report, however, the German government unilaterally recognized both republics. The following month, the other member states agreed to recognition and a consensus was restored but at great cost in at least two senses. Although Germany was not as isolated on this issue as has sometimes been suggested, German policy dramatically undermined the whole CFSP project. With the ink scarcely dry on the Maastricht Treaty, 'bulldozer' tactics of this sort were not what most observers understood by a common foreign and security policy. More directly, German unilateralism undermined the ongoing mediation effort and, with recognition of Bosnia following in April 1992, Community policy (which it had become) arguably made a significant contribution to the escalation of the Balkan crisis (see Peterson and Bomberg 1999: 242–3; Peterson and Sjursen 1998: 172, 191 fn. 2; Kintis 1997: 178–9).

Although these initial factors were crucial, the context within which the Community operated in the Balkans continued to change, hence policy was framed in different ways. For example, the focus of the Community attempt to mediate diplomatically began with the mission under Lord Carrington established by the Hague Conference in September 1991, which sought to negotiate a Yugoslav-wide settlement. The failure of the Carrington team led 12 months later to a more permanent 'conference diplomacy' vehicle based in Geneva. This was a joint EC–UN enterprise under the co-chairmanship of David Owen (EC) and Cyrus Vance (UN), which sought to establish and promote a political settlement specifically in Bosnia. Various peace plans promoted by Vance–Owen and Owen–Stoltenburg (Vance's successor) dominated the international mediation effort in 1993 but they failed to achieve agreement 'on the ground' or to attract outside support, particularly from the United States and Russia. It took the context-changing Sarajevo market massacre in February 1994 to persuade all outside parties to renew efforts to achieve peace, leading ultimately to the Dayton agreement at the end of 1995.

Reference to various outside parties underlines the point that a key contextual element throughout the crisis was what might be called the changing face of multilateralism. From the outset, the EC/EU had to work with a growing range of different actors and was increasingly dependent upon them to achieve success. This inevitably weakened a distinctive EC/EU contribution to the peace process. The key problem here was that the more high profile other actors became, the more the interests of particular EU member states rather than any sort of collective policy were magnified. The involvement of the UN, NATO and particularly the creation of the ad hoc Contact Group in April 1994 highlighted the roles of Britain, France and Germany in the policy process and effectively downgraded the contribution of other member states and the collectivity. Indeed, it has been argued that the establishment of the Contact Group as an important framework for action, with senior officials of only three member states meeting regularly with US and Russian officials to try to negotiate a ceasefire, marked the point at which 'the EU essentially ceased to function as a single entity on policy towards Bosnia' (Peterson and Bomberg 1999: 243).

As a final illustration of a dynamic policy context, the changing situation in 1994–95 was far more propitious for a political settlement in the Balkans that it had been in the previous three years. We have already noted the importance of the siege of Sarajevo and particularly the February 1994 market massacre as stimulating renewed efforts from all outside parties to make peace. This included the United States, which began a determined diplomatic effort in the spring of 1995, led the sustained NATO bombing of Serb positions after another mortar attack on the ill-fated Sarajevo market place at the end of August, and brokered the settlement at Dayton, Ohio in November. But it was not a matter of simply waiting for the 'cavalry' to arrive and a political settlement would follow. After all, the Dayton agreement differed little from the Owen–Stoltenburg plan of August 1993 in terms of the percentage of Bosnian territory to be controlled by each ethnic group. As Piening argues, 'the war had to run itself out before the parties could be brought to the negotiating table' (Piening 1997: 63). Rather more specifically, Soetendorp cites two key contextual factors in explaining the US success at Dayton:

> the readiness of the Serbian leadership to impose a settlement on the Bosnian Serbs to remove the sanctions against Serbia and Montenegro, and the Bosnian Serbs' loss of territory as a consequence of the shift in the military balance between the Croatian-Bosnian coalition and the Bosnian Serbs in favour of the former. (Soetendorp 1999: 144; see also Gow 1997: 276–87)

Process and Action

Having analysed the context within which policy towards the former Yugoslavia was made, we move on to review the interaction between process and output. The many and varied elements of action (or at least output) over five years are difficult to organize for analytical purposes but this section will be structured around Geoffrey Edward's broad distinction between the civil and the military dimensions of European policy (Edwards 1997: 184–9). There is no rigid distinction to draw, however, and, as we shall see, there are overlaps and interactions between these two categories. We start nevertheless with the military dimension, arguably the most controversial aspect of intervention but we will find that the nature of the military or quasi-military instruments used in the Balkans will preclude any simple conclusions about success or failure.

Military intervention

This sub-section draws a distinction between 'peacekeeping' – trying to provide or maintain the conditions for peace and security – and 'peacemaking' – trying to impose peace and security by force of arms. The initial Community contribution to peacekeeping took two forms, establishing the European Community Monitoring Mission (ECMM) and contributing to the United Nations Protection Force (UNPROFOR). Reviewing the roles of these two bodies, however, the overlap between military and civil intervention immediately becomes apparent. Both originally had a military rationale that quickly merged with a set of civil functions. ECMM – a novel instrument for the Community – was originally established in July 1991 to broker and try to maintain ceasefires between different sets of combatants. By 1992–93, however, the work of ECMM was increasingly coordinated with UNPROFOR and the UN in various humanitarian operations – for example, helping the UN High Commission for Refugees (UNHCR) deal with the evacuation of the wounded and monitoring the exchange of prisoners (Edwards 1997: 184). UNPROFOR was initially set up to provide the conditions for peace and security in the context of the 1991 Conference on Yugoslavia primarily by maintaining a ceasefire in Croatia. A second UNPROFOR operation (UNPROFOR 2) was set up in the spring of 1992 with a mandate extended to providing support and protection for the delivery of aid and humanitarian operations. Initially set up with 6,000 troops, by the end of 1993 there were 25,000 soldiers involved in UNPROFOR in Bosnia and Croatia with at least half that number provided by EU member states (the French, followed by the British, providing the largest number of troops).

However valuable the civil role of these two bodies, their lack of success in maintaining a real peace on the ground soon led to a lengthy and divisive debate about 'peacemaking' – the use of military force to compel the combatants to cease fighting and negotiate a political settlement. While the deployment of ECMM and UNPROFOR posed significant operational problems – not least the possibility (and on occasion the reality) of their being dragged into a combatant or hostage role – the potential use of large-scale military force by the EC/EU raised fundamental problems of principle as well as serious procedural and operational problems. The problems first surfaced in a couple of WEU meetings in August–September 1991 in the form of how best to strengthen the ECMM operation. While it was agreed to ask WEU to draw up a range of military options (illustrating incidentally the 'military arm' role envisaged in the TEU), agreement was not possible on any of them. A pattern quickly emerged on this issue with the French strongly in favour, the British strongly against and other member states taking up varying positions in between. A repeat performance of the debate took place again in a WEU context in the autumn of 1992. Another failure to agree led to the debate transferring (largely at French insistence) to the Security Council of the UN. It was this failure to agree in the WEU rather than the setting up the Contact Group 18 months later, that arguably marked 'the end of an independent EU intervention in former Yugoslavia' (Soetendorp 1999: 142).

A series of Security Council Resolutions through late 1992/1993 saw the international community (rather than the EC) edge closer towards the use of force. The establishment of a 'no fly zone' was followed in turn by authorization to enforce the zone and then by an agreement to enable UNPROFOR to take all necessary measures to defend itself. But if the use of air power against Serbia was agreed at least implicitly by mid-1993, a number of constraints – including strategic disagreements with the United States, continuing divisions between member states, a fear of endangering both troops and the aid effort on the ground – made it a theoretical possibility only. By the beginning of 1994, it took a French threat to withdraw its forces from UNPROFOR to stimulate the EU Council to call for an early NATO Council meeting. Meanwhile, the UN Secretary-General formally requested the use of NATO airstrikes, attached for the first time to an ultimatum to the Serbs to lift the siege of Sarajevo. The first albeit limited use of force followed in April 1994 with an airstrike around Gorazde under UN auspices.

The significant point here from an analytical perspective is that the EU Council in February 1994 could have requested the WEU to organize a military response under Article J.4 (1) of the TEU. The fact that the request went instead to NATO was a clear recognition that ultimately only NATO had the infrastructure, the resources and the instruments to deliver on the significant use of military force (Collester 1998: 495). This became apparent at the end of the following year when, under the terms of the Dayton settlement, UNPROFOR was replaced by a projected 60,000 strong implementation force (IFOR) in Bosnia and later IFOR was replaced by a 'stabilization' force (SFOR), both under NATO control. The same point was underlined more recently with the controversial deployment of NATO forces in Kosovo.

Civil intervention

If military intervention in the Balkans was always likely to expose the weaknesses in ECP/CFSP, civil intervention should arguably have played to the strengths of the EC/EU. This sub-section reviews action in the civil field, which includes various restrictions on economic and financial relations with Yugoslavia and a contribution through the new 'joint action' process to the humanitarian aid/political stability/reconstruction effort, in Bosnia in particular. In the early days, the potential for using economic instruments to influence the crisis in Yugoslavia seemed high, given the status the Community was acquiring as a major economic player in Central and Eastern Europe, combined with the simple fact that over 50 per cent of Yugoslav trade was with the Community (Salmon 1992: 248–9). As early as the spring of 1991, Belgrade was being warned that, in the absence of a peaceful settlement of the crisis, credits and other forms of assistance were threatened and, more significantly, the Community would not negotiate a privileged association agreement with Yugoslavia. An optimistic arms embargo in July was followed by the suspension of an existing trade and cooperation agreement in November 1991 after the breakdown of the Hague peace conference.

More comprehensive economic sanctions specifically targeted against Serbia and Montenegro were agreed in June 1992 in the context of a UN Security Council resolution. Sanctions, however, posed problems of both credibility and effectiveness. Their credibility suffered each time a tightening of sanctions was threatened without implementation in increasingly fraught attempts to compel the Belgrade Serbs to put pressure on the Bosnian Serbs to settle. Sanctions also lacked effectiveness, certainly in the short term, although, as indicated earlier, they appeared to be having an impact on Serbian behaviour by 1995. In procedural terms, however, the attempt to police sanctions saw the innovative decision of July 1992 to deploy naval forces under the auspices of the WEU in the Adriatic and on the Danube to try to make the blockade of Serbia more effective. Again we see a blurring of the distinction between civil and military instruments/action.

The WEU was also involved in the first joint action taken under the new CFSP in October 1993. Given the disagreements between member states on the use of force, a political consensus on explicitly civil action in Bosnia was fairly easily achieved.

On the basis of that consensus, the European Council was able to instruct the Council of Ministers to increase its contributions for use by UNHCR and to support by all necessary means the convoying of humanitarian food aid to Bosnia following consultations with both UNPROFOR and UNHCR. There was considerable urgency attached to this policy as food needed to reach the population before the winter made their plight considerably worse. But when it came to implementing this first joint action the problem immediately faced was who would pay for it and on what basis? As Spence and Spence note, 'the Council spent four months discussing whether to cover the cost of the operation through the Community budget or on a shared national basis'. While eventually agreeing to split the earmarked 48 million ECU, 50:50, the winter was now over and there was no urgent need for additional aid. The money was later transferred to the administration of Mostar in a renewal/extension of the joint action (Spence and Spence 1998: 52; Monar 1997b: 38–9).

Following the temporary cessation of fighting in the area, an EU civil administration was established in the Bosnian city of Mostar in July 1994 with the ambitious 'peace-building' objectives of providing public order, reconciling Croat and Muslim inhabitants, and rebuilding the infrastructure of the city. The aim was to create 'a single administration of a single, multi-ethnic city' (Spence and Spence 1998: 55). A former mayor of Bremen, Hans Koschnick, was appointed Administrator and given two years to do the job. The WEU was requested to send police officers who would help to create a single unified city police force to ensure public safety and freedom of movement. But again procedural and operational problems undermined the effectiveness of the action. Even the setting up of the EU administration with a Memorandum of Understanding required a complex legal formula because neither the EU nor the two local communities in Mostar had any legal standing (see Edwards 1997: 185).

After the signing of the Memorandum, 32 million ECU of the unspent allocation for humanitarian aid was transferred to provide initial support for the Mostar administration. But this created at least two procedural problems, one intra-, the other inter-pillar in nature. First, a proportion of this money was to come from member states, but by October 1994 only three member states had paid up. Second, drawing on the Community budget for a CFSP action should also have meant drawing the Commission and the European Parliament into the decision-making process because of their legal rights to scrutinize and control Community spending. The Council decided, however, that it would control the release of funds to the Mostar Administrator and he would be accountable only to the Council, reporting regularly to the presidency. The paucity of funds from member states, however, forced the Council to compromise and to seek a regularization of the budgetary procedure. The European Parliament approved a Community budget for Mostar in October 1994 but many battles on finance still lay ahead (see Monar 1997b).

Meanwhile the operational situation on the ground was fraught with difficulties, which should have been apparent in advance if the EU had had any sort of independent planning and analysis capability. It soon became clear as Serb shelling of the city intensified that there was no peace to build upon. Moreover, the local Croat leadership would not support reconciliation, or a unitary local authority, or WEU attempts to establish a single police force. The EU 'authority' in Mostar had no means of compelling more cooperative behaviour and even fell out with WEU personnel, who would take orders only from the WEU authorities – another illustration of inadequate advance planning. Obstruction and non-cooperation came to a head in February 1996 when an attempted assassination of Koschnik led to his resignation (Spence and Spence 1998: 55–6).

Conclusion

How effective was EC/EU policy in the former Yugoslavia? What were its strengths and weaknesses? What general conclusions can we draw about Union foreign policy from this case study? Clearly, for reasons discussed at the beginning of this chapter, more powerful expectations of success surrounded this case than, say EPC in South Africa. From this perspective, the weaknesses rather than the strengths of CFSP have been magnified. It was this case, more than any other perhaps, that fuelled concerns about a dangerous gap developing between capabilities and expectations, although the failures in the Balkans also appear to have contributed disproportionately to a more recent scaling down of those expectations of what the EU can or might do in world politics (see Hill 1993, 1998a).

The case study nevertheless underlines weaknesses that are not restricted to the area of military intervention, where problems might have been predicted. With respect to the decision-making process several problems are underlined by this case. The need to maintain a consensus on policy created huge problems here. It not only produced 'bad' decisions on occasions, such as the recognition of the breakaway republics, but drove the larger member states in particular to seek either unilateral solutions to problems or ad hoc coalitions with non-EU partners such as the Contact Group. The unanimity 'rule' served only to erode further the patent lack of political will to seek collective EU solutions to problems in the Balkans. Once decisions were made, two institutional weaknesses are revealed by this case study, the absence of a strategic planning and analysis capability to underpin effective action and also (although not highlighted in the analysis here) the limitations of a revolving presidency in providing firm, constant leadership for the Union (see Edwards 1997: 190–2). But it was in the operational area that the most serious weaknesses are revealed. Diplomatic and economic instruments were simply inadequate to resolve the Yugoslav crisis. An effective military capability was required to create and maintain peace on the ground. Despite the rather creative use of the WEU in various EU activities in the region, substantial use of military force in Yugoslavia required the use of NATO, and this had significant implications for both institutions (see Chapter 7).

What does Yugoslavia reveal about the strengths of CFSP? Not surprisingly perhaps, these emerge from the less dramatic civil rather than military area of activity. The EU was able to play a significant role in civil reconstruction where and when the peace held. In Mostar, for example, the intervention at least helped to keep a fragile peace between Croats and Muslims and, more significantly perhaps, EU money contributed to economic and technical reconstruction producing tangible benefits particularly for the Muslim part of the city (Peterson 1998: 13; Spence and Spence 1998: 56). But specific contributions apart, it was the overall scope, intensity and persistence of the European action in Yugoslavia that perhaps reveals the real strengths of CFSP in this most difficult of cases. Piening provides a useful list of the variety of joint efforts undertaken and concludes that 'in numerous areas they made a substantial contribution to alleviating suffering and to preparing the way for the eventual accord reached at Dayton' (Piening 1997: 195). Dayton did not, of course, bring the Balkan crisis to an end, as further instability and conflict in Albania and Kosovo have demonstrated all too clearly. But Kosovo in particular underlines the limitations as well as the strengths of military force in producing a lasting political settlement in the Balkans (and elsewhere) and, in that sense, it puts the EU's lack of a military capability into context. Conflict resolution requires a range of different instruments and the EU clearly has a contribution to make on the basis of its existing 'civilian power' capabilities (see Chapter 8).

Whatever the problems of evaluating performance and whatever the limitations of Union policy in the former Yugoslavia, what can be claimed here is that our analytical framework has provided a useful way of understanding CFSP in general and its particular performance in the Balkans by seeing action as the product of a policy system in which context, actors, process, and instruments all interact with each other to produce output. We have now applied this analytical framework to two of the three sub-systems of European foreign policy. We turn in the next chapter to test the effectiveness of the framework by applying it to the third sub-system, national foreign policy in a European context, taking British foreign policy as our case study.

6

The Europeanization of National Foreign Policies: The Case of Britain

It will be apparent from earlier chapters, particularly from the case studies of European foreign policy in action that, however qualified the intergovernmental nature of the policy-making processes involved, we cannot understand European foreign policy-making without looking at the separate foreign policies of member states. Embedded within the concept of European foreign policy, however, is the notion that the foreign policies of member states have been significantly changed, if not transformed, by participation over time in foreign policy-making at the European level. This process of change can be referred to as the 'Europeanization' of national foreign policies.

This chapter explores the idea of Europeanization by applying it to the case of one member state: Britain and British foreign policy. Two objections may be raised immediately. First, an analysis of one member state's foreign policy is no substitute for a full-blown comparative analysis of the impact of the EU on the foreign policies of all 15 member states (Peterson and Sjursen 1998: 177–8). This is accepted and the analysis here is intended only as modest contribution to the more or less comparative research projects that are beginning to emerge. Having conceded that, however, detailed analyses of particular member states' foreign policies over time have an important place in such a project. A second, possibly more telling objection is that, for a variety of reasons, Britain is perhaps the least appropriate member to analyse in this context, successive governments having staunchly resisted the whole process of Europeanization ever since Britain become a member of the European Economic Community (EEC) in 1973. While noting Britain's singularity, the argument here is that the British case is interesting in this context precisely because prima facie it looks so unpromising. To the extent that British foreign policy has been 'Europeanized' despite apparently strong resistance from British governments, it can be said to be a significant process indeed in the construction of a European foreign policy.

The main objective of this chapter, however, is to test out an FPA analytical framework on the foreign policy systems of member states, identified collectively as the third sub-system of European foreign policy. To this end, 'Europeanization' will be defined in terms that are consistent with our analytical framework. Assuming again that policy can be explained broadly in terms of the interaction between context, process and implementation, Europeanization will be 'measured' here in terms of changing (or not) the context in which British foreign policy is made; changing the way in which policy is made; and finally, changing the operational environment in which policy is implemented. We start in the next section, however, with further discussion of the appropriateness or otherwise of British foreign policy as a case study of Europeanization.

Britain: The Exceptional Case?

While more research is needed to assess the general impact of European integration and more specifically the impact of growing foreign policy cooperation on the policies of member states, work done to date emphasizes change as a result of Europeanization. The smaller members in particular are seen to have changed most, whether in terms of gaining additional resources and instruments or change in terms of overall foreign policy orientations – Dutch foreign policy becoming less global and more European in orientation, Portuguese foreign policy less 'Atlanticist' and more focused on Mediterranean issues, for example. In terms of foreign policy autonomy, all member states are seen as increasingly constrained by membership, with the possible exception of the 'big three' – Britain, France and Germany – who are regarded as having more options in terms of respecting collective positions or not (see, for example, Tonra 1997; Hill 1996b; Stavridis and Hill 1996).

Most commentators, however, regard Britain as a special case as far as resisting Europeanization is concerned. The one area in which British governments have positively welcomed 'Europeanization' is in the defence sphere. But this is a very different notion of Europeanization that predates membership of the EEC and is more about strengthening the European contribution to NATO in order to maintain a US commitment to European security than about creating a collective defence dimension to the EU (see Clarke 1998: 128ff.). In this sense

'Europeanization' is a variant of 'Atlanticism'. If post-war British foreign policy is seen as a struggle in terms of orientation between 'Europeanism' and 'Atlanticism', with the latter denoting a core commitment to NATO and a very close if not a 'special relationship' with the United States, then Europeanism has arguably come a poor second over the last 50 years (see White 1991, 1992a).

The resistance to Europeanism (developing closer links with Europe) can also be seen to predate the emergence of the EEC. It is rooted in thinking derived from Churchill's 'three circles' doctrine, arguably the most significant conceptual framework to have influenced the making of post-war British foreign policy. Articulated in a famous 1948 speech to the annual Conservative Party Conference, Churchill located Britain metaphorically at the intersection between three 'circles' of activity; the Empire/Commonwealth, the USA and Europe respectively. Three key assumptions were built into this most pervasive image of an appropriate role for Britain to play in the post-war world (White 1992a: 9–10). First, it depicts Britain as a global power with global interests to defend rather than as a regional power pursuing essentially regional interests. Second, it raises pragmatism and flexibility almost to a guiding principle. The object of British foreign policy is to play a leading role in all three areas of activity but not to become committed to any one 'circle' at the expense of the other two. It is for this reason that Hugo Young refers to the three circles doctrine as almost a 'biblical text for the justification of strategic indecision' (Young, 1998: 32). Finally, Churchill's notion that the British 'have the opportunity of joining them [the three circles] all together' provided a rationale for a freewheeling, 'bridge-builder' role for Britain, which has continued to be a powerful self-image throughout the post-war period.

The influence of this sort of thinking on successive British governments can be seen at each stage of an evolving relationship with Western Europe. In the 1950s it predicated intensive cooperation, particularly on defence-related issues, but detachment from the process of economic integration. As Hill and Wallace argue, Britain excluded itself from the two related post-war 'bargains' struck by the other West European states. The external bargain was to accept US protection and leadership, the internal deal was economic growth through economic integration. Britain, on the other hand, underlined its sense of separateness by retaining 'the illusion of greater autonomy, at the cost both of accepting a greater degree of dependence on the USA and of gaining less benefit from the surge of economic growth that the creation of the EEC promoted' (Hill and Wallace 1996: 10).

By the early 1960s, as the economic costs of detachment from the EEC became apparent, the Macmillan Government took the decision to join. But membership was seen as a pragmatic necessity only to shore up a fragile economy and to augment other foreign policy options. There was no special commitment to the European 'circle' and the application certainly did not imply any British conversion to the merits of European integration (Duff 1998: 36). Even after eventually joining in the early 1970s, the British determination to renegotiate the terms of entry and, more broadly, to retain an independent foreign policy, created the impression at least that Britain was less than committed to its new European role. If Britain remained, in Roy Jenkins' phrase, '*semi-detached*' from the Community through the 1970s, by the beginning of the Thatcher era, Britain was being described as 'an *awkward partner*' with a distinctively different approach to the Community (see George 1998). A succession of negative labels – *detached, semi-detached, awkward* – underlines the point that for British governments the decisions to join and later to upgrade relations with the Community were equivocal and essentially instrumental, always resisting the necessity to choose between the Atlantic and European 'circles'. With the removal of Mrs Thatcher in 1990, the situation appeared to change, at least in rhetorical terms. Both the Major and later the Blair Governments committed themselves to locating Britain 'at the heart of Europe'. The Blair Government in particular took the view after 1997 that it had established appropriate relations with both the USA and the EU and argued that there was now no need to choose between them. These relationships will be explored further towards the end of this chapter in a case study of British foreign policy in action from the Thatcher period onwards.

If this brief history of Britain's relations with the Community reveals much delayed and then hesitant adaptation at best to the demands of the European circle, there are more fundamental problems in the relationship that both reinforce the singularity of the British case and raise serious questions about the limits of further adaptation. These problems lie at a more conceptual level, relate to conceptions of national identity in particular and appear to be deeply embedded within domestic political attitudes towards Europe. Negative labels to describe the relationship *with* Europe extend more significantly to negative images as revealed by language used *about* 'Europe'. The key elements within both the dominant elite and a wider popular discourse about Europe over the last 40 years or more have remained remarkably consistent in the absence of any serious domestic debate. Critically, the concept of 'Europe' has been and continues to be suffused with almost wholly negative connotations. To select some important strands: 'Europe' is seen as a threat to independence, autonomy and the very idea of 'Britishness'; the idea of 'Britain-in-Europe' as linked to ideas about decline, declinism and failure; 'Europe' as an 'optional extra' to be embraced – or not; 'Europe' as a business arrangement, an economic necessity even, but not central to Britain's wider political interests (see, for example, Wallace, W. 1986, 1991; Tugendhat and Wallace 1988; Larsen 1997a; Young 1998).

Interestingly, Helen Wallace notes that initial membership of the Community was not accompanied by 'a conversion to the concept or the symbolism of integration' and that membership over time has not been characterized – as might have been expected – by further adaptation to Europe through a process she calls 'retarded Europeanization'. But significantly, 'Atlanticism' continues to attract a strong symbolic attachment in popular discourse. Compared to other member states, as she puts it,

> the British pattern is quite different. The symbolic dimension to integration is either absent or negative for large sections of British opinion. Only a minority of the British feel strong symbolic attachment to European integration as defined by the EU, while NATO attracts positive symbolic resonance, as does 'Atlanticism'. There persists a sense of a distinct British political identity and of distance from the European institutional framework. (Wallace 1997: 686)

All of this suggests that the other member states (with the possible exception of Denmark) have a more positive approach to European integration, are less detached from 'Europe', and that arguably any of them would serve as a more appropriate case study to test the impact of Europeanization on national foreign policies. However unpromising a British case study appears to be, we shall nevertheless apply our analytical framework, beginning in the next section with the impact of membership of the EU on the context within which British foreign policy is made.

Context

What might be called the traditional context of British foreign policy can be simply characterized, first in constitutional terms, then by the relationship between policy process and policy issues and finally in terms of the relationship between domestic politics and foreign policy. This provides a framework within which the impact of membership of the EU on foreign policy context can be evaluated. It will also help to contextualize many of the apparently entrenched attitudes to Europe discussed in the last section. Constitutionally, foreign policy in Britain is or at least was (never entirely clear in an unwritten constitution resting upon tradition and precedent!) a crown prerogative. The importance of this policy domain, on the other hand, is clearly indicated by the fact that it was the last area of government to be conceded by the monarchy in the nineteenth century and that it was handed down not to Parliament but to the Executive or, strictly speaking, to His or Her Majesty's ministers.

As Michael Clarke comments, British foreign policy has never been controlled by Parliament except in the indirect sense – although crucial to the notion of parliamentary sovereignty – that ministers are accountable to Parliament. Foreign policy 'has always been directed from the centre; whether that centre has been expressed through royalty or through a powerful political executive' (Clarke 1992: 73). This special location of foreign policy – constitutionally at the heart of the machinery of the state – helps to explain why foreign policy traditionally has been so closely identified in symbolic terms with statehood and in particular with the concept of sovereignty and associated concepts (in Britain) of national identity, freedom and independence. (A useful discussion, which contrasts British 'parliamentary sovereignty' with other European conceptions of sovereignty in terms of different histories of internal struggles for political authority, can be found in Clarke 1992: 5–8, 247–9.)

The assumed distinctiveness and centrality of foreign policy also links in highly prescriptive ways to other elements of the traditional British context. The policy process is expected to match the substance of this 'high' policy arena in terms of control. If foreign policy is central to the fundamental concerns of the state, to its security in particular and possibly to its survival, then foreign policy is literally too important to be left to the 'cut and thrust' of domestic politics. As David Vital put it, 'foreign policy, then, is the business of the Executive and for almost all practical purposes the Executive is unfettered in its exercise of this function' (Vital 1968: 49). If the making of foreign policy requires the Executive – formally the Cabinet, which constitutionally shares collective authority – to play a sort of 'gatekeeper' role within the state, the management of policy at the bureaucratic level, Vital suggests, also requires the traditional 'lead' department in foreign policy, the Foreign and Commonwealth Office (FCO) – albeit appearing historically in different institutional manifestations – to play a sort of 'gatekeeper' role in Whitehall, thus ensuring effective co-ordination of policy. The last element is the relationship between foreign policy and domestic politics. From a traditional perspective, it is already apparent that the two areas are assumed to be clearly differentiated and that foreign policy tends to be regarded as the more important sphere of governmental activity. The important final point to add is the expectation, for all the reasons touched on above, that foreign policy will not be undermined by domestic politics, that in this sense the major elements of foreign policy at least will normally be supported by a bipartisan approach if not underpinned by a broader domestic consensus.

If this is accepted as a necessarily brief characterization of the traditional context of British foreign policy, how has membership of the EU changed this context? We should start with a caveat. Clearly there have been many different sorts of challenge in the post-war period to what might be called a 'constitutional model' of British foreign policy-making. These include the changing nature of foreign policy resulting *inter alia* from the emergence of interdependence, the growth of multi-lateralism and transnationalism. All these trends have had significant implications for every aspect of foreign policy-making and they extend across very much the same time frame as Britain's membership of the EU. So we must avoid overstating the particular significance of membership in changing the context of British foreign policy (see also Wallace 1974). Nevertheless, if we now revisit the traditional context, it is difficult not to be struck by the contribution that membership has made to a radically transformed context over a period now approaching 30 years.

The most obvious contextual change – a genuine transformation – immediately followed the signing of the Treaty of Rome in 1972. At that point, Britain, in common with all new member states, accepted the accumulated rules and obligations derived from EC treaties, laws and regulations. Even more significantly, the Heath Government signed up to a new system of international law – Community law – which, in the event of conflict, takes precedence over relevant national (English, Scottish, Northern Irish) systems of law. As the distinguished English judge, Lord Denning later summarized a not entirely unambiguous new situation, Community law 'is not supplanting English law. It is part of our law which overrides any other part which is inconsistent with it' (quoted in Clarke 1992: 205).

Although commentators have continued to argue over the implications of this, most have accepted that if sovereignty is defined in narrow legal terms (admittedly a rather 'unBritish' approach to take) Britain, in common with all other members, is no longer a sovereign state with the final court of appeal located within its territorial frontiers. The real arguments, however, that continue to rage in Britain are normally framed, implicitly at least, in terms of political sovereignty, where 'sovereignty' tends to be a synonym for 'independence' or 'freedom' – highly emotive symbolic issues as we have already noted. From this perspective, there is room for different views about whether or not Britain as a member of the EU is or is not 'sovereign'. What is indisputable, however, is the real rather than symbolic loss of control, consequent upon membership, with respect to certain foreign policy issues – trade most obviously and to some extent aid, although not formally at least with respect to foreign policy and defence. Whether or not membership overall has provided benefits as well as costs in terms of the capabilities and instruments available to British foreign policy-makers is an important question to which we will return in a later section.

Picking up the comment about issues, a second area of dramatic change lies in the range of issues that now constitutes the foreign policy agenda, largely although not exclusively a result of the ever-widening purview of EU activities. This agenda has so blurred the boundaries between foreign policy and domestic politics that it raises the question of whether a distinctive area of 'British foreign policy' exists any more. 'In a sense', William Wallace has argued, 'foreign policy has now disintegrated within the widening agenda of intergovernmental business' (Wallace 1990: 241). Certainly, it is no longer appropriate to try to analyse European policy as a 'foreign policy' issue area only. Nevertheless, the demands posed by having to deal with a widening agenda of foreign policy issues have been felt within the foreign policy process as in other areas of policy-making.

Most obviously, an expanding foreign policy agenda has drawn more domestic actors and institutional players into the foreign policy process – to the extent that a distinctive foreign policy process can still be identified. Although some government departments have been closely involved with the Community for many years, by the mid-1990s it could be said that every government department is involved in networks of transgovernmental and transnational relations with other actors and institutions across the EU (Smith 1999: 232–3). As David Spence succinctly puts it, the 'omnipresence of the European context' means that 'the reach of the EU now covers every domestic ministry and all levels of government, be they local, regional or national' (Spence 1999: 249). It is apparent, then, that Europeanization now impacts upon domestic politics as much as on foreign policy. Equally clearly, the challenge posed for national policy systems is to devise effective systems of coordination and control. The vast increase in cross-border activity across the EU poses particular challenges to traditional conceptions of the government (and within a narrower sphere) the FCO as 'gatekeepers'.

The particular demands upon the FCO have increased enormously. It is now the focus of a wide range of domestic as well as external pressures that emanate from a domestic political system which has itself been radically transformed by membership. Assumptions that informed the traditional context about bipartisanship and a domestic consensus with respect to foreign policy have been seriously undermined since the 1970s. The 'European issue' has increasingly come to dominate domestic politics in Britain, it has created major fault lines within as well as across the two major political parties and, in its various manifestations, it remains a highly controversial issue for the general public. The clear absence of anything approaching a consensus on 'Europe' means that policy-making must take place within a domestic context that is fraught with difficulties for policy-makers.

It is clear then that dramatic changes have occurred in the context of foreign policy-making in Britain and, even allowing for the influence of other change factors, membership of the EU can be seen as the most significant factor overall. The EU does not, however, provide the only context that frames British foreign policy. If we revisit Churchill's three circles, both the global and transatlantic 'circles' remain as contexts at least in residual form. Indeed, as Hill notes, some issues over the last 20 years or so, particularly those perceived as successes, have actually reinforced a predisposition to look beyond a European context and have offered tempting opportunities to play a wider international role (Hill 1996c: 70). These issues include the Falklands War in 1982, an influential East–West role in the mid-1980s, and the Gulf War in 1991. From a longer perspective, however, it is clear to most observers not only that the context of British foreign policy has been changing but that Britain's traditional extra-European roles have been in decline for many years (Bulmer 1992: 17–22; Bulmer et al. 1992: 255). In this sense, the European context provides a new framework for British foreign policy and a context that is now so pervasive that, as David Allen comments, it has been necessary 'to adjust both the procedures and the substance of British foreign policy to the growing importance of the European Union' (Allen 1999: 208). How this has been done and with what consequences are discussed in the next two sections of this chapter.

Actors and Policy-making

In response to dramatically increased European activity, Britain, like other member states, has attempted to strengthen coordination mechanisms within and across its national policy-making machinery. While this has not involved substantial institutional change at the centre, what has emerged, Martin Smith suggests, is 'an informal, yet powerful, elite' that attempts to control all aspects of European policy-making (Smith 1999: 233). This section identifies the key actors within this elite and then focuses in more detail on a debate that is beginning to emerge about how effectively control has been retained at the centre. This will serve as a measure of the degree to which the policy process in Britain has been 'Europeanized' and the consequences for the workings of the policy machinery.

The relevant 'core executive' here consists of six sets of players. At the centre of the centre, as it were, is the prime minister's office and, within the Cabinet Office, the European Secretariat. At Cabinet level, there are two key Cabinet Committees involved; the Defence and Overseas Policy Committee (DOP) and the Sub-Committee on European Issues ((E)DOP). These committees are 'shadowed' by several official committees, known generically as the European Questions (EQ) system of committees, which look after different aspects of European issues. At departmental level, the Foreign and Commonwealth Office (FCO) is effectively the 'lead' department on European policy not least because it gives instructions to the final set of actors, the UK permanent representation (UKREP) in Brussels.

From a coordination perspective, three sets of actors – the European Secretariat, the FCO and UKREP – can be regarded as particularly important in the policy process, constituting 'the central triad of the Whitehall policy-making machine' (Bulmer and Burch 1998: 612). Strategic coordination of all aspects of European policy is provided by the European Secretariat. This body coordinates the responses of Whitehall, resolves any conflicts between departments and, through its close links with the prime minister's office, ensures that policy is in tune with wider governmental objectives. Operational coordination, on the other hand, is provided by the FCO and its external arm, UKREP.

Most issues can be handled smoothly in this way. If there are any problems, they can be dealt with at the weekly meeting between representatives of all three institutions. The purpose of this meeting, usually held on a Friday in the Cabinet Office, 'is to iron out any problems or conflicts and any unresolved issues go to the relevant cabinet committee' (Smith 1999: 234).

There is some dispute, nevertheless, about just how effectively policy is coordinated and controlled. Most commentators would have no problem with the brief description of the process offered above. They argue that the system works well, is essentially unchanged in form since Britain joined the EEC, that effective control is retained at the centre and, moreover, that the system demonstrates the traditional strengths of the 'Whitehall model' of government. Institutions have been skilfully and smoothly adapted over time rather than radically changed. Central control is effective but exercised with a 'light touch', departments retaining much operational control of the policy process. The FCO, in particular, still keeps its 'gatekeeper' role. Unlike the French Foreign Office for example, it has retained control of the permanent UK representation in Brussels. So successful is the British system thought to be in terms of producing agreed, coherent, cross-departmental European policy that it has been regarded as a model for other member states to follow. As for 'Europeanization', this has obviously occurred but its impact on the UK policy process has been limited. There have been significant changes in the operation of the machinery but these have been subsumed within a robust traditional system of central state administration (see, *inter alia*, Spence 1993, 1995; Wright 1996; Bulmer and Burch 1998; Allen 1999).

Some recent research, though, has tended to question the assumptions that underpin these conclusions, and points to a rather different account of the impact of Europeanization on the UK policy process. Smith, for example, challenges the Whitehall model from a 'policy networks' perspective, which in turn rests upon a very different and much more limited conception of core executive power. With respect to the coordination of European policy, he identifies two countervailing trends: a centralizing trend that is consistent with the analysis above; but he also notes that there are 'strong centripetal forces' at work, based upon departmental interests. In recent years, he argues, 'as departments have become more adept and better resourced in dealing with Europe, they have relied much less on either Cabinet Office or FCO support. As a result, the role of the coordinating bodies has become less important' (Smith 1999: 232). Despite high levels of departmental satisfaction with coordination at the centre and the continuing FCO belief that it alone controls contacts with Brussels, the centripetal forces appear to be at least as significant in explaining the impact of the EU on the policy process. 'The reality', Smith argues, 'is that as EU business increases, the FCO and the Cabinet Office are losing control, and departments are increasingly conducting business with the Commission, and other states, *directly*' (Smith 1999: 234, my italics).

With central control apparently diluted at best, Smith goes on to reveal a differential pattern of both coordination and Europeanization at the level of departments. Some departments, such as the Ministry of Agriculture (MAFF) and the Department of Trade and Industry (DTI) are at the highly 'Europeanized' end of a spectrum, with a considerable degree of autonomy over 'their' issue areas and actively geared up to exploit relevant transnational networks across the EU. At the other end of the spectrum are departments such as the Department of Social Security (DSS) and the Home Office, who are much more ambivalent about the opportunities that EU policy networks offer to increase their role and autonomy (Smith 1999: 234–42). But if some departments at least are becoming increasingly autonomous (and locked into transnational policy networks that are structurally difficult for national governments to control), this must surely challenge the FCO's traditional 'gatekeeper' role? What are the limits to the FCO's ability to play an effective and controlling coordinating role?

One response is to say it depends upon what is meant by 'coordination'. David Spence reminds us that there are different types of coordination. Day-to-day coordination in the form of ensuring effective information flows is clearly important – indeed it constitutes one of the alleged strengths of the British coordinating system – but it is a very different activity from 'coordination as mediation and conciliation between rival ministerial interests'. The latter, Spence argues, is normally 'drawn into the ambit of prime ministerial offices or other forms of central, non-foreign ministry coordination' (Spence 1999: 254). Spence also suggests, by implication, that it is misleading to regard UKREP as simply an extension of the FCO in Brussels. Not only is UKREP increasingly staffed by officials from domestic ministries but, in common with all other member states' permanent representations:

> over time, the balance has switched from foreign ministry staffing of such posts to the lead ministries, itself arguably a trend underlining the foreign ministry's failure in the historic endeavour to retain a gatekeeper role.

The 'extension' view also understates the growing role of permanent representations collectively in the policy process. As Spence notes, they 'mirror, on the spot, the coordinating role of the EU departments in national ministries of foreign affairs, while providing the main actors in the negotiating and lobbying framework' (Spence 1999: 253). From this perspective, UKREP is not simply an extension of the FCO or even an extension of national government, but arguably part of a transnational if not supranational policy process that, as we have already noted, is becoming increasingly 'Brusselized' (see Chapter 5). In this context, coordination has a rather different meaning again. As Spence (1999: 262) explains:

> the fact of daily collaboration is doubtless creating a 'European reflex', which clearly provides a context for national foreign ministry action and an incentive to seek administrative and policy-making synergies and cost-effectiveness.

If the FCO-as-gatekeeper is challenged both 'vertically' (by the European Secretariat) and 'horizontally' (by other lead departments also connected to transnational policy networks across the EU), there is some evidence that the FCO itself is becoming increasingly Europeanized in structure and operation. In formal organizational terms, the FCO has an EU command that consists of three departments: EU (External), which deals with external economic policy; EU (Internal), which covers other EC/EU issues and shadows the European dimensions of the work of domestic departments; and CFSP, which covers all Pillar 2 work and briefs the Political Director (Smith 1999: 241).

Reference to the Political Director indicates more explicit convergence, given that the FCO, like other member states, has adopted the organizational changes that followed the establishment of European Political Cooperation and have continued under CFSP. As we noted in Chapter 4, these include a Political Director who represents the minister on the Political Committee and a Political Correspondent who monitors working groups and oversees direct communications between desk officers across member states through the COREU network. Even more overt signs of convergence are evident in operational terms where working practices have been transformed by operating over many years with other member states within an EPC/CFSP framework. Often stimulated by the need to cut costs and improve efficiency, the activities that are increasingly shared with other foreign offices across the EU include joint reporting, joint training, some exchange of personnel on secondment (to the Commission as well as to other foreign offices), comparisons of staff conditions and performance indicators, and some sharing of embassy facilities in third countries (Forster and Wallace 1996: 416–17; Spence 1999: 262).

But there are limits to how far the FCO to date has been prepared to go in fundamentally changing structures and working practices to accommodate the EU. As David Allen argues, the FCO has maintained an organizational structure that maximizes its ability to monitor and coordinate the external work of 'domestic' departments. More directly, it has successfully managed to head off occasional calls for a separate European Ministry that would 'separate EU business from the overall responsibilities of the FCO'. Abroad, it has successfully preserved the 'pivotal role of the ambassador' and the embassy structure, not least in UKREP where it has resisted the argument that the increasing number of domestic specialists based there should report directly to their home departments. While the FCO may have 'gone along with' increasing Brusselization, it has resisted proposals to establish joint embassies (as opposed to sharing facilities) and has strongly opposed the wholesale pooling of resources abroad that would logically result in a European diplomatic service. It has fought valiantly both to maintain a national diplomatic service and to retain, insofar as this has been possible, its own gatekeeper role (Allen 1999: 211–12, 217–23).

So, to what extent has the foreign policy process in Britain been 'Europeanized'? No categorical answer has been given here. Instead two rather different perspectives have been presented. What might be called the orthodox view suggests limited Europeanization only, with changes essentially assimilated into the traditional Whitehall process. A second view, however, questions this conclusion and points to a differential, a more extensive and, in terms of effective central control, a potentially more disruptive impact of Europeanization on the policy-making process. From an analytical perspective, this discussion about a changing foreign policy process in Britain has established linkages back to policy context and forward to operational issues to which we now turn. How has the operational environment of British foreign policy changed as a result of membership of the EU?

Capabilities and Instruments

We have already noted how British diplomatic practices have been changing as a result of operating within an EU context. But arguably the operational environment has been radically transformed in more fundamental ways. EU membership has transformed the nature of relations both with other member states and with non-member states and international organizations. An increasing range of issues have to be negotiated with partner states and with Community institutions. On a day-to-day basis, British representatives are locked into a complex, well-established, multilateral *and* multileveled process of foreign policy-making: the UK government with other member governments in bilateral and multilateral fora; the FCO and other departments with their opposite numbers in state and Community institutions; UKREP with other permanent representatives and relevant Directorate-Generals of the Commission; British embassies abroad with other member state embassies and the external representatives of the Commission. Reference to the growing external representation of the Commission serves as a reminder that 'Brusselization' has not only affected the foreign policy process, it has also impacted upon the operational environment. As Spence notes, member states 'increasingly entrust the Commission with much of the operational side of European foreign policy'. Although, as we have observed, this has been an incremental and a controversial process over many years, the Commission has now become, in Spence's assessment, 'a powerful actor on the world stage' (Spence 1999: 263).

The key question here is whether membership overall has augmented the capabilities and instruments available to British foreign policy-makers or whether the costs have outweighed the benefits as far as policy output is concerned. To date, there has been only one extensive survey that addresses this question. This was the study carried out by Bulmer et al., *The UK and EC Membership Evaluated*, published in 1992 as part of a series of studies addressed to each member state. The findings of this study are nevertheless still broadly relevant. Their conclusions (rather crudely summarized here) are that, in terms of autonomy, British foreign economic policy has been most Europeanized, foreign policy less so, and defence policy least Europeanized. In terms of evaluating the costs versus the benefits of differential Europeanization, they conclude that overall the benefits outweigh the costs, particularly given a general decline in independent capabilities. The benefits accrue mainly from what Roy Ginsberg calls the 'politics of scale' (Ginsberg 1989). Membership has in different ways added to the UK's 'weight' and extended the UK's 'reach'. Interestingly, this augmentation is most marked in areas in which the UK has lost most autonomy. For example, they argue that membership of the largest trading bloc in the world has added considerable 'leverage' to Britain's trading policy – a particularly significant benefit given Britain's declining influence in the global economy over many years.

They also argue that EPC as a multilateral foreign policy framework added particular benefits to British foreign policy. It provided both capabilities and opportunities to handle issues such as international economic management and post-cold-war aid to Russia and the CEECs that simply would not have been available bilaterally. It provided a useful framework to advance specifically British interests such as the Falklands or Rhodesia/Zimbabwe. Where a unilateral policy on, for example, the Middle East or Central America might have generated costs in terms of attracting US displeasure, the 'collective mechanism' of a multilateral approach has provided useful protection (Hill 1996c: 75). Finally, multilateralism through EPC did not constrain British policy-makers in terms of preventing an extra-European policy on occasion from being pursued whether at the UN, in relation to Washington, or elsewhere. Indeed, aid policy through Lomé enabled historical contacts with Commonwealth states and former colonies to be maintained, albeit within a different framework. For all these reasons, the Bulmer et al. study argues that EPC 'served as an important anchor' for British foreign policy (Bulmer et al. 1992: 158). British governments were able to steer EPC in 'acceptable' – that is, intergovernmental – directions, which neither threatened sovereignty in formal terms nor attracted the sort of domestic controversy that certain other Community areas such as the Common Agricultural Policy did. EPC provided a useful framework for solving shared problems through common solutions and a useful vehicle for managing interdependence in a regional context (Bulmer 1992: 25).

While Britain appeared to be getting 'the best of both worlds' through the Thatcher period – gaining the benefits of multilateral diplomacy through EPC without the costs of relinquishing an independent foreign policy – by the early 1990s the dangers of a 'pick and mix' approach – what Hill calls a 'selective approach to European diplomacy, supporting many joint endeavours, ignoring others and at times complaining loudly about "European" spinelessness' – had become apparent (Hill 1996c: 76). It left Britain distinctly vulnerable to her partners demanding further integration in the area of foreign and defence policy. Having played a leading role in the development of EPC, the Thatcher and then the Major Governments found themselves playing a 'damage-limitation' role with respect to what became the

Common Foreign and Security Policy. In Hill's analysis, the 'contradictions' between an Atlanticist and a Europeanist orientation had now been 'sharpened... to the point where something will soon have to give, and where the traditional ability of the British elite to manage change from above will come under even greater pressure than has been evident since 1945'. His basic argument, though, is that the Thatcher period was 'little more than the dramatic interruption of a longer trend towards the Europeanization of British foreign policy' (Hill 1996c: 70–1). It is worth updating and testing out Hill's thesis here as a case study of British foreign policy in action. To what extent has Britain now finally rejected Atlanticism in favour of Europeanism? Or, do these two orientations co-exist uneasily and provide a continuing source of tension at the heart of contemporary British foreign policy? Is it still necessary to make fundamental strategic choices about the future of British foreign policy – or not?

A Europeanized British Foreign Policy?

After the painfully slow and hesitant reorientation of British foreign policy towards Europe from the 1960s onwards, the Thatcher period after 1979 witnessed an apparent return to 'Atlanticism' with some residual 'globalism' thrown in. Three decisions taken in her first year in office revealed Thatcher's priorities. The decision to replace Polaris by purchasing the Trident nuclear missile system from the United States underlined the 'special relationship' with Washington and symbolized the Prime Minister's determination to restore Britain to a position of international influence and global status. Her fundamental commitment to the Atlantic alliance was illustrated by her support for the NATO decisions to increase defence spending and to deploy Cruise and Pershing missiles in Europe. After the election of Ronald Reagan, the personal relationship between the two leaders ensured that that the transatlantic connection would continue to underpin a Thatcherite foreign policy. One issue above all can be taken to illustrate the dominant orientation of British foreign policy in the 1980s – the conflict with Argentina over the Falkland Islands in 1982. Extensive US assistance was crucial to the successful outcome but, significantly, this was underplayed in Britain at the time. The victory was presented as a British victory and taken as evidence not only of a restored relationship with the US but also of restored global influence and respect for Britain. After a second electoral victory in 1983, assisted although not assured by the 'Falklands factor', the Prime Minister sought to build upon this by using her relationship with both Reagan and Gorbachev to play a key bridge-building role in improving the climate of East–West relations between 1983 and 1987 (White 1992b).

Meanwhile, the Thatcher approach to Europe was beginning to clarify. The first five years were dominated by the budgetary rebate issue – securing the return of 'our' or 'my money', as Thatcher referred to it. Thereafter, her relations with the Community appeared to improve as completing the Single European Market (SEM) – a Thatcherite objective – took centre stage. After the signing of the Single European Act in 1986, however, relations rapidly plummeted, the control of money again being largely responsible. Three interrelated issues combined to test the Prime Minister's patience to breaking point: the pressures to move towards Economic and Monetary Union (EMU); the particular pressure on Britain to join the Exchange Rate Mechanism (ERM) of the European Monetary System (EMS) and, finally, the launch of a social dimension to the proposed SEM (Bradbury 1996: 75). The result was an unprecedented attack on the EC in Thatcher's speech to the College of Europe, Bruges in September 1988. Despite FCO attempts to water down the contents, this speech gave full vent to her anti-Community prejudices and again underlined her Atlanticist priorities – referring to the Atlantic community as 'our noblest inheritance and our greatest strength' (quoted in Young 1998: 348). With hindsight, this speech can be seen as the beginning of Thatcher's end and, two years later, she was removed from office by her senior Cabinet colleagues.

But an analytical focus on the rhetoric and the personal prejudices of Margaret Thatcher is misleading if it suggests that the process of Europeanization came to a halt during the Thatcher period. Indeed, the best evidence for the continuing dominance of what Jonathan Bradbury calls an 'accommodationist' approach to Europe comes from the eventual removal of Thatcher before she could do more damage to Britain's standing with her European partners (Bradbury 1996: 78–9). Not only did the process of Europeanization continue through the 1980s but, arguably, it accelerated despite the Prime Minister's increasingly strident views. 'In her time', Young argues, Thatcher 'took Britain further into Europe than anyone except Heath. Institutions and markets and laws became far more deeply imbued with the Europe effect' (Young 1998: 306).

By the 1980s, in terms of policy outputs, Britain was gradually becoming a more mainstream player in Community affairs, moving, in

Allen's phrase, 'from the periphery of the Community towards the middle ground' (Allen 1988: 52). This could be seen in the leading role Britain was playing in developing EPC. By the mid-1980s, it is striking how far the main lines of British policy on many issues had come to resemble those pursued collectively by her partners. On occasions – with respect to the Siberian gas pipeline issue in 1981–82, for example – this even saw the British Government taking up a position in opposition to the United States (Smith, M. 1988: 15). But it is British support for the Single European Act that best illustrates an accelerating Europeanization process during this period. This has led to considerable debate about what the Thatcher Government was doing in supporting a piece of legislation that introduced the idea of the qualified majority vote into Community business and thus constituted 'the most practical advance towards the abolition of national frontiers and national powers that the Community had undertaken in the whole period of British membership' (Young 1998: 333ff.).

But at least her exit from office spared Margaret Thatcher from the final stages of the negotiations that led up to the Maastricht Treaty, which, despite the opt-outs negotiated by the new Prime Minister John Major, committed Britain to political and economic union and even deeper integration as a result. The first foreign policy issue that John Major had to deal with, however, was the Gulf War, an issue that underlined again the continuing resonance of both the Atlantic and global 'circles'. But on Europe the rhetoric at least had changed. His oft-quoted and (thereafter) frequently deconstructed statement on the subject came on a visit to Germany shortly after the Gulf War. 'I want us to be where we belong. At the very heart of Europe. Working with our partners in building the future' (quoted in Young 1998: 424). But any desire to implement that objective failed after the 1992 election delivered a very small Conservative majority and enabled a group of 'Euro-sceptic' MPs to derail his European policy, although he did eventually get the Maastricht Treaty ratified in 1993.

New Labour, New Europeans?

After winning the sort of overwhelming parliamentary majority in May 1997 that John Major could have only dreamed of, the new Blair Government appeared to be sufficiently detached from party constraints to succeed where Major had failed – in placing Britain at the heart of Europe. Perhaps the most dramatic illustration of a new

European approach to foreign and defence policy to date has been the transformed British position on European defence that emerged after 1998. The British view through the 1990s, maintained by the Major Government and initially supported by the incoming Blair Government, had been to oppose Franco–German attempts to promote a coordinated EU approach to defence. The objective (consistent with the special meaning of Europeanization outlined at the beginning of this chapter) was to avoid any policy that might weaken the American commitment to European security. But, initially floated at a European summit meeting and confirmed in principle at the St Malo summit with the French in December 1998, the Blair Government now sought to give a lead in establishing a European defence force. As the idea has developed, discussions have focused on establishing an integrated force up to 60,000 strong that will be capable of handling international crises independently of the United States.

Sceptics may argue, of course, that these plans will take years to come to fruition. Meanwhile, a positive British approach on this issue usefully serves to distract attention from the negative connotations associated with the decision to opt out of the first wave of member countries joining the Euro currency system in January 1999. It is certainly true that the new policy had its origins in the concern that the British presidency of the EU in the first half of 1998 had failed to serve as a turning point in establishing Britain's European credentials. A request to the FCO towards the end of that period for ideas about how to maximize the potential of Britain's future in Europe produced *inter alia* a recommendation to use Britain's military assets to develop 'a European capacity to act independently in the defence field' (FCO memorandum, quoted in *The Economist*, 10 October 1998). But the significance and the symbolism of this issue should not be underestimated. Given that Britain controls a large proportion of Europe's usable military capacity, defence is an issue on which Britain can credibly give a lead. Indeed without British participation, there could be no effective European military force. A new, agenda-setting British approach to this issue also powerfully symbolizes the fact that Britain can be a valuable and effective partner in the European integration process.

But there is a more fundamental conceptual problem that is highlighted by the defence issue. The Blair Government has chosen to locate European policy within a conception of Britain's role in the world that explicitly maintains that there are no longer any contradictions within the basic orientation of British foreign policy and therefore no necessity for strategic decisions about choosing between Atlanticism and Europeanism. Pulling together various ideas developed in earlier speeches, Blair delivered a major speech on foreign policy at the London Guildhall in November 1999. 'We have a new role', he announced. 'It is to use the strengths of our history to build our future not as a superpower but as a pivotal power, as a power that is at the crux of alliances and international politics which shape the world and its future. Engaged, open, dynamic, a partner and, where possible, a leader in ideas and in influence, that is where Britain must be.' Thus positioned, Blair went on to argue, the British should not 'continue to be mesmerized by the choice between the US and Europe. It is a false choice… my vision for Britain is as a bridge between the EU and the USA.' From this perspective, Blair sought to downplay the radical nature of the new British approach to European defence. The objective, as he put it, was to 'shape European Defence Policy in a way designed to strengthen [the] transatlantic bond by making NATO a more balanced partnership, and by giving Europeans the capacity to act whenever the United States, for its own reasons, decides not to be involved' (see http://www.fco.gov.uk/text/news).

This conception of Britain's role is not to be rejected lightly. It offers an explicitly internationalist position that contrasts with rather narrow nationalist postures offered elsewhere in the UK. It also serves as a timely reminder (to the French in particular) that US–EU relations should not be regarded as a zero-sum game. The speech itself was part of an explicit attempt by the government to give a much needed lead in stimulating a national debate about the significance of European developments for Britain's future. The very general and rather vague nature of the conception may also be useful in domestic political terms although that is a reminder that Blair too is highly constrained from adopting an overtly European posture by the ingrained domestic political attitudes towards Europe discussed in an earlier section of this chapter.

But there clearly are problems both with this conception of Britain's role and with the prescription about avoiding strategic choices that is extracted from it. Although Blair in his speech dismisses Churchill's three circles image in passing, linking it to other failed attempts to establish a new role for Britain such as 'Mrs Thatcher's call to repel a European federal state', his concept has an evident Churchillian lineage, even if the three 'circles' have now effectively become two after 50 years of decolonization. Apart from introducing a new metaphor – Britain-as-pivot – this conception appears to be an extension of traditional thinking rather than a new approach. The idea of Britain-as-pivot is also weakened by many of the same problems that undermined Churchill's conception. The pivot image connotes a form of magisterial detachment, as if Britain is somehow 'above' rather than immersed 'within' world politics. The ethnocentric assumption that everything turns around Britain-as-pivot – as with being at the centre of the three interlocking circles – is also likely to lead to an overestimation of British influence. Finally, as Hugo Young observes, the pivot image suggests equal closeness to, as well as equal distance from, the United States and Europe, which might predispose Britain to support particular American positions that might in turn damage European interests (*Guardian*, 25 November 1999).

This last point links to problems with the view that choices do not need to be made about the predominant orientation of British policy. Most significantly, perhaps, it assumes a degree of commonality of interests and positions across the Atlantic that the evidence, particularly since the end of the cold war, suggests is unlikely to be sustained. It may well be that Britain can, on certain issues at certain times, act effectively as a 'bridge-builder' with the United States. In May 1998, for example, the Blair Government as EU President did help to broker a deal with the US that resolved the trade dispute over the Helms-Burton extra-territorial legislation. This in turn helped to pave the way for the Trans-atlantic Economic Partnership to boost US–EU trade. On other issues at other times, however, choices may well need to be made. Defence, for example, the issue increasingly highlighted by Blair, may well become an increasingly problematic issue area. In the recent past, over Iraq and Kosovo for example, the British Government has tended almost instinc-tively to defer to and to support the American line. Following the crisis over UN inspections, British involvement in the military action against Iraq in February 1998 was particularly damaging because at the time the expectation in Europe was that Britain as Council President would be organizing and leading an EU response to the crisis. This led to sharp criticism of British policy from her EU partners.

A new British approach to European defence that seeks to maintain a balance between Atlantic and European interests may well be difficult to sustain in the future, particularly if neo-isolationist tendencies in the United States, as illustrated by the refusal of the US Senate to ratify the Comprehensive Test Ban Treaty, continue or even intensify under a possible Republican leadership. Current concerns in Europe (at the time of writing) are focused on the proposed space-based defence system (SBIRS – Space-Based Infra-Red System), which is designed to protect the United States but not Western Europe from missiles fired by 'rogue states'. Implementation of this system will involve the United

States breaching the terms of the 1971 Anti-Ballistic Missile (ABM) Treaty. An even-handed British approach to this issue is seriously complicated by reported plans for US bases in Britain to serve as relay stations in Europe, which will be crucial to the operation of the system (*Guardian* 18 November 1999). The question that may well be asked at some stage is, will the European partners trust Britain not to take a US rather than a European line on defence issues?

Finally, the bridge-builder image understates the impact of Europeanization on British foreign and defence policy discussed at some length in this chapter. We have established that the traditional policy-making context has been transformed by membership. The EU now constitutes the most important framework of British foreign policy and a European role has gradually replaced other traditional roles. The policy-making process has been extensively although not wholly Europeanized and there is some debate emerging about the impact of this on the workings of the policy machinery and on the possibility of retaining control of the process at the centre. Policy outputs have also been radically affected by membership and, given developments since 1998, more extensively so than Bulmer et al. concluded in 1992. It would now appear that we need to revise the idea that defence as an issue area has been restricted to the transatlantic (NATO) sphere and all but excluded from the Europeanization process.

From this perspective, the 'new' Blairite location of Britain is revealed as a very conservative approach, as if role can somehow be detached from policy context, process, instruments and outputs. To this extent it continues a tradition dating back to the early 1960s whereby important decisions with respect to Europe are taken and trends followed that produce major transformations over time. But, at the same time, the impression at least is created that nothing of great significance is actually changing (see Young 1998: 129ff.). As a result, not only are the British people left in ignorance of the real extent of change but they are led to believe that British governments are less constrained and have more room for manoeuvre than is the case. Arguing persistently that no choices need to be made itself suggests that the parameters of choice are wider than in fact they are. Such an approach, it may be argued, is more likely to reinforce rather than to change ingrained attitudes towards 'Europe'.

Conclusion

Three brief points can be made here by way of a conclusion both to the case study and to the chapter as a whole. First, of the positions offered at the beginning of the case study, the argument presented here suggests that both European and Atlantic orientations continue to coexist rather uneasily in British foreign policy and that, if we assume increasing Europeanization, what Hill refers to as the 'contradictions' are likely to become even 'sharper'. More than any other issue perhaps, the debate in Britain about the Euro, culminating in the promised referendum, will show whether or not the Blair Government's attempted reorientation of Britain has been successful in terms of changing popular attitudes towards the EU.

Second, the process of Europeanization itself has been extensive in the British case as revealed by our common analytical framework. The significance of this process as a more general phenomenon across member states is underlined by its application to Britain, for reasons discussed at the beginning of this chapter. The process of Europeanization has continued apace under the Blair Government but, while relations between Britain and her partners have improved dramatically since 1997, the Prime Minister, like his predecessors, still insists on the importance of avoiding making strategic choices between the Atlantic and Europe. This may well become an increasingly problematic position. Crucially, the one significant gap in the process of Europeanization in Britain is now with respect to generating more positive domestic attitudes towards Europe. As Bradbury puts it, if we define 'Europeanization as a means of fostering new attitudes to EU membership [it] clearly has a long way to go' (Bradbury 1996: 86). This suggests that even more positive leadership from government is required in stimulating a real, informed, popular debate.

Finally, the discussion in the latter part of this chapter about changing British attitudes to European defence has highlighted a possible gap in our definition of European foreign policy. To what extent does European defence now merit consideration not simply as a dimension of other sub-systems but as a fourth sub-system of European foreign policy in its own right? This question provides the focus of the next chapter.

7

Security and Defence: Towards a Common European Defence Policy?

This chapter looks at the possible criticism that the analysis of European foreign policy developed so far in this book, constructed around three sub-systems of activity, is incomplete in that it fails to include a fourth sub-system – relating directly to European security and defence – which merits separate analysis. A brief introduction clarifies important definitional issues with significant political implications, focusing on the particular issues surrounding the changing notion of security. The second section reviews in some detail the substantive progress made since the 1950s towards the establishment of a common defence policy in Europe. Finally, we reflect on the debate about whether or not a defence capability in common is essential to the idea of Europe as a significant player in world politics.

The underlying definitional problem here is that the key terms 'security' and 'defence' have become increasingly differentiated over the last 30 years or so, largely because security has been defined in ways that have transported the notion into a range of non-defence areas, denoted by terms such as 'economic security', 'environmental security' and, more generically, 'common security' (Palme 1982). Security has come to mean a concern to reduce or eliminate threats, risks or merely uncertainties in a number of different areas of activity – political, economic, environmental, and so on – as well as dealing with threats of a strictly military nature (Buzan et al. 1990: 4–5; Stainier 1995: 17). This contrasts sharply with an earlier period when references to security were usually implicit references at least to military security, and the terms 'security' and 'defence' were essentially linked and indeed often used interchangeably. Frequent US references in the cold war period to national security policy, for example, suggest a close interrelationship not only between security and defence but also, more broadly, between these terms and foreign policy as a whole. While defence, too, has undergone some conceptual revisions, its essential linkage to the use or threatened use of organized military force has remained unchallenged. Security, on the other hand, has become such an 'essentially contested concept' (Buzan 1983: 6) that reference to it usually requires some further clarification that addresses the 'what sort of security?' challenge.

Given this 'contestation', one way of reconnecting the ideas of security and defence has been to refer to security in the defence domain as 'hard security' and to other meanings of security as 'soft security'. While this distinction is useful analytically, despite the many 'grey areas' in between, it is important to note here that this sort of language implicitly privileges defence over security. By implication at least, the adjective 'soft' denotes a less significant area of activity than 'hard' and suggests a hierarchy of security-related activities. We shall return to this important point later but, while we are dealing with the use of language, it is also worth noting again the political use of language in a European context – something of a recurring theme in this book. In this context, maintaining a distinction between security and defence has been useful to national policy-makers because of the relationship between defence and national sovereignty, which, if anything, is even closer in symbolic terms than the link between foreign policy and sovereignty. While it has been difficult for this reason to discuss defence in a European integration context, the same sort of political constraint has not related to security. Nevertheless, as we shall see in the next section, this linguistic convenience has helped over time to facilitate discussions about defence proper, as it were, that have gradually appeared on the agenda, although significant problems still confront the idea of a common European defence policy, to which we now turn.

Towards a Common European Defence Policy?

It is necessary to preface a historical survey by clarifying what is meant by the key terms 'common defence policy' and 'common defence' in an EU context, particularly as the terms have appeared in treaty form as an explicit objective of the Union since 1991. To quote again the relevant article of the Treaty on European Union: 'the common foreign and security policy shall include all questions related to the security of the Union, including the eventual framing of a *common defence policy*, which might in time lead to a *common defence*' (Article J.4.1, Treaty on European Union 1991, my italics). We should note that there were two significant linguistic changes to this formulation in the more recent Treaty of Amsterdam (TOA). The first, the replacement of the word 'eventual' by 'progressive', suggests a shortened time frame for the achievement of these objectives, at least in aspirational terms. But the second, the addition of a rider at the end of the sentence – 'should the European Council so decide' – seems to give the whole process an even more conditional flavour (Article J.7, Treaty of Amsterdam 1997).

John Roper (1995) offers useful definitions of both 'common defence policy' and 'common defence' and suggests appropriate linkages between them. A common defence policy (CDP) is defined as 'a common policy with respect to the use of the armed forces of the member states of the European Union'. A CDP should also set out, he suggests, a 'conceptual framework to provide some coherence for the development of a common defence', to include ways in which 'human, equipment and financial resources for military action will be developed', together with 'operational aspects of the organization of armed forces, their training and the conduct of military operations'. The 'full' development of a CDP would also necessitate at some stage (as with national defence policies) a common assessment of possible threats and appropriate responses, identification of missions for the armed forces, agreement on budgetary issues and a common armaments procurement policy. Roper goes on to offer two ways of defining 'common defence': a stronger version, 'the organization of the armed forces of the member states in common'; and a weaker version, 'the organization of *the activities* of the armed forces of the member states in common' (my italics). The stronger version 'in its ultimate form', he suggests, would imply 'common procurement, logistics, training... budget, communications, intelligence and command structures'. Significantly, a common European defence is also likely 'to mean very considerable restrictions on the scope for national defence policies'. Finally, Roper draws parallels between the stronger version of a common defence and the 'ill-fated' European Defence Community (EDC), which provides a useful link to and starting point for our historical review (Roper 1995: 8–10).

From European Defence Community to the Single European Act

The idea of a common European defence policy in an institutionalized form has its post-war origins in the EDC treaty signed by all six members of the European Coal and Steel Community (ECSC) in May 1952. As Anne Deighton notes, 'the treaty had emerged out of a French proposal in October 1950 for a European army, which was itself a response to the US demand that West Germany should enter NATO' (Deighton 1997: 14). As we noted in an earlier chapter, it was envisaged that EDC would be followed by a more inclusive European Political Community that would have contained both a common European foreign and defence policy. After two years of intense negotiations over ratification, however, the EDC was rejected, ironically by the French National Assembly in August 1954, producing a major crisis in both European and transatlantic relations. The crisis was resolved by some impressive and inventive bridge-building diplomacy by the British Foreign Secretary Anthony Eden. Eden managed to persuade all the major parties to agree to the creation of the Western European Union (WEU) within NATO by expanding first the membership of the 1948 Brussels Treaty and then the membership of NATO to include West Germany and Italy (see Deighton 1997: 11–24). This clever solution (invented, Eden claims, in his bath!) facilitated a rearmed West Germany (thus meeting American demands), provided a credible, institutionalized constraint on German military power (thereby alleviating French concerns), secured West German sovereignty (Chancellor Adenauer's preoccupation), and strengthened the intergovernmental transatlantic alliance structure (the clear British preference).

While defence integration in Europe was not explicitly ruled out by the WEU-in-NATO solution, it was clear by the mid-1950s that a supranational defence option was simply not available for the foreseeable future and the Six turned their attention to integration in other fields. There was no further progress towards a European defence policy until the creation of European Political Cooperation (EPC) in the 1970s. Defence remained firmly barred from discussions within EPC, but it was soon found to be impossible to separate foreign policy coordination from security concerns broadly conceived (Hill 1992: 136). Within an EPC context, it gradually became necessary and legitimate to discuss security issues and this was helped by the expanding conception of security that we have already noted. One important development here was the major contribution made by EPC to the 'Helsinki process' in the first half of the 1970s, a multilateral set of negotiations concerned *inter alia* with enhancing the political and economic aspects of security, which eventually produced the Conference of Security and Cooperation in Europe (CSCE, later the Organization for Security and Cooperation in Europe (OSCE)) in 1975.

By the early 1980s, security had formally become part of the EPC agenda. There were two 'motors' driving this forward, one internal and the other external. The external factor was growing concern in Europe about the direction of US foreign policy particularly after the election of Ronald Reagan and the renewal of East–West tensions, usually referred to as the 'new' or the 'second' cold war (Halliday 1983). In this context, the British Government pushed for a distinction between defence and security and took a lead in securing agreement to what became the 1981 London Report (Forster 1997: 31). Significantly, this referred to continuing the 'flexible and pragmatic approach that has made it possible to discuss in Political Cooperation certain important foreign policy questions bearing on the political aspects of security' (quoted in Hill 1992: 137). This enabled discussions within EPC on issues such as arms control, confidence-building measures, armaments and terrorism.

The second internal factor, however, was the revived momentum of the European integration process through the first half of the 1980s, which in this context meant that there was continuing pressure after the London Report to extend the parameters of 'allowable' areas of security in EPC (see Hill 1992: 137; Forster 1997: 31). An important although ultimately abortive effort came from the West German and Italian foreign ministers in what became known as the Genscher–Colombo Plan, which explicitly sought to include defence issues in EPC. Resistance to this proposal from certain member states, however, eventually lead to a compromise agreement – the 1983 'Solemn Declaration of Stuttgart' – which added only a reference to economic as well as political aspects of security. But more substantial progress from an integrationist perspective was made in the negotiations which led to the Single European Act (SEA). The SEA not only underlined in treaty form the need to coordinate political and economic aspects of security and to maintain what it called 'the technological and industrial conditions for security', but it asserted that 'closer cooperation on questions of European security would contribute in an essential way to the development of a European identity in external matters' (Article 30. 6, Single European Act 1986).

Reference in SEA to developing an external European identity in a security context suggests a link to the reactivation of the WEU in 1983–84, although any linkage between the WEU and the Community was only implicit at that stage. As we have noted, progress towards a European defence rather than a security identity in EPC had not proved possible but there was continuing pressure – from the French in particular – to move towards a European defence identity, preferably one that was independent of NATO (and US) control. Although, as Forster comments, the British took the opposite view – that the WEU could provide an intergovernmental forum for discussing defence issues but *without* damaging the integrity and the primacy of NATO by introducing a separate defence organization – 'British and French interests thus converged onto WEU, though for different reasons' (Forster 1997: 32). This opened the way for the WEU Rome Declaration of October 1984, which identified a number of areas for defence cooperation and institutional mechanisms to support it. This was followed by the Hague Platform of October 1987, which acknowledged that 'the construction of an integrated Europe will be incomplete as long as it does not include security and defence'. But, while it was agreed that the WEU might play a useful role in coordinating 'out of (NATO) area' operations, the limits of agreement about the future role of the WEU and the whole question of what was now being called a European security and defence identity (ESDI) had been reached. There was effectively a stalemate between the 'Europeanists' led by France and the 'Atlanticists' led by Britain until the dramatic change in the external environment after 1989 (Forster 1997: 32–4).

After the cold war: ESDI and NATO

If the period up to the reactivation of the WEU and the SEA suggests that security but not defence was on the integrationist agenda, the period immediately after the end of the cold war appeared to open up the possibility of extending that agenda to include *both* security and defence. Clearly both the wider security and defence environments had been radically transformed almost at a stroke and neither a continuing US commitment to West European defence nor the future of NATO itself could now be guaranteed. A unique opportunity for the new EU to become *the* security and defence organization in Europe appeared suddenly to have presented itself. As Helene Sjursen comments, 'although the idea of a European security and defence identity was not "invented" by the end of the cold war it was given new life with the breakdown of bipolarity in Europe' (Sjursen 1998: 95).

This opportunity was clearly recognized by the urgency that was injected into the intergovernmental debates in 1990–91 about the reform of the Community. As we have seen, the resulting Maastricht Treaty contained the aspiration to include defence as well as security on the Union (although not the EC) agenda and to link WEU explicitly to the EU as its 'defence arm'. Indeed, it can be argued that the CFSP actually required the 'eventual incorporation of a defence and security identity to complete its external dimensions' (Deighton 1997: 170). Any expectation of rapid progress, however, in terms of translating aspiration into action was undermined by what Deighton calls the 'institutional resilience' of NATO and the strength of continuing opposition to including defence in the integration process. The more successful NATO was in 'Atlanticizing' ESDI and the WEU, the more attention in Europe turned to other issues such as Economic and Monetary Union (EMU) and enlargement, which were either seen as more pressing or upon which agreement could more easily be attained. Interestingly, having been staunchly resistant to the ESDI idea, the Americans came round to supporting it and NATO collectively had endorsed the concept by 1994.

In fact, the 'rebranding' of NATO for a post-cold-war era began as early as 1991 with the adoption of a new strategic concept at the Rome summit that identified three important areas of future activity. The first acknowledged the widening definition of security and envisaged an increased role for cooperation and dialogue in NATO activities. The second area foreshadowed a restructuring of military capabilities with more emphasis on crisis management. Finally, it was agreed in Rome that the European allies would in future take greater responsibility for their own security. Thereafter, a rapid series of agreements and actions had by 1997 repositioned NATO, in Sjursen's phrase, 'at the apex of a network of new security arrangements in Europe' (Sjursen 1998: 101). The restructuring of military capabilities particularly relevant to both NATO and European roles in the new strategic environment was the Combined Joint Task Forces (CJTFs) proposal agreed at the NATO Brussels summit in 1994. These forces were intended to improve NATO's ability to act 'out of area' but they also raised political questions about who would have access to and control these forces. This was resolved, in principle at least, at the Berlin NATO Council meeting in June 1996 when it was agreed that CJTFs could be made available to WEU in military operations that *may* not involve the United States.

Rather than strengthening a European-based defence identity, however, this agreement had the effect of further binding WEU and ESDI into the NATO framework, underlining as it did the dependence of WEU upon NATO for military capabilities. The precise institutional role of the EU in these new arrangements was far from clear (Hill 1998b: 45). This was scarcely clarified by the TOA. Apart from adding the tantalizing linguistic ambiguities noted earlier, it offered little clarity on defence. Whether intended or not, however, what the TOA did say appeared to reinforce the institutional primacy of NATO in the defence field and to 'map out' an appropriate security rather than defence role for the EU. Significantly, a decision to incorporate WEU into the EU was deferred but, for the first time in an EC/EU treaty, NATO was explicitly mentioned. Any EU decisions on defence must 'respect the obligations of certain member states, which see their common defence realized in NATO' (Article 17, Treaty of Amsterdam, quoted in Peterson and Bomberg 1999: 292 fn. 13). It was also agreed that the so-called Petersburg Tasks – defined as 'humanitarian and rescue tasks, peacekeeping tasks and tasks of combat forces in crisis management, including peacekeeping' – would be brought within the scope of CFSP and incorporated into the Treaty. These tasks – arguably more related to a security rather than defence role for WEU – had emerged originally at the WEU meeting of foreign and defence ministers in June 1992, which issued the Petersburg Declaration. To carry out these operations, the EU would 'avail itself of the WEU', the TOA declared loftily but without comment on practical problems (see Dinan 1998: 386–7; Deighton 1997: 5).

Security and defence?

An interested observer reviewing the defence scene in Europe after the signing of the TOA could be forgiven for thinking that the European defence issue was now firmly located within a NATO framework, that the 'Atlanticists' led by the UK had triumphed over the 'Europeanists' led by France and that the EU was restricted to playing a 'soft' security role. This view appeared to be reinforced by some sober thinking in Europe about the costs of providing separate defence capabilities outside NATO. By the end of 1998, however, even before the TOA could be ratified, the possibility of developing a common European defence had dramatically reappeared on the European agenda. There were two interrelated reasons for this, one political, the other military.

In political terms, the sudden change in British defence policy discussed in the last chapter was crucial. As the member state who had most staunchly resisted the idea of a European defence policy for fear of damaging the transatlantic alliance, the 'conversion' of Britain was crucial, although the Blair Government still wanted to maintain the view that a European defence policy did not and should not threaten the cohesion of NATO. The fact that Britain joined up with France – the other major military power within the EU but with a very different view of the political and symbolic implications of a European defence identity – to present a common defence initiative at the St Malo summit in December 1998 was also highly significant. Their combined political and military weight was sufficient to carry the support of the other EU members and to reopen the question of developing a genuine European defence identity.

The other more overtly military stimulus to this process was the evidence 'on the ground' in Kosovo in the spring of 1999 that the Europeans remained woefully dependent upon the Americans for any sort of serious, sustained military intervention – even in Europe. The Balkans was, of course, a particularly sensitive region for the Europeans for reasons that were detailed in Chapter 5. European embarrassment was further underlined in the Kosovo crisis. Not only did the Americans mount the air war on Serbia almost single-handedly, but the Europeans struggled to provide and maintain a modest number of troops for the ensuing military intervention in Kosovo itself. It would be difficult to imagine a more telling illustration of the need for the Europeans to develop a more effective defence force to deal with yet another crisis 'in their own backyard'. It now became commonplace for political leaders in Europe to compare the shortfall between spending inputs and 'firepower' outputs in Europe with the ratios achieved by the United States. For approximately two-thirds of the US spending, the Europeans collectively were achieving a small fraction of the military 'punch'. These statistics provided powerful ammunition for an integrated European defence policy if only in terms of economic efficiency. In sum, a combination of political, strategic and economic arguments was now pointing towards a renewed attempt to develop an effective ESDI – or EDI as it was often being referred to – as if to underline the renewed focus on defence. But again, translating aspiration and political rhetoric into realistic action proved problematic.

Some progress was made through 1999 and into the new century. This consisted of beginning the process of replacing WEU by setting up EU political and military institutions in Brussels, and outlining plans for European force structures. In May 1999, the ten member countries of the WEU agreed in principle to merge WEU and EU. A detailed framework for the 'progressive framing of a common defence policy' was agreed at the Cologne European summit in June. A clear objective was established that, interestingly, borrowed much of the language of the St. Malo agreement. To undertake the Petersburg tasks, it was agreed that 'the Union must have the capacity for autonomous action, backed up by credible military forces, the means to decide to use them, and a readiness to do so'. The General Affairs Council was given until the end of 2000 to take the decisions necessary and, more dauntingly, to find the means to meet this objective. By this date, it was assumed that the 'WEU as an organization would have completed its purpose' (Presidency Conclusions, Annex 111, Cologne European Council, Press Release 4 June 1999). It was also agreed to hold regular meetings of EU defence ministers, and to set up a permanent committee of senior military and civilian officials in Brussels (on the model of the EU Monetary Committee that set up the euro), together with an advisory military committee and a military staff.

In November 1999, a full meeting of EU foreign and defence ministers met for the first time. The proposed European force was now being discussed in terms of 60,000 troops, to be deployable within 60 days and to be sustainable in the field for at least a year. The target date for establishing this force was agreed as 2003. By March 2000, following the Cologne guidelines, an interim Political and Security Committee, a Military Committee and an embryo Military Staff had all been established in Brussels.

Apparent progress towards a common European defence policy in Brussels, however, was soon being contrasted with a marked absence of progress in national capitals and indications of further problems in Kosovo. More questions were being posed than answers provided. Where was this European force coming from? How would it be constituted? What would be its relationship to the existing Eurocorps and NATO's combined joint task force? How would it be supported? Was it just a 'paper army'? Continuing problems in Kosovo 12 months after the military intervention provided an unhappy context for contrasts to be drawn between aspiration and performance. There clearly was no peace on the ground and the EU collectively was accused, not least by an increasingly exasperated Washington, of failing to provide the promised resources, civilian as well as military, to effect that peace. Most importantly, there was no evidence at that stage that EU members were prepared to find the resources in terms of increased defence budgets to provide a realistic European defence option. Indeed, the indications were that some European states, notably Germany, were more concerned to cut their defence budgets for domestic political and economic reasons. Perhaps the only thing that was apparent was that expectations were being raised again that the EU this time would deliver a credible defence policy with appropriate military capabilities. Failure to deliver will equally clearly have serious costs both within the EU and beyond.

Security, Defence and Actorness

Having reviewed the history of the EU's attempts to develop a common defence policy, we turn in the final section of this chapter to the debate about the relationship between defence, security and actorness. The key question here is, what is the impact of the continuing absence of autonomous military capabilities on the ability of the EU to be a significant and effective international actor? We touched upon this debate in Chapter 2 when reviewing the 'EU as actor' approach to Europe's global role. The debate began in the early 1970s when François Duchène argued that superpower détente and an apparent East–West nuclear stalemate provided an opportunity for the EC to exercise 'civilian forms of influence and action' based upon its economic power. But this distinctive international role could be performed, in Duchène's view, only if the Community avoided becoming a military power. Duchène's conclusion was that the Community is and ought to be a civilian power and, as such, could serve as a non-military model of international power and influence that might help to transform international relations (Duchène 1972). Duchène's conclusions were supported from a different perspective by Johan Galtung who was becoming increasingly concerned that, if it combined resource power and what he called 'structural power', the Community was a 'superpower in the making'. For Galtung, the prospect of the Community as a potential superpower conventional or otherwise was a role model to be avoided (Galtung 1973).

The most important response to Duchène and Galtung came a decade later from Hedley Bull. From a mainstream realist perspective, Bull argued bluntly that the notion of a 'civilian power' is a contradiction in terms (Bull 1983). Only if the Community developed a military capability and became a military power could it be a successful international actor. By implication at least, to be a 'real' power and therefore to be an effective actor in world politics requires the acquisition of military capabilities. This view continues to attract support and indeed it appears to accord with views about what constitutes a 'great power' that are not restricted to tough-minded realists. At the end of the 1990s, it was not difficult to hear echoes of Bull. For example, Peterson and Bomberg, scarcely mainstream realists, were bemoaning the fact that the 'EU continued to lack one of the essential prerequisites of great-power status: a military capability that could be deployed in the pursuit of political goals' (Peterson and Bomberg 1999: 240). This view is not restricted to academic commentators. To the extent that the EU collectively regards the absence of common defence capabilities as detracting from a comprehensive external identity, arguably the members themselves see this as detracting from effective actorness (see, for example, Van den Broek 1996: 4). And, whatever may now be in the planning stage, Hill's comment is still apposite: 'the defence dimension of the Union... has notably failed to develop... thus defence is more a theoretical than practical addition to the EU's armoury'. 'If the EU is a power', he goes on to say, 'it is still a civilian power' (Hill 1998a: 25).

Whatever the continuing strengths of arguments about the relationship between a defence capability and credible actorness, there is another view that builds upon the expanded notion of security. This suggests that important dimensions of the EU's evolving security role are missed if the focus on actorness is too narrowly restricted to defence in a traditional sense. It can be argued that in the new post-cold-war environment, 'soft' security is at least as important as 'hard'. Helene Sjursen develops the argument that this environment has further exposed the limitations of the traditional definition of security and has also led to a heightened recognition of the limits of military power to secure desired outcomes If we add that the EU faces no serious military threats but rather more diffuse 'risks' and 'challenges', it can be argued that the forms of civilian power deployed by the EU are a very useful element of 'actorness' and that the EU has made and continues to make significant contributions to security by helping to provide stability and peace in Europe and beyond (Stainier 1995: 13; Sjursen 1998: 97–8. See also Smith, K.E. 1998: 78–80).

To illustrate, the EU has effectively 'domesticated' security within the Union in the sense that it is now extremely unlikely that member states would use military force to resolve disputes with fellow members. Further expansion of the EU to include formerly East European states has the potential to provide stability across Europe although, as Sjursen notes, the enlargement process has to be handled carefully to avoid creating a less rather than a more stable European environment. 'The enlargement question... raises difficult and sensitive issues of inclusion and exclusion in the part of Europe that is outside the EU, and could create new dividing lines in Europe... The way in which the EU deals with enlargement will have a very serious impact on European security and stability' (Sjursen 1998: 98). Beyond Europe, the EU has also contributed significantly to the development of a more stable international environment by creating 'dense networks' of agreements with a large number of third parties (see Chapter 1).

An important dimension of the civilian power role noted by several commentators is the EU's ability to project and foster particular values in world politics. This shades into the idea of the EU as a 'civilianizing' or even as a 'civilizing' actor (Hill 1990; Whitman 1998). Sjursen, for example, suggests that the EU can be seen as the 'embodiment of a cooperative approach to security' (Sjursen 1998: 97). Article 11 of the TOA now makes it explicit in treaty terms that the EU should stand in world politics for a range of values, such as democracy, liberalism, human rights, dialogue and international cooperation (Peterson and Bomberg 1999: 240). This position does, of course, create problems if the EU wants to have the option of using military means to support (impose?) those values. As the United States has discovered on more than one occasion, there is a risk that using traditional defence capabilities to support broader security objectives may undermine the very values that legitimize the action. This suggests that it might be more consistent with a civilian power role for the EU to act by using its existing and growing 'armoury' of diplomatic and economic instruments (Smith, K.E. 1998: 78–80). Nevertheless, the Union itself clearly wishes to maintain the position, at least at an aspirational level, that there are occasions when defence capabilities are an essential part of actorness.

Conclusion

Drawing together the various threads of the argument here, we can conclude that, despite some progress towards a common defence policy, the EU remains essentially a civilian power although it plays a significant security role in Europe and beyond. While ambitious plans are being developed and institutions are being created, defence proper remains, in Hill's phrase, only a 'theoretical addition' to the EU's capacity to act and is likely to remain so for some time. Seeking to detach a European defence identity 'separate but not separable' from the NATO framework will remain fraught with political and practical difficulties. Indeed, from an integrationist perspective, the pessimistic view continues to be that no amount of 'institutional tinkering' will take responsibility for Europe's defence away from national capitals unless or until the EU becomes a sovereign state. At the very least, commentators argue, a credible 'common defence' must await a coherent 'common foreign policy' (Sjursen 1998: 111; Martin and Roper 1995: 1). An updated progress report on this prospect is the subject of the next chapter.

To reflect finally upon the important question that has provided the focus of this chapter, should defence and security be regarded for analytical purposes as a fourth sub-system of European foreign policy? The negative case with respect to defence is much clearer than that with respect to security, to the extent that they can be separated. Unless or until defence moves from aspiration to concrete form along the lines indicated earlier by Roper's definitions, it is still appropriate to discount defence as a separate sub-system of European policy. But a much stronger case can be made for the inclusion of security, despite the problem with the notions of 'hard' and 'soft' security. Certainly a case has been made here for not understating the impact of the EU collectively as an increasingly significant actor in the security arena, broadly conceived, particularly since the end of the cold war.

8

After Maastricht and Amsterdam: A Common European Foreign Policy?

This is the first of two chapters that attempt to draw different conclusions from this study. More theoretical conclusions about the consequences for FPA of applying an FPA approach to the study of European foreign policy will be drawn in the next chapter, but the focus here is on European foreign policy itself. What is the status of European foreign policy at the beginning of the twenty-first century? The two EU treaties in the 1990s were intended *inter alia* to improve consistency between and coordination of Community and Union foreign policy. Given also the extensive Europeanization of national foreign policy systems, have our three sub-systems of policy activity now become so interwoven that we can refer to a 'common' or even a 'single' European foreign policy? If not, what problems remain and what are the future prospects?

To help us to draw appropriate conclusions, our analytical framework will be deployed for a final time here to characterize the most recent changes. What has contextualized developments? In particular, what sorts of expectations have framed them? What is the relationship between context, process and action? In terms of the policy process, have the introduction of new actors and institutions together with procedural changes enhanced or set back the prospects of a common EFP? Have the capabilities that might support EFP been strengthened? Does EFP now have at its disposal effective policy instruments to implement policy? Did European foreign policy activity in the second half of the 1990s justify the conclusion that a common policy is now being pursued or is at least in the process of emerging?

Context

Jan Zielonka reminds us that improvements in three areas directly or indirectly related to European foreign policy were expected to follow the signing of the Treaty of Amsterdam (TOA) in 1997. First, it 'was supposed to create a foreign policy structure that would allow Europe to act efficiently when faced with conflicts such as the one in the Balkans'. Second, the TOA 'was intended to restructure EU institutions in preparation for Eastern enlargement'. Finally, 'it was supposed to create a diplomatic – if not military – machinery in proportion to its ever-increasing economic might' (Zielonka 1998: 1). In the event, as Zielonka concedes, the fundamental choices necessary to achieve these objectives were avoided. We will review the results of the TOA more fully in the following sections, but the point to stress here is that the expectations that framed Amsterdam were of a fundamentally different order from those that preceded Maastricht. We need to understand this very different context if we are to begin to explain what most observers regard as the disappointing results at Amsterdam.

While the intergovernmental negotiations that preceded the Treaty on European Union (TEU) were injected with both high expectations and urgency by the sudden end of the cold war, together with the unprecedented acceleration of European integration from the mid-1980s, there was no comparable context to frame the Intergovernmental Conference (IGC) that preceded the Amsterdam Treaty. Indeed, after the TEU was ratified in 1993, the apparent inability of the new EU to translate the much heralded changes in foreign policy regime into improvements in policy output had the opposite effect of lowering expectations of what could be achieved at Amsterdam. In an influential 1993 article, Christopher Hill was warning about the dangers of a growing gap between expectations of what the EU would deliver after Maastricht and its capacity to deliver in policy terms. As early as 1997, however, he was revising his central argument largely on the basis of lowered expectations following a widely felt sense of disappointment at the record of EU achievement in the intervening period (Hill 1993, 1998a: 18–23).

One of the important reasons for a different climate of expectation, as Hill and other commentators have noted, is that alternative multilateral vehicles to CFSP coordination of foreign policy were emerging on an ad hoc basis. These clearly indicated weaknesses in CFSP, and the evident utility of these alternative vehicles detracted from the centrality of Union foreign policy. To illustrate, we noted in Chapter 5 the establishment of the five-member Contact Group in April 1994 set up to try to negotiate a ceasefire in Bosnia. The operation of this Group inevitably highlighted the roles of Britain, France and Germany (whose officials met regularly with US and Russian officials) in the policy process and downgraded the contribution of the other EU member states and the collectivity. It has been argued that the establishment of this Group marked the final point at which 'the EU essentially ceased to function as a single entity on policy towards Bosnia' (Peterson and Bomberg 1999: 243).

Another Balkan example of an alternative vehicle was Operation Alba, which was constituted, Hill suggests, by 'an Italian initiative, UN legitimacy and OSCE [Organization for Security and Cooperation in Europe] support' (Hill 1998b: 45). This was set up in 1997 to deal with the crisis in Albania following the inability of the EU to establish a peacekeeping force through CFSP/WEU. An Italian-led multinational force, unattached either to the EU or WEU, eventually helped to establish order in a country that was rapidly descending into civil war. Thereafter, the OSCE took a lead role in overseeing elections and the emergence of a new government. What is interesting about this episode is the contrast between the 'gung-ho' attitude in 1991, when the EC had originally discussed sending a peacekeeping force to Yugoslavia, and the much more cautious approach to the prospects of intervention in Albania in early 1997 (Peterson and Sjursen 1998: 173). Expectations had clearly changed within the EU as well as without.

Given also the developments in European defence detailed in Chapter 7, it is possible to argue, as David Allen does, that, by 1997, as Amsterdam was being signed, the EU had already 'lost its central role in the creation of a new European architecture. The policy lead had shifted, in a way that would have been hard to predict in the early 1990s, to NATO and the United States.' As Allen suggests, this seems to have generated a degree of complacency in Europe and to have made the task of creating a common European foreign policy seem less important and certainly less vital than it had at the beginning of the decade (Allen 1998: 57). Other priorities also pushed foreign policy down the agenda. In particular, the timetables established to bring about an enlarged Union and a single currency combined to provide a compelling focus for the TOA. Although both these issues have major implications, of course, for future European foreign policy, they provided a distraction from undertaking extensive reforms of existing foreign policy structures and processes. Although even in terms of achieving other priorities, it must be said, Amsterdam was deemed a failure by most observers.

An interesting indicator of a general dissatisfaction with Amsterdam was the speed with which a follow-up IGC was agreed. It took about two-and-a-half years after the ratification of the TEU in October 1993 to establish a follow-up IGC (the Westendorp Reflection Group began preparatory work in the Summer of 1995 and the IGC began in Turin in March 1996). Less than 12 months after the ratification of the TOA in May 1999, however, a follow-up IGC began in February 2000, scheduled to finish by the end of that year. The focus of this Conference is the work that Amsterdam failed to complete, notably to agree revised institutional procedures for an enlarged Union as the pressure of ongoing and scheduled negotiations with 12 different applicants increases.

Actors and Policy-making

Such changes in foreign policy-making as were made were largely agreed before Amsterdam and then incorporated into the TOA. The main change in the policy process that affects the existing relationships between actors is the enhanced role given to the European Council. The Council is now tasked to lay down 'guidelines' for foreign policy action and, more importantly, to adopt 'strategies' that define in broad terms the goals to be achieved and the means to be used. Thereafter, it is the job of the General Affairs Council (GAC) to implement guidelines and strategies via three possible types of decision-making. With respect to implementing guidelines, the unanimity rule applies, although up to one third of members may abstain from voting without blocking a decision. This has become known as 'constructive abstention', allowing action to be taken by, as it were, a 'coalition of the willing'. Proposed action relating to agreed strategies, however, may be taken by qualified majority vote (QMV) as long as at least ten member states constitute the majority. But the vote may be opposed and effectively blocked by any member state 'for important and stated reasons of national policy'. The GAC may thereafter return the issue to the European Council, but a decision there will require unanimity. Finally, any decision with military implications must be taken unanimously (Peterson and Bomberg 1999: 230).

The role of the European Commission is not essentially changed by the TOA. In particular, there is no upgrading of its role in Pillar 2 activities. There is, however, some potential, as Cameron notes, for underlining its contribution to the continuing objective of ensuring consistency of foreign policy action across the three-pillar structure that remains in place. Article C of the TEU, for example, has been amended to reinforce the .point that it is the duty of both the Council and the Commission to cooperate to ensure consistency. A new Article J.4 has been added to enable the Council to request the Commission to submit proposals on CFSP to ensure the implementation of joint actions (Cameron 1998: 69). Overall, the Commission remains well positioned to be a significant actor in the foreign policy process after Amsterdam. It remains a key player in Pillar 1 external activities even if it failed to add trade in services and intellectual property to its exclusive external economic competences (Allen 1998: 54). It remains 'fully associated' with both Pillars 2 and 3. The real problem for the Commission with respect to actorness, as with the EU as a whole, is coherence and effectiveness. As the Delors Commission recognized even before the TEU was ratified, the Commission is not organized in such a way as to maximize its impact on the European foreign policy process.

This recognition stimulated a series of internal reorganizations of the external affairs portfolios and the associated Directorate-Generals through the 1990s, culminating in a fundamental restructuring under Romano Prodi as the new Commission President in 1999. As we noted in an earlier chapter, this began with Jacques Delors' overt attempt to create a Commission-based 'foreign ministry' by creating a separate DG1A responsible for CFSP and controlling an integrated 'foreign policy machinery'. A second attempt under Delors' successor Jacques Santer went for a regional rather than functional subdivision of external responsibilities, in part to accommodate new commissioners from the three new members states (Austria, Sweden and Finland). Control of foreign policy was now spread across four different commissioners (and the President) and four different Directorate-Generals – scarcely a distinguished organizational contribution either to coherence or consistency! (Allen 1998: 52; Cameron 1998: 62–3).

Not surpringly perhaps, the Commission attached a declaration to the TOA that gave notice of a further reorganization planned to be in place by the time the next Commission took office in 2000. This was to be built around the designation of a senior commissioner – referred to as a Commission vice-president at that stage – who would coordinate foreign policy activity on behalf of the Commission. Before these plans could be finalized, however, the whole context of Commission activity was transformed by the accusations of cronyism and financial mismanagement that led to the resignation en masse of the Santer Commission in March 1999. Clearly, much hinged thereafter on the ability of the new Commission under Romano Prodi to revive the reputation of the

Commission as a credible policy player and on the latest reorganization being a success. The external policy machinery was unified in October 1999 under a new Commissioner, Chris Patten, who heads a new Directorate-General for External Relations that replaces DG1, DG1A and DG1B.

But, however successful the latest reorganization of the Commission turns out to be in restoring its reputation and making it a more effective foreign policy actor, the Commission now operates under new constraints in this arena resulting from two related institutional innovations agreed at Amsterdam. These provide new capabilities for CFSP but, as we shall see in the following sections, they are clearly located under Council rather than Commission control.

Capabilities and Instruments

The TOA ostensibly added to the capabilities and instruments available to support CFSP. First, it added a potentially significant new actor, the 'High Representative' (HR) for CFSP who will also serve as the Secretary-General of the Council of Ministers. Responding directly to the long-felt need to give the EU a 'single voice' in external representation, the HR is given three related functions: to 'assist the Council in matters coming within the scope of the CFSP, in particular through contributing to the formulation, preparation and implementation of policy decisions'; to conduct political dialogues with third countries 'when appropriate and acting on behalf of Council at the request of the Presidency'; and to assist the presidency in representing the EU abroad and with respect to implementing CFSP decisions (Treaty of Amsterdam, Articles 18 and 26). The former Secretary-General of NATO, Javier Solana, was appointed to this post for five years in October 1999.

The HR also heads up a second institutional innovation, a Policy Planning and Early Warning Unit (PPEWU) established within the Council Secretariat to provide a much needed capacity for policy analysis that is nominally independent of member states. Its mandate includes monitoring, analysis and assessment of international developments and events, including early warning on potential crises. But its envisaged role goes beyond policy analysis. Either at Council request or on its own initiative, it may contribute to policy formulation by drafting policy options that may contain recommendations and strategies for presentation to the Council under the responsibility of the presidency.

As touched on earlier, a third innovation at Amsterdam is the addition of a new policy instrument, the common strategy. An important part of the expanded role of the European Council is to 'decide on common strategies to be implemented by the Union in areas where the Member States have important interests in common'. This involves establishing objectives, duration, and the means to be made available for implementation of a strategy. A significant feature of this instrument from a common European foreign policy perspective is that it is intended to be an improved mechanism for ensuring consistency across the range of external policies. A common strategy may cover issues across the pillars rather than CFSP alone and, crucially, may draw upon capabilities and instruments from the EC, the EU and member states. The role of the GAC here is to recommend strategies to the European Council and to implement those agreed in their CFSP aspects. Other extant but now more clearly delineated instruments come into play at this point. Strategies may be implemented (by decision-making mechanisms discussed earlier) either by 'joint actions' – legally binding operational actions with financial means – or by 'common positions'. These are legal, binding 'acts' that clarify the Union position towards a situation but without specifying action. Finally, the Treaty goes some way to resolving a major problem that had clearly weakened CFSP – namely how it would be funded. After a long period of dissension on this issue, Amsterdam confirmed that there would in future be a specific CFSP 'line' in the Community budget. The only exceptions are operations with military implications or if the Council unanimously decides upon a different charging method.

Towards a Common European Foreign Policy?

To what extent did the specific changes agreed at Amsterdam, in the context of a long process of development over nearly 30 years, represent further progress towards the achievement, more narrowly, of a common foreign and security policy and, more extensively, a common European foreign policy? Some positive evaluation of Amsterdam is warranted but of a very conditional type. The two institutional innovations, the HR and the PPEWU, *may* improve the quality of CFSP decisions and action, both by being better informed and by being more effectively coordinated by one central figure (the HR). CFSP *may* in future be more flexible and effective with action by 'coalitions of the willing' less likely to be blocked by intransigent member states. It is difficult, however, for integrationists to be very optimistic. Certainly, there was no great leap forward at Amsterdam towards an integrated foreign policy that might be compared to say, the Common Agricultural Policy or the Common Commercial Policy.

Perhaps the most neutral comment that can be made is that Amsterdam is unlikely to make much difference either to policy-making or policy implementation (Peterson and Sjursen 1998: 169). While subscribing to this judgement, Hill also notes a serious potential problem. Enhanced flexibility may improve effectiveness, but it may also serve to reduce expectations that the EU will act together. In which case, Amsterdam might actually undermine the idea of both a CFSP and a common European foreign policy (Hill 1998a: 30). David Allen goes further, suggesting that 'constructive abstention' might be better labelled 'destructive abstention' to the extent that the treaty actually 'sets out the conditions in which a member state may disassociate itself from a CFSP decision' (Allen 1998: 54–5). Claims by EU institutions that Amsterdam will facilitate more 'effective', more 'efficient', or simply 'improved' foreign policy decision-making are difficult to sustain. In particular, weak institutions at the European level remain a serious problem. If decision-making actually looks more complicated as a result of compromises at Amsterdam, the capacity for action at the operational end still looks inadequate. Without rehearsing again here the arguments about European security and defence, the continuing absence of a credible European defence capability to augment other available instruments will continue to detract from the overall credibility of European foreign policy – at the level of internal and external perceptions at least (Bonvicini 1998: 73).

In more general terms, we can conclude that Amsterdam confirmed and extended the trend towards an increasingly 'Brusselized' policy – with more and more decisions taken in Brussels-based institutions – rather than towards a 'Communitized' policy necessary for an integrated European foreign policy to emerge. Indeed, it can be argued that, in this sense, the TOA represented a setback for the integration process. Certainly, Amsterdam strengthened the Council machinery and to that extent weakened Community control of the foreign policy process. The location of the HR and the PPEWU within the Council and the member state-dominated composition of the PPEWU leads Allen to conclude that these institutional innovations are likely to enable 'the Council and EU member states to exert firm control over the Commission's input into CFSP' (Allen 1998: 55; see also Peterson and Bomberg 1999: 248).

But it is also important to note, as does Allen, that the Commission is part of a reconstructed 'troika' that emerged from Amsterdam at the representational and operational level – what might be called the 'sharp end' of European foreign policy (Allen 1998: 52, 54). While the presidency remains the representational focus of CFSP (assisted 'if need be' by the next member state to hold the presidency), it will now be aided much more substantially by the HR. Indeed, it is likely that more and more representational and operational tasks will be taken over by the HR's staff in the Council Secretariat. But the 'full association' of the Commission with the activities of all three pillars, its access to PPEWU, and not least its control of the Community's extensive representational machinery abroad must mean that the External Affairs Commissioner will be a third member of the new 'troika' (together with the Council and the presidency). Within the Commission, it was certainly envisaged that the new commissioner would be its interface with the GAC and its 'interlocutor' with the HR.

It remains to be seen how well these new relationships work and whether or not they will contribute to a more coherent and effective European foreign policy in operational terms. Early indicators were quite promising. Concerned to respond to growing criticisms of the EU's post-conflict role in the Balkans (see Chapter 7), the March 2000 EU summit in Lisbon mandated both Javier Solana and Chris Patten to 'get a grip' on a situation there characterized 'by overlapping authority, underperforming agencies and poor delivery of help'. Their joint report quickly led to a conference of donors that agreed to inject extensive funding for civilian projects to help stabilize the region (*Guardian*, 30 March 2000). But it is difficult to imagine that there will not be future personal and institutional battles for control of European foreign policy if, rather than working harmoniously together, both Council and Commission (under more focused leadership) play bureaucratic politics and attempt to extend their roles. Who controls the extensive Community representational machinery abroad, for example, could constitute one important issue in a future 'turf war' (*The Economist*, 8 April 2000).

If the TOA merits at best a neutral evaluation, more fundamental problems continue to hamper the development of a 'genuine' European foreign policy; these are problems that were not addressed or at least not addressed adequately by Amsterdam. A list might include interrelated problems associated with identity, interests, representation and legitimacy. As several commentators have noted, institution-building at an elite level does not of itself build a European identity, create European interests, or provide representational mechanisms at the European level that are widely perceived to be legitimate. Without all these things, arguably, the necessary 'substructure' to underpin a common European foreign policy will be absent. While certain developments might help to rectify these shortcomings in the short term, such as more extensive involvement by the European Parliament in foreign policy-making, nothing less than a distinct European polity is what is fundamentally required over the longer term (see Guehenno 1998). This means going beyond decision-making by an essentially techno-cratic elite towards involving the peoples of Europe in a popular debate about the construction of Europe as a political entity. Popular support is what is ultimately required to underpin a 'genuine' EFP. John Peterson puts it bluntly, 'It is plausible to suggest that a "common" foreign policy cannot, by definition, exist as long as there is no "Euro-pean public"' (Peterson 1998: 3).

Whether or not these shortcomings will be rectified and, equally importantly, how, divides analysts. What might be called a 'revolu-tionary' approach is offered by Christopher Hill. 'Unified actorness', he argues, simply will not happen without a great constitutional leap forward from what he sees as the current impasse. The process cannot go much further forward 'without the creation of a significant execu-tive to mobilize the foreign policy resources of the member states, to impose discipline and to implement policy through a single machinery'. But he remains sceptical about that possibility at least in the short to medium term. 'That very jump into foreign policy supra-nationalism is unlikely to take place without a prior convergence of attitudes, interests and policies in other issue areas on the part of the Member States – and such convergence is always a matter of the longue durée' (Hill 1998b: 40–1; see also Hill 1993: 316–17).

But Hill appears to be talking here about a 'single' rather than a 'common' European foreign policy and this provides an important opportunity at this point to clarify the difference between them. A 'single' EFP suggests a fully integrated, supranational foreign policy rather like the 'single' market or the 'single' currency. From this perspective Bonvicini, for example, talks prescriptively about the 'single voice of the Union', which, he argues, 'should be represented in both the foreign (and security) policy dimension and the economic dimension, and coordination between the two must be close and auto-matic' (Bonvicini 1998: 74). A 'common' European foreign policy, on the other hand, is taken here to refer to the coordination and growing harmonization of foreign policy emerging from the different policy systems within the EU. Significantly, this avoids any assumption of 'singleness' or 'unitariness' and the criteria for 'success' or even for progress is less demanding than that required for a 'single' foreign policy. Indeed, as Hill's criteria illustrate, a fully integrated, supranational European foreign policy remains very far in the future and may well be an unattainable objective.

The View from Foreign Policy Analysis

This clarification enables us to identify a more 'evolutionary' approach to the possibility of a common (rather than a single) European foreign policy that focuses on more modest, less dramatic but apparently inexorable changes over time. This approach better reflects the perspective adopted here and the findings revealed by this study, to which we now turn in the final section of this chapter. The first and arguably the most important conclusion that can be drawn is that, from a 30-year perspective, the progress made towards a common foreign policy, given the strength of member states' 'national interests', has been remarkable, even if there is still a long way to go. As Ben Soetendorp argues, 'a large leap forward has already been made' (Soetendorp 1994: 118). It can be argued that an FPA approach that has analysed the development of policy over time and has focused on the relationship between policy processes and policy output has highlighted the more evolutionary trends at work in European foreign policy (see White 1989: 15; Peterson 1998: 15–16).

Second, our three sub-systems of European foreign policy remain separate and European foreign policy can still, in the language of systems analysis, be referred to as 'sub-system dominant'. But, as this study shows, there has undoubtedly been a growing interaction between them. Community, Union and national foreign policies are increasingly intertwined at both policy-making and policy implementation levels. While Union and national foreign policies may still be described as intergovernmental in form – apparently reinforced structurally by changes agreed at Amsterdam – the development of transnational policy networks operating increasingly across both the pillar framework and our sub-systems make control of the process by governments, individually or collectively, difficult although not, of course, impossible (after all, the national veto now appears explicitly in treaty form). The more established these networks have become, the more the members of them have become socialized into accepting particular sets of values and norms. The resulting 'coordination reflex' means that there is a more or less collective commitment to reach agreements and to push the process of coordination further forward.

Growing linkages across different foreign policy systems are perhaps most apparent at the operational end of the process. In this context, it will be particularly interesting to track the development of the new common strategies that, we have already noted, are intended explicitly to link cross-pillar decision-making to capabilities and instruments drawn from all three types of European foreign policy. A useful way of characterizing the impact of piecemeal changes to the policy process over time, particularly at the 'sub-systemic' or 'policy-shaping' level of decision-making (see Peterson 1995) is to deploy the 'ratchet' metaphor. Peterson, for example, gives the establishment of the PPEWU as an illustration of the 'ratchet effect' on foreign policy coordination (Peterson 1998: 16). The more recent establishment of the various interim political and military committees in Brussels, noted in Chapter 7, might serve as examples from the defence/security field of institutional mechanisms that are likely to 'ratchet up' cooperation and foster incremental change.

Third, within European foreign policy, the individual foreign policies of member states remain very important, possibly still more important than either Community or Union foreign policies in terms of their overall impact on world politics (Peterson and Sjursen 1988: 169). It is important to stress that member states' foreign policies have not been replaced by European foreign policy. But, as illustrated in Chapter 6 by the detailed case study on Britain, the foreign policies of member states are scarcely recognizable as traditional foreign policy. The context in which they operate, the processes through which they are made and their outputs all show very clearly the growing impact of Europeanization. One common element of that impact on all members is that the distinctiveness of 'foreign policy' has been progressively eroded. The traditional boundary between foreign policy and domestic politics, already blurred by interdependence, has been fundamentally breached by the evolving processes of the EU as the range and number of 'domestic' actors and institutions involved in the European policy process has multiplied.

Fourth, despite the focus in much of the literature and the media on specific policy failures and the ineffectiveness of European foreign policy more generally, it is surely now possible to review policy output over time and begin to talk of some policy successes that might be set against a more negative appraisal? Alhough, consistent with our FPA approach, this study has concentrated more on process than outputs,

EFP and specifically CFSP have arguably had a number of successes, although criteria for establishing success and failure are not easily established (see Jorgensen 1998). One obvious candidate from the case studies undertaken here is European policy towards South Africa since the 1970s (see Chapter 4). Other cases suggested by Peterson as 'at least partial successes' include the 'stability pacts' initiative to stabilize Central and Eastern Europe, the administration of the Bosnian city of Mostar (see Chapter 5) and the 'EU salesmanship' of the Nuclear Non-Proliferation Treaty. In his view, member states have moved from 'nominally' adjusting their foreign policies in the 1970s and 80s to a point 'where something which deserves the name "common" has been created in the 1990s' (Peterson 1998: 4, 16). If high profile failures have done damage in the headlines, a focus on low profile issues, which rarely attract media coverage, may well tell a different story. To illustrate, Karen Smith has produced an interesting study which suggests that the EU has used its range of instruments on a global stage very effectively indeed. Reworking the 'EU as civilian power' theme, she argues that these instruments have been used effectively to promote particular values such as human rights and, more often than not, used to promote international dialogue and cooperation rather than conflict (Smith, K.E. 1998).

Fifth, although progress is being made albeit haltingly towards a common European foreign policy, there are continuing pressures from within the EU and without to present a united face to the outside world and thus to move even further, beyond a common and towards a single European foreign policy. These pressures are unlikely to go away, indeed, they are likely be reinforced by precisely the issues that currently preoccupy the EU (see Chapter 1). In particular, economic and monetary union has major implications for the future of EFP. The adoption of the Euro as the single currency in 2002, Bonvicini argues, means that the EU 'will inevitably be forced to play a bigger international role. As a "global currency", the euro will require a [single] policy towards the dollar and the yen, with unavoidable repercussions for the Union's foreign policy' (Bonvicini 1998: 73; see also Peterson and Bomberg 1999: 264).

Finally, we can conclude that the use of the term 'European foreign policy' rather than any of the more commonly used alternative labels has been justified by this study as a focus of description and analysis. European foreign policy is not simply a convenient shorthand for the collective foreign policies of member states. Nor is it simply 'EU foreign policy', which appears to be the preferred label of most commentators. We have established that there are different types of foreign policy system in the EU and that these different types increasingly overlap. We therefore need a term that encompasses them but goes beyond a narrow focus on any one of them. There are, however, different ways of conceptualizing European foreign policy.

One possible criticism of the particular way EFP is conceptualized here is to say that it is a too EU-centred or possibly too 'Eurocentric'. Hill develops the·argument that European foreign policy gets 'made' in a variety of ways that increasingly involve what he calls a 'mixity of organizations and actors' that extend beyond the EU family of players. These other actors – non-EU states, non-European states such as the US, other non-EU organizations (governmental and non-governmental) all overlap the EU's areas of activity. His general point is that contemporary world politics as a whole is characterized by 'overlapping institutionalism' and that separating out the activities of different regional players for analysis is increasingly problematic (Hill 1998b: 43–6). This is an important argument and we have seen examples throughout this study of the role played by non-EU actors in ostensibly European foreign policy activities. But, as Hill himself comments, he is talking about 'foreign policy in Europe' rather than 'European foreign policy' and, to the extent that these terms have different connotations, his argument does not undermine the way that European foreign policy has been conceptualized here with an FPA focus on the different actors and policy processes within the EU.

If, as has been suggested, the study of CFSP remains at the 'pretheoretical stage', the same comment is even more justified with respect to European foreign policy (Peterson and Sjursen 1998: 180). At this stage, a variety of theoretical approaches is to be welcomed. A case has been made in this study that an FPA approach, suitably adapted, has a useful contribution to make to an understanding of European foreign policy and, more widely, to an understanding of Europe's global role. If valuable insights into European foreign policy have resulted from applying an FPA approach, what have we learned from it about FPA itself? We turn in the final chapter of this book to draw more theoretical conclusions in the light of this study about the status of FPA as a distinctive field of international relations.

9

European Foreign Policy and Foreign Policy Analysis[1]

A useful 'spin-off' from developing an FPA framework for analysing European foreign policy is that it provides a perspective from which to evaluate the effectiveness of FPA. If FPA provides, as it were, a 'lens' through which to analyse European foreign policy, that 'lens' can be repositioned to reflect back on FPA itself. It was argued in Chapter 8 that the FPA approach used in this study has produced valuable insights into the nature of European foreign policy. But if we stand back a little from this study, we can see that the European case poses wider theoretical challenges to foreign policy analysts with implications that go beyond a European focus.

Three related challenges can be identified. First, making sense of European foreign policy offers a fundamental challenge to 'state-centric realism' as the organizing focus of this field. It is clear from this study that states and governments remain key players in European foreign policy, but they are not the only significant policy actors. We have established that while Union and national foreign policy-making can be explained in intergovernmental terms, the broader focus here on European foreign policy has confirmed that intergovernmentalism is too limited as an explanation. European foreign policy processes as a whole are also characterized by other types of process in operation, such as transnational policy networks, which require explanations of policy that go beyond a realist account of what is going on.

Second, European foreign policy powerfully illustrates a different actor focus for analysing policy at the international level. The assumption that this non-unitary actor is unique also poses particular problems for the foreign policy analyst who has been traditionally concerned to produce a comparative analysis of policy, comparing the foreign policy of one actor (usually a state) with that of one or more other actors. The apparent absence of an analogous entity to 'Europe' in world politics at least raises wider questions about the role and function of the foreign policy analyst. This is not a new insight. It was recognized as early as the 1970s that foreign policy-making in an EC context was unique and that foreign policy analysts should beware of simply transposing the traditional analytical categories of FPA to a European context (see Allen 1978). Finally, the attempt to understand this complex phenomenon, European foreign policy, should encourage foreign policy analysts to think carefully about what they study and how they study it. In this spirit, the final chapter of this book reviews the current status of FPA in the light of the present study. What are its continuing strengths but which aspects of the study of foreign policy need to be re-examined at the beginning of the twenty-first century?

Foreign Policy Analysis in Crisis?

A case was made in Chapter 2 that FPA has adapted and changed considerably over the last 50 years in the light of a changing international system and new ways of understanding those changes. But the particular challenges to FPA posed by developments in the new Europe need to be located within an intellectual climate in which FPA is already under fire from other colleagues in international relations (IR). At issue is whether this area of study remains a major sub-field of IR or whether it has become anachronistic, either subsumed or replaced by other approaches to understanding and explaining state behaviour. FPA has always been a controversial field but commentaries in the 1990s, particularly by European scholars, suggest that something of a crisis point has been reached. One indicator of this is neglect. While there were a number of attempts up to the mid-1980s to review the status of FPA as an approach (see, for example, Smith 1986; Hermann et al. 1987), there have been few attempts since then. The commentaries on FPA that have been produced in recent years have ranged from the hostile through the sceptical to those that recognize that whatever the continuing strengths of this analytical perspective, it remains beset by problems.

In one of the most sympathetic commentaries, Margot Light attempts to defend FPA against attack from a variety of foes but even she is forced to concede that there has been 'a steady erosion of a separate concept of foreign policy and a consequent undermining of FPA as a discrete field of investigation' (Light 1994: 100). Her litany of problems with FPA begins with the failure of a general theory of foreign policy to emerge after many years of study, although, she observes, many foreign policy analysts of the predominantly American

Comparative Foreign Policy (CFP) school are themselves disappointed about this. Second, Light makes the point that FPA does not fit neatly within existing IR theories although it is most frequently associated (unfairly in Light's view) with traditional realism. Other problems with this field relate to an allegedly excessive concern with the domestic processes of foreign policy-making and the inner workings of the state.

An important set of problems associated with the conventional state-centric focus of FPA is highlighted in Chris Brown's recent introduction to IR theory (Brown 1997). First, he notes that traditional realism – and by implication FPA – offers a state-centric account of the world but no explicit theory of the state. He argues that there is a problem in trying to understand foreign policy if we have no 'clear sense of what it is that states are motivated by, what their function is, how they work' (Brown 1997: 69). Second, as Brown, Light and others note, state behaviour in contemporary IR is assumed to be so highly circumscribed by the nature and the operation of the international system that many scholars have concluded that the international system itself is the appropriate level of analysis from which to explain state behaviour. As a result, to the partial exclusion at least of FPA, with its 'micro' focus on highlighting differences between states, IR has been dominated in recent years by 'macro' structuralist approaches – variants of neo-realism and neo-liberalism in particular (see the discussion of institutionalist approaches in Chapter 2). Brown's conclusion with respect to the current status of FPA is ambivalent. On the one hand, FPA may still be regarded as one of the most established areas of IR. On the other hand – and Brown appears to veer towards this view – it can be argued that FPA is a rather sterile field that has been devoid of innovation for a number of years. As Brown puts it, 'most of the work being done takes the form of empirical case studies which shuffle and reshuffle a small number of ideas rather than create new theories' (Brown 1997: 79).

In this rather hostile context, this study offers an encouraging response. It has demonstrated the adaptability of FPA and the relevance of this approach to an understanding of the important new area of European foreign policy. From a theoretical perspective, it shows very clearly that FPA does not need to be located within a traditional methodology. One of the other strengths of the field underlined by this study is its eclecticism. It can be argued that the 'flowering' of this field in the 1960s and 70s, when some of its most important work was done, occurred partly at least because foreign policy analysts incorporated into FPA insights and methods from other subjects, particularly from other social sciences such as sociology, psychology and political science. Work on belief systems, for example, was developed from psychology, bureaucratic politics was developed from both sociology and political science and applied to foreign policy-making. Arguably again, problems have emerged in recent years because FPA has become disconnected from other theoretical work in cognate fields both within IR and in other subjects. To some extent this has been a 'self-inflicted wound' as some analysts have wanted to put up barriers, suggesting that FPA as an approach should and must remain locked within a US-dominated, positivist approach (Smith, S. 1994). This means that important new work, largely done by European scholars, which has taken up what is broadly called a 'post-positivist' position in analysing foreign policy is necessarily excluded from FPA 'proper' ('positivism' here refers to the view that there are objective truths about the social world that can be revealed by reference to the facts. 'Post-positivists' reject this view. For a clear introduction to positive and post-positivist approaches to international theory, see Smith, S. 1997).

This study has suggested that a more open, eclectic position can be adopted. There are links here, for example, to policy analysis from which insights about policy networks are built into the analysis of the European foreign policy process. The focus on the importance of negative discourses about 'Europe' in Chapter 6 on British foreign policy illustrates a link to post-positivist, constructivist work that attempts to show how foreign policy is 'constructed' from social interaction and language. The importance of language as a key indicator of political sensitivities in Europe has been a recurring theme in several chapters of this book. The general argument developed in the rest of this chapter is that further connections to these and other approaches concerned to analyse policy-making at the international level can help to address if not to resolve some of the problems with FPA identified earlier. Three problem areas are reviewed in the following sections to illustrate the argument: the inadequacy of the traditional FPA focus on the state; the related need to focus more extensively on what might be called the politics of identity; and the limitations of FPA analyses of the policy process.

Foreign Policy Analysis and the State

One of the main weaknesses of traditional FPA is its attempt to explain state behaviour without addressing directly the nature of statehood. One consequence of the contested nature of statehood in Europe is that foreign policy analysts can no longer avoid confronting this issue (see Smith, M.

1994: 29ff.). At an empirical level, this means confronting head on the variety of states in contemporary world politics and recognizing that different types of state are likely to produce different types of foreign policy behaviour. This also has major implications for the comparativist ethos of FPA and must limit expectations about the ability of FPA to produce generalizations about 'state behaviour'. At a theoretical level, there are two related types of recent work here to which FPA might usefully connect. First, there is interesting work elsewhere that develops typologies of states and tries to relate their behaviour to type. In particular, the notion of the 'post-modern state' offers a promising route to explaining state behaviour in an EU context (Sorenson 1997). The second type of work offers a more fundamental critique by making no prior assumptions at all about the existence of 'states'. Robert Cox's idea of 'forms of state' has been developed to produce the notion of the 'international state', which can usefully be applied to the problem of conceptualizing the EU as a foreign policy actor (see Cox 1983, 1986; Caporaso 1996).

Engaging with this literature, however, requires a serious attempt to get to grips with what is meant by the 'state'. IR as a whole and FPA in particular needs to connect to the extensive debates about the state that have been running for many years now in other disciplines, notably in sociology and historical sociology. What is underlined in, for example, Fred Halliday's useful summary of these debates for an IR audience is an implicit adherence by most IR theorists to what Halliday calls the state as 'national [social] – territorial totality', which 'comprises in conceptual form what is denoted visually on a political map'. The alternative socio-logical conception of the state 'denotes not the social-territorial totality but a specific set of coercive and administrative institutions, distinct from the broader political, social and national context in which it finds itself'. As Halliday concedes, FPA is one of the few areas of IR that by impli-cation at least has begun to explore a more limited conception of the 'state', but alternative conceptualizations need explicitly to be built into analyses. From this perspective, in Halliday's words, 'the argument is not about whether we are or are not "state-centric", but what we mean by the state' (Halliday 1994: 77–9, 255, fn. 16).

Foreign Policy Analysis, Identity and Social Meanings

The contested nature of statehood in Europe also highlights important questions about identity and legitimacy that have not traditionally excited the attention of foreign policy analysts or occupied a major place on what might be called the FPA agenda. If these questions have not been addressed extensively, however, it is not because they are regarded by analysts as unimportant but rather because they are assumed to be answered by the conjunction of state with nation – just one of the unexplored consequences of the 'totality' concept of the state noted above. 'Effective foreign policy rests upon a shared sense of national identity, of a nation-state's "place in the world", its friends and enemies, its interests and aspirations' (Hill and Wallace 1996: 8). When national identity becomes contested, however, as in Europe, and is not replaced by a strong sense of identity in the EU, it follows, as we noted in Chapter 8, that one of the crucial underpinnings of an effective European foreign policy is missing. The key question, therefore, of how the new Europe as an international actor might develop a strong collective identity and how that identity might be conceptualized should become one that concerns foreign policy analysts to a much greater extent than has hitherto been the case. There is an emerging literature on 'collective identity formation' outside the field, largely from a constructivist perspective, which has an important contribution to make to understanding European foreign policy-making as well as a much wider application beyond (see Wendt 1994).

A closer look at the nature of statehood in the new Europe not only reveals an arena of contested identity but also the realization that the whole European 'project' is difficult to understand outside the contestation of ideas between and among those engaged in the project. Again, there is an important new literature beginning to emerge that clearly separates 'state' and 'society' and starts from the assumption that social meanings lie at the heart of European governance in general and European foreign policy in particular (Jorgensen 1997a; Larsen 1997a). This work, from an avowedly 'reflectivist' perspective, poses a significant challenge to FPA, grounded as it has traditionally been in a positivist epistemology. It offers a 'critical' critique of established FPA approaches such as belief systems and bureaucratic politics, highlighting the social origins and meaning of decision-makers' beliefs and the relationship between knowledge, ideas and the formulation of policy.

Henrik Larsen, for example, uses a 'political discourse' approach to compare British and French policies towards European integration in the 1980s and provides a useful illustration here of the difference between positivist and post-positivist approaches to foreign policy analysis. He starts by identifying the limitations of the FPA literature on belief systems, which characteristically adopts an individualistic perspective located within a positivist approach. 'Beliefs are often seen as intervening variables not as necessary meaningful references for the actors by which they make sense of the world' (Larsen 1997b: 110). Put rather crudely, what has interested foreign policy analysts about studies of perception is the possibility of relating 'misperception' to policy outcomes rather than understanding the social and linguistic bases of perception as a framework of meaning. Larsen goes on to argue that the beliefs systems approach in FPA is limited to the extent that it is unable to reveal the 'general lines in a country's foreign policy' where 'individualist beliefs give way to social beliefs and those beliefs constitute a central framework within which policy-making takes place' (Larsen 1997a: 10). From this perspective, discourse(s) constitute a very significant part of the domestic structure of foreign policy-making at the macro-social level, a dimension that is not only largely absent from the belief systems literature but also from more conventional FPA studies of the role of political culture and domestic public opinion in foreign policy-making (Larsen 1997a: 22).

Two further points emerge from Larsen's study that are important to the discussion here, one methodological and the other more substantive, although they are related. First, the discourse approach offers an actor-centric rather than state-centric account of policy-making. Even if aspects of a political discourse reflect material and other structural factors, as Larsen puts it, 'the political discourse is still highly relevant as it provides insights into the framework of meaning of the actors in foreign policy' (Larsen 1997a: 23). Given that the political discourse approach operates at a high level of abstraction, however, Larsen goes on to argue that positivist FPA approaches such as bureaucratic politics remain more appropriate for explaining specific foreign policy decisions rather than understanding general orientations. This is crucial because it explicitly acknowledges that FPA is a 'broad church' and can contain positivist *and* 'post-positivist' approaches. To use Robert Cox's widely accepted theoretical categories, FPA can offer both 'problem-solving' (positivist) and 'critical' (post-positivist) theories (Cox with Sinclair 1996: Ch. 6).

The other important substantive finding of Larsen's work is that he manages successfully to test his hypothesis that political discourses on Europe and other key concepts tested are essentially national discourses. In his comparative case studies on British and French policies towards Europe in the 1980s, he discovers that both sets of policies were underpinned by some elements of shared or overlapping discourses, but concludes that the relevant discourses had national 'borders' and that state borders 'still define the primary borders of identity' (Larsen 1997a: 199). If the results of this empirical study are replicated in other work, two major consequences follow. First, a traditional state-centric approach to (European) foreign policy analysis is reinforced from an unexpected source. Second, the persistence of national discourses on Europe may well delay if not prevent the construction of a European political identity which, as argued above, is necessary to underpin an effective European foreign policy.

Foreign Policy Analysis, Ideas and the Formulation of Policy

The reflectivist focus on the contestation of ideas in a macro-social context not only underlines the limitations of cognitive approaches and analyses of other elements of the domestic context of policy-making, it also raises questions about the adequacy of established FPA approaches to understanding the nature of the foreign policy process itself. It might be argued, for example, that the traditional emphasis on the making and, more recently, on the implementation of foreign policy has meant that the important initial stages of the policy process have been neglected by foreign policy analysts. Both the reflectivist/constructivist literature and policy analysis approaches as applied to the EU have potentially much to offer with respect to understanding the ways in which policy is formulated, in particular the relationship between knowledge and ideas, and the process whereby ideas are translated into policy proposals and move onto the policy agenda.

Possible ways forward in this context need only be sketched out here, but both literatures contain concepts and approaches that are instructive in the context of understanding and explaining European foreign policy. If we begin by assuming that the relationship between ideas, interest formation and agenda setting is crucial to the formulation of policy and, ultimately, to policy outcomes, policy analysts offer important sets of related ideas associated not only with policy networks, but also with 'stakeholders' and 'epistemic communities' that might usefully be applied to European foreign policy (see, for example, Richardson 1996). It would be instructive to develop hypotheses about actors in the European foreign policy process as constituting networks of stakeholders, rather than 'simply' as members of different political elites or as bureaucratic actors with specific sets of interests tied to their institutional affiliations. If these stakeholder networks are also assumed to contain 'communities' of experts, we might learn much about the process whereby new knowledge and ideas are introduced into the policy process and translated into specific policy proposals.

From a post-positivist position, as we have seen, reflectivists offer concepts and approaches that focus on the importance of discourse, ideas and also socialization, which might in turn make a significant contribution to understanding the way ideas are communicated and (in common with policy analysts) the processes of interest formation and agenda setting in the EU and elsewhere. From this perspective, hypotheses might be developed that test the importance of language and discourse in the European foreign policy process, specifically with respect to the forms in which ideas are communicated. Interesting work is already beginning to emerge that analyses European foreign policy-making as a social process in which actors are socialized over time into an official EU discourse, and within that process learn both the 'rules of the game' and the norms for appropriate action, which are then 'internalized' at national levels (Jorgensen 1997b: 167–81).

Conclusion

If we accept that FPA can be adapted from its traditional state-centric realist methodology, European foreign policy has provided a very productive arena for testing out the techniques and the analytical methods of the foreign policy analyst. This approach should at least augment other more established approaches in this area discussed in Chapter 2. The European case, however, has revealed broader theoretical challenges to the foreign policy analyst that require further consideration about what is to be studied and how. The argument here has underlined the need for more effective linkages between FPA and other approaches to the study of policy-making at the international level. FPA has a long tradition of eclecticism, the 'borrowing' of ideas and approaches from other subject areas and applying them creatively to the foreign policy arena. The extent to which FPA has become disconnected from important debates elsewhere in recent years helps to explain why this approach has become rather unfashionable. Hopefully this study will help to counter the view that FPA is a sterile field devoid of innovation.

Note

1. This chapter draws extensively upon White, B. (1999) The European Challenge to Foreign Policy Analysis, *European Journal of International Relations*, **5**(1): 37–66.

Bibliography

Allen, D. (1978) Foreign Policy at the European Level: Beyond the Nation-State. In W. Wallace and W. Paterson (eds) *Foreign Policy-Making in Western Europe*, pp. 135–54. Westmead: Saxon House.

Allen, D. (1988) British Foreign Policy and West European Cooperation. In P. Byrd (ed.) *British Foreign Policy Under Thatcher*, pp. 35–53. Oxford: Philip Allan.

Allen, D. (1996) The European Rescue of National Foreign Policy? In C. Hill (ed.) *The Actors in Europe's Foreign Policy*, pp. 288–304. London: Routledge.

Allen, D. (1998) 'Who Speaks for Europe?': the Search for an Effective and Coherent External Policy. In J. Peterson and H. Sjursen (eds) *A Common Foreign Policy for Europe?*, pp. 41–58. London: Routledge.

Allen, D. (1999) United Kingdom. The Foreign and Commonwealth Office: 'Flexible, Responsive and Proactive?'. In B. Hocking (ed.) *Foreign Ministries: Change and Adaptation*, pp. 207–25. Basingstoke: Macmillan.

Allen, D. and Byrne, P. (1985) Multilateral Decision-Making and Implementation: the Case of the European Community. In S. Smith and M. Clarke (eds) *Foreign Policy Implementation*, pp. 123–41. London: Allen & Unwin.

Allen, D., Rummel, R. and Wessels, W. (eds) (1982) *European Political Cooperation*. London: Butterworth.

Allen, D. and Smith, M. (1990) Western Europe's Presence in the Contemporary International Arena. *Review of International Studies*, **16**(3): 19–38.

Allison, G. (1971) *Essence of Decision: Explaining the Cuban Missile Crisis*. Boston, MA: Little, Brown.

Allison, G. and Zelikow, P. (1999) *Essence of Decision: Explaining the Cuban Missile Crisis* (2nd edn). Harlow: Longman.

Bainbridge, T. (1998) *The Penguin Companion to European Union* (2nd edn). London: Penguin.

Baldwin, D. (ed.) (1993) *Neorealism and Neoliberalism: The Contemporary Debate*. New York: Columbia University Press.

Bonvicini, G. (1998) Making European Foreign Policy Work. In M. Westlake (ed.) *The European Union Beyond Amsterdam*, pp. 61–75. London: Routledge.

Bradbury, J. (1996) The UK in Europe. In R. Bideleux and R. Taylor (eds) *European Integration and Disintegration*, pp. 66–92. London: Routledge.

Bretherton, C. and Vogler, J. (1999) *The European Union as a Global Actor*. London: Routledge.

Brown, C. (1997) *Understanding International Relations*. Basingstoke: Macmillan.

Buchan, D. (1993) *Europe: The Strange Superpower*. Aldershot: Dartmouth.

Bull, H. (1983) Civilian Power Europe: A Contradiction in Terms? In L. Tsoukalis (ed.) *The European Community: Past, Present, Future*, pp. 149–70. Oxford: Blackwell.

Bulmer, S. (1992) Britain and European Integration: Of Sovereignty, Slow Adaptation and Semi-Detachment. In S. George (ed.) *Britain and the European Community: The Politics of Semi-Detachment*, pp. 1–26. Oxford: Clarendon.

Bulmer, S. and Burch, M. (1998) Organizing For Europe: Whitehall, the British State and European Union. *Public Administration*, **76** (Winter): 601–28.

Bulmer, S., George, S. and Scott, A. (eds) (1992) *The UK and EC Membership Evaluated*. London: Pinter.

Buzan, B. (1983) *People, States and Fear*. Brighton: Wheatsheaf.

Buzan, B., Jones, C. and Little, R. (1993) *The Logic of Anarchy: Neorealism to Structural Realism*. New York: Columbia University Press.

Buzan, B., Kelstrup, M., Lemaître, P., Tromer, E. and Waever, O. (1990) *The European Security Order Recast*. London: Pinter.

Cameron, F. (1997) Where the European Commission Comes In: From the Single European Act to Maastricht. In E. Regelsberger, P. de Schoutheete de Tervarent and W. Wessels (eds) *Foreign Policy of the European Union*, pp. 99–108. Boulder, CO and London: Rienner.

Cameron, F. (1998) Building a Common Foreign Policy: Do Institutions Matter? In J. Peterson and H. Sjursen (eds) *A Common Foreign Policy for Europe?*, pp. 59–76. London: Routledge.

Caporaso, J. (1996) The European Union and Forms of State: Westphalian, Regulatory or Post-Modern. *Journal of Common Market Studies*, **34**(1): 30–52.

Clarke, M. (1992) *British External Policy-Making in the 1990s*. Basingstoke: Macmillan.

Clarke, M. (1998) British Security Policy. In K. Eliassen (ed.) *Foreign and Security Policy in the European Union*, pp. 124–46. London: Sage.

Clarke, M. and White, B. (eds) (1989) *Understanding Foreign Policy: the Foreign Policy Systems Approach*. Aldershot: Elgar.

Collester, J. (1998) Yugoslavia. In D. Dinan (ed.) *Encyclopedia of the European Union*, pp. 493–7. Basingstoke: Macmillan.

Collinson, C. (1999) 'Issue-Systems', 'Multi-Level Games' and the Analysis of the EU's External Commercial and Associated Policies: a Research Agenda. *Journal of European Public Policy*, **6**(2): 206–24.

Cox, R. (1983) Gramsci, Hegemony and International Relations: An Essay in Method. *Millennium*, **12**(2): 162–75.

Cox, R. (1986) Social Forces, States and World Orders: Beyond International Relations Theory. In R. Keohane (ed.) *Neorealism and Its Critics*,
pp. 205–54. New York: Columbia University Press.

Cox, R. with Sinclair, T. (1996) *Approaches to World Order*. Cambridge:
Cambridge University Press.

Deighton, A. (1997) Introduction. Britain and the Creation of Western
European Union, 1954. Conclusion. In A. Deighton (ed.) *Western European Union 1954–97: Defence, Security, Integration*, pp. 1–10, 11–28,
169–78. Oxford: European Interdependence Research Unit, St Antony's
College, Oxford.

Destler, I. M. (1992) *American Trade Politics*. Washington DC: Institute
for International Economics/Twentieth Century Fund.

Devuyst, Y. (1995) The European Community and the Conclusion of the
Uruguay Round. In C. Rhodes and S. Maizey (eds) *The State of the
European Union: Building a European Polity*, Vol. 3, pp. 449–68.
London: Longman.

Dinan, D. (1994) *Ever Closer Union?* London: Macmillan.

Dinan, D. (ed.) (1998) *Encyclopedia of the European Union*. Basingstoke:
Macmillan.

Duchène, F. (1972) Europe's Role in World Peace. In R. Mayne (ed.) *Europe
Tomorrow: Sixteen Europeans Look Ahead*, pp. 32–47. London: Fontana.

Duff, A. (1998) Britain and Europe: Their Relationship. In M. Westlake (ed.)
The European Union Beyond Amsterdam, pp. 34–46. London: Routledge.

Edwards, G. (1996) National Sovereignty vs Integration?: The Council of
Ministers. In J. Richardson (ed.) *European Union: Power and Policy-
Making*, pp. 127–47. London: Routledge.

Edwards, G. (1997) The Potential and Limits of the CFSP: The Yugoslav
Example. In E. Regelsberger, P. De Schoutheete de Terverant, and
W. Wessels (eds) *Foreign Policy of the European Union*, pp. 173–96.
London: Rienner.

Eliassen, K. (1998) Introduction: The New European Foreign and Security
Policy Agenda. In K. Eliassen (ed.) *Foreign and Security Policy in the
European Union*, pp. 1–8. London: Sage.

European Commission (1995) *Report of the Commission for the Reflection
Group*. Brussels: Intergovernmental Conference, May.

Foreign Ministers (1976) Foreign Ministers of the European Community.
Statement on the Situation in Southern Africa. 23 February, Luxembourg, European Community.

Forster, A. (1997) The Ratchet of European Defence: Britain, and the
Reactivation of Western European Union 1984–91. In A. Deighton (ed.)
Western European Union 1954–97: Defence, Security and Integration,
pp. 29–46. Oxford: European Interdependence Research Unit, St
Antony's College, Oxford.

Forster, A. and Wallace, W. (1996) Common Foreign and Security Policy: a New Policy or Just a New Name? In H. Wallace and W. Wallace (eds) *Policy-Making in the European Union* (3rd edn), pp. 411–35. Oxford: Oxford University Press.

Galtung, J. (1973) *The European Community: A Superpower in the Making?* London: Allen & Unwin.

George, S. (1998) *An Awkward Partner: Britain in the European Community* (3rd edn). Oxford: Oxford University Press.

Ginsberg, R. (1989) *Foreign Policy Actions of the European Community.* Boulder, CO: Rienner.

Ginsberg, R. (1997) The EUs CFSP: the Politics of Procedure. In M. Holland (ed.) *Common Foreign and Security Policy*, pp. 12–33. London: Pinter.

Gomez, R. (1998) The EU's Mediterranean Policy: Common Foreign Policy by the Back Door? In J. Peterson and H. Sjursen (eds) *A Common Foreign Policy for Europe?*, pp. 133–51. London: Routledge.

Gow, J. (1997) *Triumph of the Lack of Will: International Diplomacy and the Yugoslav War.* London: Hurst.

Guehenno, J.-M. (1998) A Foreign Policy in Search of a Polity. In J. Zielonka (ed.) *Paradoxes of European Foreign Policy*, pp. 25–34. The Hague: Kluwer Law International.

Haas, E. B. (1958) *The Uniting of Europe: Political, Economic and Social Forces 1950–57.* London: Stevens; Stanford, CA: Stanford University Press.

Halliday, F. (1983) *The Making of the Second Cold War.* London: Verso.

Halliday, F. (1994) *Rethinking International Relations.* Basingstoke: Macmillan.

Hallstein, W. (1962) *United Europe.* Oxford: Oxford University Press.

Hermann, C., Kegley, C. and Rosenau, J. (eds) (1987) *New Directions in the Study of Foreign Policy.* Boston, MA: Allen & Unwin.

Hill, C. (1974) The Credentials of Foreign Policy Analysis, *Millennium*, **3**(2): 148–65.

Hill, C. (ed.) (1983) *National Foreign Policies and European Political Cooperation.* London: Allen & Unwin.

Hill, C. (1990) European Foreign Policy: Power Bloc, Civilian Model – or Flop? In R. Rummel (ed.) *The Evolution of an International Actor*, pp. 31–55. Boulder, CO: Westview.

Hill, C. (1992) The Foreign Policy of the European Community: Dream of Reality? In R. Macridis (ed.) *Foreign Policy In World Politics* (8th edn), pp. 108–42. Englewood Cliffs, NJ: Prentice Hall.

Hill, C. (1993) The Capability–Expectations Gap, or Conceptualizing Europe's International Role. *Journal of Common Market Studies*, **31**(3): 305–28.

Hill, C. (1996a) Introduction: The Falklands War and European Foreign Policy. In S. Stavridis and C. Hill (eds) *Domestic Sources of Foreign Policy: West European Reactions to the Falklands Conflict*, pp. 1–18. Oxford: Berg.

Hill, C. (ed.) (1996b) *The Actors in Europe's Foreign Policy*. London: Routledge.

Hill, C. (1996c) United Kingdom: Sharpening Contradictions. In C. Hill (ed.) *The Actors in Europe's Foreign Policy*, pp. 68–89. London: Routledge.

Hill, C. (1997) The Actors Involved: National Perspectives. In E. Regelsberger, P. de Schoutheete de Tervarent and W. Wessels (eds) *Foreign Policy of the European Union*, pp. 85–97. London: Rienner.

Hill, C. (1998a) Closing the Capabilities–Expectations Gap. In J. Peterson and H. Sjursen (eds) *A Common Foreign Policy For Europe?*, pp. 18–38. London: Routledge.

Hill, C. (1998b) Convergence, Divergence and Dialectics: National Foreign Policies and the CFSP. In J. Zielonka (ed.) *Paradoxes of European Foreign Policy*, pp. 35–52. The Hague: Kluwer Law International.

Hill, C. and Wallace, W. (1996) Introduction: Actors and Actions. In C. Hill (ed.) *The Actors in Europe's Foreign Policy*. London: Routledge.

Holland, M. (ed.) (1991) *The Future of European Political Cooperation*. Basingstoke: Macmillan.

Holland, M. (1995a) Bridging the Capability–Expectations Gap: A Case Study of the CFSP Joint Action on South Africa. *Journal of Common Market Studies*, **33**(4): 555–72.

Holland, M. (1995b) *European Union Common Foreign Policy*. Basingstoke: Macmillan.

Holland, M. (1997a) Introduction: CFSP – Reinventing the EPC Wheel? In M. Holland (ed.) *Common Foreign and Security Policy*, pp. 1–11. London: Pinter.

Holland, M. (1998) South Africa. In D. Dinan (ed.) *Encyclopedia of the European Union*, pp. 428–9. Basingstoke: Macmillan.

Ifestos, P. (1987) *European Political Cooperation*. Aldershot: Avebury.

Jorgensen, K. (ed.) (1997a) *Reflective Approaches to European Governance*. Basingstoke: Macmillan.

Jorgensen, K. (1997b) PoCo: The Diplomatic Republic of Europe. In K. Jorgensen (ed.) *Reflective Approaches to European Governance*, pp. 167–80. Basingstoke: Macmillan.

Jorgensen, K.E. (1998) The European Union's Performance in World Politics: How Should We Measure Success? In J. Zielonka (ed.) *Paradoxes of European Foreign Policy*, pp. 87–101. The Hague: Kluwer Law International.

Kegley, C. (ed.) (1995) *Controversies in International Relations Theory: Realism and the Neoliberal Challenge*. New York: St. Martins Press.

Keohane, R. and Nye, J. (1974) Transgovernmental Relations and International Organizations. *World Politics*, **27**(1): 39–62.

Keohane, R. and Nye, J. (1977) *Power and Interdependence*. Boston, MA: Little, Brown.

Keohane, R and Nye, J. (1988) *Power and Interdependence* (2nd edn). Boston, MA: Little, Brown.

Kintis, A. (1997) The EU's Foreign Policy and the War in the Former Yugoslavia. In M. Holland (ed.) *Common Foreign and Security Policy*, pp. 148–73. London: Pinter.

Krasner, S. (1995/96) Compromising Westphalia. *International Security*, **20**(3): 115–51.

Laffan, B. (1992) *Integration and Cooperation in Europe*. London: Routledge.

Larsen, H. (1997a) *Foreign Policy and Discourse Analysis*. London: Routledge.

Larsen, H. (1997b) British Discourses on Europe: Sovereignty of Parliament, Instrumentality and the Non-mythical Europe. In K. Jorgensen (ed.) *Reflective Approaches to European Governance*, pp. 109–27. Basingstoke: Macmillan.

Light, M. (1994) Foreign Policy Analysis. In A. Groom and M. Light (eds) *Contemporary International Relations: A Guide to Theory*, pp. 93–108. London: Pinter.

Lister, M. (1997) *The European Union and the South*. London: Routledge.

Lowi, T. (1964) American Business, Public Policy, Case Studies and Political Theory. *World Politics*, **16** (July) 677–715.

Luxembourg Report (1970) Collected in *Texts Relating to European Political Cooperation*. German Government, Press and Information Office, 1977.

Martin, L. and Roper, J. (1995) Introduction. In L. Martin and J. Roper (eds) *Towards a Common Defence Policy*, pp. 1–6. Paris. Institute for Security Studies, WEU.

Meny, Y., Muller, P. and Quermonne, J.-L. (eds) (1996) *Adjusting to Europe: The Impact of the European Union on National Institutions and Policies*. London: Routledge.

Monar, J. (1997a) Political Dialogue with Third Countries and Regional Political Groupings: The Fifteen as an Attractive Interlocutor. In E. Regelsberger, P. de Schoutheete de Tervarent and W. Wessels (eds) *Foreign Policy of the European Union*, pp. 263–74. London: Rienner.

Monar, J. (1997b) The Financial Dimension of the CFSP. In M. Holland (ed.) *Common Foreign and Security Policy*, pp. 34–51. London: Pinter.

Moravcsik, A. (1991) Negotiating the Single European Act: National Interests and Conventional Statecraft in the European Community. *International Organization*, **45**(1): 651–88.

Moravcsik, A. (1993) Preference and Power in the European Community: A Liberal Intergovernmentalist Approach, *Journal of Common Market Studies*, **31**(4): 473–524.

Morgan, R. (1973) *High Politics, Low Politics: Towards a Foreign Policy for Western Europe*. London: Sage.

Morse, E. (1970) The Transformation of Foreign Policies: Modernization, Interdependence and Externalization. *World Politics*, **22**(3): 371–92.

Morse, E. (1976) *Modernization and the Transformation of International Relations*. London: Collier-Macmillan.

Muller, H. and van Dassen, L. (1997) From Cacophony to Joint Action: Successes and Shortcomings of the European Nuclear Non-Proliferation Policy. In M. Holland (ed.) *Common Foreign and Security Policy*, pp. 52–72. London: Pinter.

Nugent, N. (1994) *The Government and Politics of the European Union*. Basingstoke: Macmillan.

Nuttall, S. (1992) *European Political Cooperation*. Oxford: Clarendon Press.

Nuttall, S. (1996) The Commission. In C. Hill (ed.) *The Actors in Europe's Foreign Policy*, pp. 130–47. London: Routledge.

Nuttall, S. (1997a) Two Decades of EPC Performance, In E. Regelsberger, P. de Schoutheete de Tervarent and W. Wessels (eds) *Foreign Policy of the European Union*, pp. 19–39. Boulder, CO: Rienner.

Nuttall, S. (1997b) The Commission and Foreign Policy-making. In G. Edwards and D. Spence (eds) *The European Commission* (2nd edn), pp. 303–20. London: Cartermill.

Nye, J. (1975) Transnational and Transgovernmental Relations. In G. Goodwin and A. Linklater (eds) *New Dimensions of World Politics*, pp. 35–53. London: Croom Helm.

Palme, O. (1982) *The Palme Report. Common Security: A Programme For Disarmament*. London: Pan.

Peterson, J. (1995) Decision-making in the European Union. *Journal of European Public Policy*, **2**(1): 69–93.

Peterson, J. (1998) Introduction: The European Union as a Global Actor. In J. Peterson and H. Sjursen (eds) *A Common Foreign Policy For Europe?*, pp. 3–17. London: Routledge.

Peterson, J. and Bomberg, E. (1999) *Decision-making in the European Union*. Basingstoke: Macmillan.

Peterson, J. and Sjursen, H. (1998) *A Common Foreign Policy For Europe?* London: Routledge.

Piening, C. (1997) *Global Europe*. Boulder, CO: Rienner.

Potter, W. (1980) Issue Area and Foreign Policy Analysis. *International Organization*, **34**(3): 405–27.

Puttnam, R. (1988) Diplomacy and Domestic Politics: the Logic of Two-level Games. *International Organization*, **42**(2): 427–60.

Regelsberger, E. (1991) The Twelve's Dialogue with Third Countries: Progress Towards a Communauté d'Action. In M. Holland (ed.) *The Future of European Political Cooperation*, pp. 161–79. Basingstoke: Macmillan.

Regelsberger, E., De Schoutheete de Terverant, P., and Wessels, W. (eds) (1997) *Foreign Policy of the European Union*, Boulder, CO: Rienner.

Richardson, J. (1996) Policy-making in the EU. In J. Richardson (ed.) *European Union: Power and Policy-making*, pp. 3–23. London: Routledge.

Risse-Kappen, T. (1996) Exploring the Nature of the Beast: International Relations Theory and Comparative Policy Analysis Meet the European Union. *Journal of Common Market Studies*, **34**(1): 53–79.

Rittberger, V. (ed.) (1993) *Regime Theory and International Relations*, Oxford: Clarendon Press.

Roper, J. (1995) Defining a Common Defence Policy and Common Defence. In L. Martin and J. Roper (eds) *Towards a Common Defence Policy*, pp. 7–12. Paris: Institute for Security Studies, WEU.

Rosenau, J. (1967) Foreign Policy as an Issue Area. In J. Rosenau (ed.) *Domestic Sources of Foreign Policy*, pp. 11–51. New York: Free Press.

Rosenau, J. (1992) Governance, Order and Change in World Politics. In J. Rosenau and E.-O. Czempial (eds) *Governance Without Government: Order and Change in World Politics*, pp. 3–6. Cambridge: Cambridge University Press.

Salmon, T. (1992) Testing Times for European Political Cooperation: the Gulf and Yugoslavia. *International Affairs*, **68**(2): 233–53.

Salmon, T. (1998) European Political Cooperation. In D. Dinan (ed.) *Encyclopedia of the European Union*, pp. 217–19. Basingstoke: Macmillan.

Sedelmeier, U. and Wallace, H. (1996) Policies Towards Central and Eastern Europe. In H. Wallace and W. Wallace (eds) *Policy-Making in the European Union* (3rd edn), pp. 353–87. Oxford: Oxford University Press.

Sjursen, H. (1998) Missed Opportunity or Eternal Fantasy?: The Idea of a Common European Security and Defence Policy. In J. Peterson and H. Sjursen (eds) *A Common Foreign Policy for Europe*, pp. 95–112. London: Routledge.

Smith, H. (1998) Actually Existing Foreign Policy – or Not?: the EU in Latin and Central America. In J. Peterson and H. Sjursen (eds) *A Common Foreign Policy For Europe?*, pp. 152–68. London: Routledge.

Smith, K.E. (1998) The Instruments of European Union Foreign Policy. In J. Zielonka (ed.) *Paradoxes of European Foreign Policy*, pp. 67–86. The Hague: Kluwer Law International.

Smith, M. (1988) Britain and the United States: Beyond the 'Special Relationship'? In P. Byrd (ed.) *British Foreign Policy under Thatcher*, pp. 8–34. Oxford: Philip Allan.

Smith, M. (1994) Beyond the Stable State? Foreign Policy Challenges and Opportunities in the New Europe. In W. Carlsnaes and S. Smith (eds) *European Foreign Policy*, pp. 21–44. London: Sage.

Smith, M. (1996) The EU as an International Actor. In J. Richardson (ed.) *European Union: Power and Policy-Making*, pp. 247–62. London: Routledge.

Smith, M. (1997) The Commission and External Relations. In G. Edwards and D. Spence (eds) *The European Commission* (2nd edn), pp. 264–302. London: Cartermill.

Smith, M. (1998) Does the Flag Follow Trade? 'Politicisation' and the Emergence of European Foreign Policy. In J. Peterson and H. Sjursen (eds) *A Common Foreign Policy For Europe*, pp. 77–94. London: Routledge.

Smith, M. J. (1999) *The Core Executive in Britain*. Basingstoke: Macmillan.

Smith, S. (1986) Theories of Foreign Policy: an Historical Overview. *Review of International Studies*, **12**(1): 13–29.

Smith, S. (1994) Foreign Policy Theory and the New Europe. In W. Carlsnaes and S. Smith (eds) *European Foreign Policy*, pp. 1–20. London: Sage.

Smith, S. (1997) New Approaches to International Theory. In J. Baylis and S. Smith (eds) *The Globalization of World Politics*, pp. 165–90. Oxford: Oxford University Press.

Soetendorp, B. (1994) The Evolution of the EC/EU as a Single Foreign Policy Actor. In W. Carlsnaes and S. Smith (eds) *European Foreign Policy*, pp. 103–19. London: Sage.

Soetendorp, B. (1999) *Foreign Policy in the European Union*. London: Longman.

Sorensen, G. (1997) An Analysis of Contemporary Statehood: Consequences for Conflict and Cooperation. *Review of International Studies*, **23**(3): 253–69.

Spence, A. and Spence, D. (1998) The Common Foreign and Security Policy from Maastricht to Amsterdam. In K. Eliassen (ed.) *Foreign and Security Policy of the European Union*, pp. 43–58. London: Sage.

Spence, D. (1993) The Role of the National Civil Service in European Lobbying: the British Case. In S. Mazey and J. Richardson (eds) *Lobbying in the European Community*, pp. 47–73. Oxford: Oxford University Press.

Spence, D. (1995) The Coordination of EU Policy by Member States. In M. Westlake (ed.) *The Council of the European Union*, pp. 353–89. London: Cartermill.

Spence, D. (1999) Foreign Ministries in National and European Context. In B. Hocking (ed.) *Foreign Ministries: Change and Adaptation*, pp. 247–68. Basingstoke: Macmillan.

Stainier, L. (1995) Common Interests, Values and Criteria For Action. In L. Martin and J. Roper (eds) *Towards a Common Defence Policy*, pp. 13–28. Paris: Institute for Security Studies, WEU.

Stavridis, S. and Hill, C. (1996) *Domestic Sources of Foreign Policy: West European Reactions to the Falklands Conflict*. Oxford: Berg.

Taylor, P. (1996) *The European Union in the 1990s*. Oxford: Oxford University Press.

Tonra, B. (1997) The Impact of Political Cooperation. In K. Jorgenson (ed.) *Reflective Approaches to European Governance*, pp. 181–98. Basingstoke: Macmillan.

Tugendhat, C. and Wallace, W. (1988) *Options for British Foreign Policy in the 1990s*. London: Routledge.

Van den Broek, H. (1996) Why Europe needs a Common Foreign and Security Policy. *European Foreign Affairs Review* **1**(1), July.

Vital, D. (1968) *The Making of British Foreign Policy*. London: Allen & Unwin.

Wallace, H. (1996) The Institutions of the EC: Experience and Experiments. In H. Wallace and W. Wallace (eds) *Policy-making in the European Union*, pp. 37–68. Oxford: Oxford University Press.

Wallace, H. (1997) At Odds With Europe. *Political Studies*, **45**(4): 677–88.

Wallace, W. (1974) British External Relations and the European Community: the Changing Context of Foreign Policy-making. *Journal of Common Market Studies*, **12**: 28–52.

Wallace, W. (1983) Introduction; Cooperation and Convergence in European Foreign Policy. In C. Hill (ed.) *National Foreign Policies and European Political Cooperation,* pp. 1–16. London: Allen & Unwin.

Wallace, W. (1986) What Price Interdependence? Sovereignty and Interdependence in British Politics. *International Affairs*, **62**(3): 367–89.

Wallace, W. (1990) The Nation State and Foreign Policy. In F. De La Serre, J. Leruez and H. Wallace (eds) *French and British Foreign Policies in Transition*, pp. 230–44. Oxford: Berg.

Wallace, W. (1991) Foreign Policy and National Identity in the United Kingdom. *International Affairs*, **67**(1): 65–85.

Wallace, W. (1996) Government Without Statehood: the Unstable Equilibrium. In H. Wallace and W. Wallace (eds) *Policy-making in the European Union* (3rd edn), pp. 439–60. Oxford: Oxford University Press.

Waltz, K. (1979) *Theory of International Politics*. Reading, MA: Addison-Wesley.

Webb, C. (1983) Theoretical Perspectives and Problems. In H. Wallace, W. Wallace and C. Webb (eds) *Policy-making in the European Community* (2nd edn), pp. 1–41. Chichester: Wiley.

Wessels, W. (1991) The EC Council: The Community's Decision-making Center. In R. Keohane and S. Hoffman (eds) *The New European Community: Decision-making and Institutional Change*, pp. 133–54. Boulder, CO: Westview.

Wendt, A. (1994) Collective Identity Formation and the International State. *American Political Science Review*, **88**(2): 384–96.

White, B. (1978/1994) Decision-making Analysis. In T. Taylor (ed.) *Approaches and Theory in International Relations*, pp. 141–64. London: Longman; Reprinted in P. Williams, D. Goldstein, and J. Shafritz (eds) *Classic Readings of International Relations*, pp. 197–26. Belmond, CA: Wadsworth.

White, B. (1989) Analysing Foreign Policy: Problems and Approaches. In M. Clarke and B. White (eds) *Understanding Foreign Policy: The Foreign Policy Systems Approach*, pp. 1–26. Aldershot: Elgar.

White, B. (1991) Britain: An Atlantic or a European Relationship? In R. Jordan (ed.) *Europe and the Superpowers*, pp. 155–74. London: Pinter.

White, B. (1992a) British Foreign Policy: Tradition and Change. In R. Macridis (ed.) *Foreign Policy in World Politics* (8th edn), pp. 7–31. Englewood Cliffs, NJ: Prentice Hall.

White, B. (1992b) *Britain, Detente and Changing East-West Relations.* London and New York: Routledge.

White, B. (1999) The European Challenge to Foreign Policy Analysis. *European Journal of International Relations*, **5**(1): 37–66.

Whitman, R. (1998) *From Civilian Power to Superpower?* Basingstoke: Macmillan.

Woolcock, S. and Hodges, M. (1996) EU Policy in the Uruguay Round. In H. Wallace and W. Wallace (eds) *Policy-making in the European Union* (3rd edn), pp. 301–24. Oxford: Oxford University Press.

Wright, V. (1996) The National Coordination of European Policy-making. In J. Richardson (ed.) *European Union: Power and Policy-making*, pp. 148–69. London: Routledge.

Young, H. (1998) *This Blessed Plot: Britain and Europe From Churchill to Blair.* Basingstoke: Macmillan.

Young, O. (1972) The Actors in World Politics. In J. Rosenau, V. Davis and M. East (eds) *The Analysis of International Politics,* pp. 125–44. New York: Free Press.

Zielonka, J. (1998) Constraints, Opportunities and Choices in European Foreign Policy. In J. Zielonka (ed.) *Paradoxes of European Foreign Policy*, pp. 1–13. The Hague: Kluwer Law International.

Internet References

http://europa.eu.int/comm.dg08/SouthAfrica/index 20 April 1999, consulted
    23 July 1999.
http://www.fco.gov.uk/text/news 23 November 1999, consulted 23 November
    1999.
http://www. europa.eu.int

Index

A
aid policy, EC 52–3
    to former Soviet countries 2, 77
Andriessen, F. 65

B
Balkans
    Albania crisis 158
    European disunity on 158
    post conflict, criticisms of EU role
        164
    Yugoslav crisis 107–10
Beyen, J.W. 5
British foreign policy
    and EMS 135
    and EMU 135
    and ERM 135
    'Atlanticism', public opinion on
        122
    Atlanticism vs pro-European 135,
        139–40
    Blair Government views on
        relations with US and EU 121
    Blairite position, examination of
        140
    Churchill, W., views on 120
    Community law, consequences on
        national law 124, 125
    Community law, differences caused
        by 126
    Community law, government
        committees involved with 127
    defence, pro-US or pro-European
        stance 139–40
    Denning, Lord 124
    EC membership, cost benefit
        analysis of 132–4
    European policy, consequences of
        1992 election on 136
    European policy, consequences of
        1997 election on 136–8
    Europeanization, impact of on UK
        policy process 128–31

    Europeanization, resistance to
        119–22
    Falklands conflict, US–UK
        relationship, effects on 134
    Iraq, military action against 139
    Jenkins, R. 121
    Maastricht Treaty 136
    Macmillan Government, views on
        121
    pro-European consensus in 136
    Reagan–Thatcher relationship 134
    symbolism, importance of 123
    Thatcher, M., effects of resignation
        on 121
Brittan, Leon, role in Uruguay Round
    1, 50, 66, 67

C
Clinton, Bill 65, 66
cold war era 1
    Berlin crisis 4
    North Atlantic Treaty 4
cold war, end of
    and European defence policy
        147–9
    and European integration 9, 36
    European foreign policy agenda
        expansion, as result of 43–4
    security interests, change in 61, 95
Committee of Permanent
    Representatives (COREPER) 6, 13,
    97, 100
Common Agricultural Policy (CAP)
    conflicts within 6
    reform of 62, 64
Common Commercial Policy (CCP)
    49
common defence policy (CDP)
    142–55
Common External Tariff (CET) 49
Common Foreign and Security Policy
    (CFSP)
    COREPER, responsibilities 97, 100
    Delors, J., role in 98

German unilateral action on
Yugoslav crisis 108–9
IFOR, establishment of 113
joint actions, examples of 103–4
Koschnick, H., appointment of 114
military capability, absence of 2,
104, 106, 107, 109, 110, 117
Mostar, civil administration of
114–15, 116
NATO, action in Balkans 110, 112,
113
NATO, future of 95, 116
NPT, EU action on 101
Santer, J., role in 98
Sarajevo massacre, effects on
peace efforts 109
SFOR, establishment of 113
Treaty on European Unity (TEU)
102
'turf wars' 99
UNPROFOR, role in Yugoslav
crisis 111–14
US, reduced reliance on 95
Vance, C., role in peace plans 109
Yugoslavia crisis 95, 104–10
Community foreign policy
and state sovereignty 48
Commission role 50
Common Commercial Policy
(CCP) 49
Common External Tariff (CET) 49
concessions by member states 48
definition of 40, 49–70
economic diplomacy 56
economic instruments used to
implement 56
expansion of, as result of cold war
ending 43–4
external, unity in 2
implementation, problems of 53
individual states' policies,
importance of 167
limitations of Community decision-
making 53
political sensitivity of 48
single policy, pressures to achieve
168
single vs common 165–6
trade policy-making process 50–1

Treaty of Rome, Articles referring
to external trade 49–50, 52
unification of 161–2
Council of Ministers 6, 12, 51
Council Secretariat 14
customs union 6, 8

D

de Gaulle, Charles, CAP conflicts 6
defence capability, as separate from
NATO 2, 3
European Defence Community
Treaty 5
failure of CFSP, in Balkans 2, 104,
106, 109, 117
defence, common European policy
(CDP) 142–55
British resistance to 149–50
cold war, effects of ending on
147–9
definition of 143–4
Eden, A., role in creation 145
European defence force, proposals
151
Kosovo, influence on 150
London Report 146
military capability, need for 152–3
NATO, German membership of
145
origins of 144–5
progress towards 150, 154
see also Common Foreign and
Security Policy
defence, transatlantic cooperation 4
North Atlantic Treaty 4
see also NATO
Delors, J. 8, 65, 98
Delors Report 8–9
Directorate-Generals (DGs) 15
responsibility for foreign policy
160

E

Economic and Monetary Union
(EMU) 3
and British policy 135
Euro 3
plans for 7, 8, 9, 10
economic policy *see* Community
foreign policy; GATT; trade

Euro, the 3
  and global currency competition 3
  British policy 135
European Atomic Energy Community
  (EURATOM) 6
European Coal and Steel Community
  (ECSC) 5–6
European Commission 14–16
  OECD, relationship with 55
  trade policy, Commission role
    50–3
  'turf wars' resulting from
    reorganization of 55–6
  WTO, relationship with 55
European Council 11
European Court of Justice 18
European Defence Community Treaty
  5
European Economic Community
  (EEC) 6
  and economic policy 49
  applications to join 6, 7
  Britain, de Gaulle veto 7
European foreign policy, definition of
  36–41
European Monetary System (EMS) 8
  and British policy 135
European Parliament 16–17
European Political Cooperation
  (EPC)
  Africa, Working Group on 86
  apartheid, condemnation of 86
  apartheid, help for victims of 88,
    92
  ASEAN 81
  British Code of Practice,
    evaluation of 87–8
  capabilities and instruments 80–4
  communism, assistance following
    collapse of 77
  Copenhagen Report 78
  definition of 71
  EPC process, conclusions about 79
  establishment of 7, 38, 40, 45
  European Council, results of
    creation of 75
  Falklands, effect of invasion 73
  Fouchet talks 72

Granada, Commission view on US
  invasion 76
Gulf Cooperation Council 81
Hungary, Europe Agreement with
  82–3
Israeli invasion of Lebanon, effects
  on 73
key elements of 74–5
London Report, agreement on
  political cooperation 76, 81
Luxembourg Report, interpretation
  of 71–2
Mandela, effects of release 86
national interests, continued pursuit
  of 78
OPEC, relationship with 73
Ostpolitik, in relation to 72
Poland, Europe Agreement with
  82–3
Poland martial law imposition,
  effects on 73, 83
Rio Group 81
Schuman Plan 72
Single European Act 74
South Africa, condemnation of
  military aggression of 76
South Africa, economic sanctions
  86–7, 89
South Africa, evaluation of EPC on
  92–3
South Africa, relations with 84–6
Soviet Union, sanctions on 76, 83
Troika system, support for 75
US/Soviet relations, EU concern at
  change in 73
Venice Declaration 80–1
European Political Union (EPU),
  plans for 9
European Union (EU)
  as international actor 22–3
  as international organization 21
  development policy, role of
    member states in 52
  enlargement 3, 10, 28
  institutions, description of role
    11–18
  Lomé Conventions 52
  role as state 19–21

Treaty of Rome, legal framework
  of 52
external relations *see* Community
  foreign policy

F
foreign policy
  agenda, expansion 42–4
  application of FPA 24–6
  standard FPA questions about 40–1
  terms, clarification of 47–8
  see also Community foreign policy
Foreign Policy Analysis (FPA)
  analysis framework 40–1
  application of 24–6
  case studies, use and value of 45–6
  challenges to 171–3
  criticisms of 32–46
  member states' foreign policy 45
  state, definition of 174–5
  techniques of, applied to EFP 178

G
General Affairs Council, limitations
  of 63
General Agreement on Trade and
  Tariffs (GATT) 1, 2
  Blair House agreement, effect on
    member states 67
  Bush Administration 65
  Cairns Group 62
  CAP, reform of 62, 64
  Clinton Adminstration 65, 66
  cold war, change in security
    interests 61
  Community policy on 58–70
  consensus, importance of 70
  Delors, J. 65
  Dunkel Text 64, 65
  ECJ ruling, effect on 18
  ECSC, merging of institutions with
    EEC 59–60
  ECSC, role within GATT rules 59
  EU Presidency, intervention in
    negotiations 70
  G7, Houston summit 63
  GAC, limitations of 63
  GATS, audio-visual services,
    exclusion from 68
  historical background 59

MacSharry resignation 65
  qualified majority vote (QMV),
    replacement of 67
  Soviet Union demise of, change in
    Europe–US relations 61
  textile industry, as part of 68
  TRIPs, as part of 69
  UR, Commission negotiations 50
  UR, increase in members 60
  UR, phases of, 1986–94 62
  UR, US concern at growth of EC
    62
  Uruguay Round, agenda 60
General Agreement on Trade in
  Services (GATS) 68
German reunification 9
global role, of EU 1, 2, 21–3, 24–46
  application of FPA 24–6
  common foreign policy, prospects
    of 25
  differing approaches in analyses of
    27–32
  enlargement of EU, as factor 3, 10,
    28
  foreign policy agenda, expansion
    of 42–4
  FPA, criticisms of 32–46
  interpreting European role within
    27
  Treaty of Rome, division of powers
    in trade policy 42
Group of Seven (G7) 2
  Houston summit 63

I
Israel, Lebanon invasion, effects on
  EPC 73
integration and cooperation,
  development 4–10
  Amsterdam Treaty (1997) 10
  Brussels Treaty 4
  CAP, conflicts 6
  common market 5–6
  customs union 6, 8
  Delors Report 8–9
  divergent views, compromise 9–10
  Dunkirk Treaty 4
  economic recovery, post-war 5
  EMS 8

EMU, plans for 7–9
enlargement, of EU 3, 10, 28
European Coal and Steel
    Community (ECSC) 5–6
European Economic Community
    (EEC) established 6
European Political Cooperation
    (EPC), establishment of 7
German reunification 9
Hague summit 7
North Atlantic Treaty 4
SEM 8
Single European Act 8
Treaty of Rome, 6, 8
Treaty of Paris 5
Treaty on European Union (1991)
    9, 10
intergovernmentalism 42

K

Kantor, Mickey, role in Uruguay
    Round 1, 50, 66

M

MacSharry, R. 65
Marshall Aid 5
Middle East war, reactions to, effects
    on oil prices 7
    Israeli invasion of Lebanon, effects
        on EPC 73
Monnet, J. 6

N

national foreign policy, of member
    states 41
NATO 1, 2, 3, 4
    British support for 134
    future of 95, 116, 147–9
    German membership of 145
    in Balkans 110, 112, 113
North Atlantic Treaty Organization
    see NATO
Nuclear Non-Proliferation Treaty
    (NPT) 101

P

Political Committee (PoCo) 14
Pompidou, G. 7
presidency 13

Q

qualified majority voting (QMV) 12,
    67

S

Santer, J. 98
security politics 33, 34
Single European Act (1986) 8, 12, 74
    and British policy 135
Single European Market (SEM),
    moves towards 8, 9, 10
    and British policy 135
South Africa
    apartheid condemnation of 86
    apartheid, help for victims 88, 92
    British Code of Practice 87–8
    Code of Conduct 90
    European relations with 84–6
    evaluation of EPC on 92–3
    Mandela, N. 91
    military aggression, European
        condemnation 76
    Netherlands, government position
        on 89, 90
    sanctions 86–7, 89
    Thatcher, position on anti-apartheid
        89
Soviet Union
    Berlin crisis 4
    cold war end, effect on European
        defence policy 147–9
    demise of, change in Europe–US
        relations 61
    East–West competition 4
    EC aid to former satellites of 2, 77
    trade sanctions 57, 76, 83
    US relations, change in 73
Spaak, Paul-Henri 6
    state, definition of within FPA
        174–5
state-as-actor 32
state-centricity 32, 33, 34

T

trade
    anti-dumping regulations 56–7
    Barcelona Declaration 3
    economic diplomacy 56
    economic favours, effect on third
        parties of 56

EU foreign policy, *The Economist* comment on 57
EU-Mercosur Agreement 3
Euro-Asian summit, Bangkok 3
New Transatlantic Agenda 3
outside Europe 3
regulatory instruments 56
Trade Barriers Regulation 57
transatlantic conflict 1–3
'turf wars' 55–6, 99
see also global role; trade sanctions; GATT
trade agreements
COREPER, role in 51
Council of Ministers, role in 51
DG, role in 51
key stages in negotiating 51
Permanent Representatives, role in 51
see also GATT
trade policy, division of powers 42
Treaty of Rome, Articles referring to external trade 49, 50, 52
trade sanctions
anti-apartheid 57, 86–7
Argentina 58
breaches of collective policy 58
disunity on 58
import bans 58
Iran 57
nuclear cooperation 58
oil exports 58
Poland 57
Soviet Union 57, 76, 83
UN arms embargo, cooperation with 58
transgovernmentalism 34
Treaty of Amsterdam, provisions of 157–62
evaluation of 162–9
Treaty of Rome 6
Articles referring to external trade 49, 50, 52
division of powers in trade policy 42
influence on third parties 54
legal framework 52
monitoring and implementation, Commission role 54

revision of 8
Treaty on European Union
and CFSP 102
decision-making under 9, 10, 13, 15, 18, 97, 98, 160

U
Union foreign policy 40
United States
Burton-Helms and D'Amato legislation 2
Bush Adminsistration 65
Clinton Administration 2, 65, 66
defence, European capability, concerns over 2, 106
economic recovery, role in post-war European 5
economic sanctions, on European companies 2
Falklands conflict 134
Grenada invasion 76
NATO alliance 1, 2, 95, 134
Reagan–Thatcher relationship 134
reduced reliance on by Europe 95
Soviet Union, change in relationship 73
'trade wars' 1, 2
Uruguay Round *see* General Agreement on Trade and Tariffs

W
World Trade Organization (WTO) 1
and European Commission 55

Y
Yugoslavia, policy towards 94, 106–17
crisis, Poos, J., comment on US ability in 108
IFOR 113
Owen, D., role in peace plans 109
Sarajevo massacre, effects on peace efforts 109
Serbs, ultimatum to by UN 112
SFOR 113
UNPROFOR, role in Yugoslav crisis 111–14